AF471277

Beningfield's
Orchards

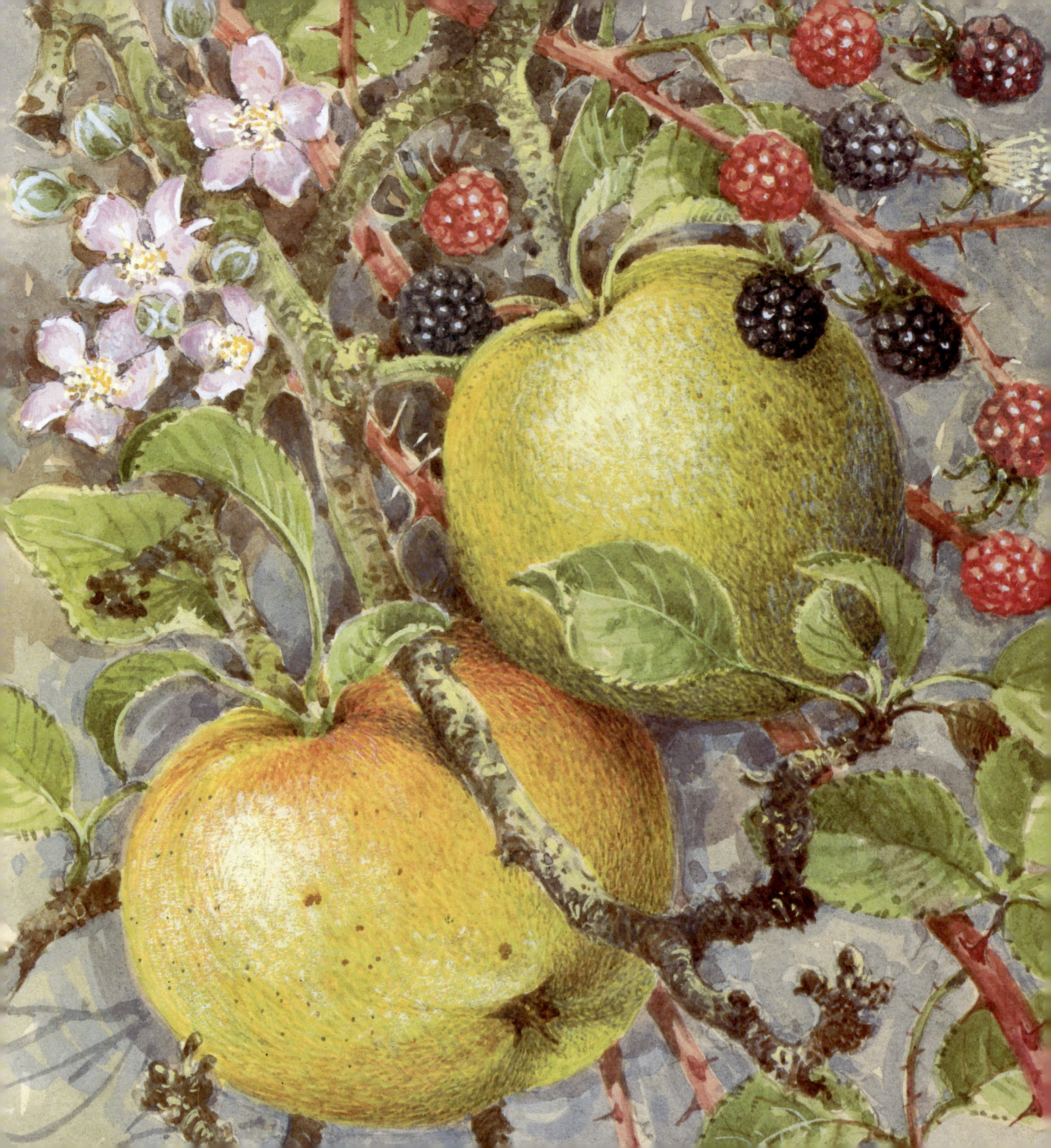

Beningfield's Orchards

Text by Betty Beningfield and Robin Page

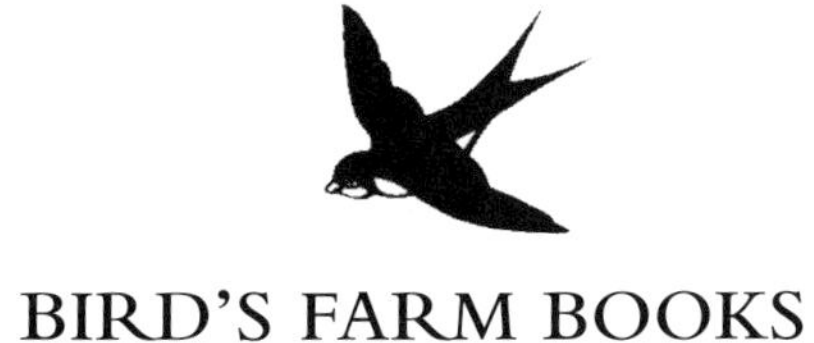

BIRD'S FARM BOOKS

Published by Bird's Farm Books, Barton, Cambridgeshire CB3 7AG
www.robin@robinpage.info
Distributed by Merlin Unwin Books, 7 Corve Street, Ludlow, Shropshire

ISBN 0 905232 24 0

Designed by Jim Reader
Design and production in association with Book Production Consultants plc,
25–27 High Street, Chesterton, Cambridge CB4 1ND
www.bpccam.co.uk

Printed and bound in Great Britain by The Burlington Press, Foxton, Cambridge

FRONTISPIECE: *Bramley apples and blackberries.*

Contents

Acknowledgements

Without the help of many people it would have been impossible to complete this final book of the work by Gordon Beningfield. Most important has been the support and active help given by Betty Beningfield and her daughters Sally and Sarah. Not only have they found pictures, but they have read proofs and supported totally a project that they believe would have met with Gordon's complete approval.

Others have helped both directly and indirectly; some have produced pictures and prints; some have photographed pictures and others have come up with information, memories and anecdotes. All have been indispensable and include: Jean Andrewartha, Derek Christopher, Joyce Christopher, Canon Alan Cole, David and Elizabeth Dawson, John and Jane Hawker, John Hayward, Professor William Hill, Brian and Annabel Jackman, Chris Knights, James Marsden, Rachael Page, Martin Smith, Oliver Tynan, 'Badger' Walker, George Warre, George Wright, The Brogdale Horticultural Trust (home of the national fruit collection), Bulmer's Cider of Hereford, Angela King and Sue Clifford of Common Ground, Adrian Barlow of English Apples and Pears Ltd, John Edgley of Pershore College, Vicki Hird of Sustain, Weston's Cider of Much Marcle and Nigel Housden of Pinsharp Photography for the Herefordshire photographs.

I am grateful to Ian Cameron and Jill Hollis of Cameron Books, who have made a generous donation to the Gordon Beningfield Memorial Appeal in lieu of any copyright payment.

Almost last, but not least, I am grateful to Roger and Maggie Smith whose wonderful Beningfield collection came to light in the nick of time. My final thanks must go to Jim Reader and Franca Holden at Book Production Consultants for all their efforts and to Margaret Taylor for typing the text and researching some of the poems.

Every effort has been made to trace copyright holders. If any have been overlooked I apologise and the fault is entirely mine.

R.P.

Introduction

There are many reasons for publishing *Beningfield's Orchards*. The first is to give all those who appreciate the art of Gordon Beningfield an opportunity to enjoy what will almost certainly be the last collection of his work – with many of the paintings and sketches being published for the first time. At the same time it is hoped that the book will introduce new people to his work – and through his work encourage them into the world of conservation and the traditional British countryside.

We hope too that *Beningfield's Orchards* will inspire gardeners to grow some traditional fruit trees in their gardens, and shoppers to ask for traditional varieties of fruit in their village shops and town supermarkets – after all, supermarkets continually boast of how they respond to the wishes of their customers – fact or fiction? Why not find out! Perhaps the odd politician may peer into this book and at last realise what an important part orchards could, and should, play in contributing quality food to a healthy and tasty national diet.

Finally a donation will be made on the sale of every book to The Gordon Beningfield Memorial Appeal. The long-term aim is to buy a working farm in Dorset, through the Countryside Restoration Trust, as a living tribute to the work and life of Gordon Beningfield. Although he lived in Hertfordshire, he loved Dorset and was a self-taught expert on the work of Thomas Hardy – so it is Dorset where his friends, family and admirers believe the Gordon Beningfield Memorial farm should be.

Any individual donations should be sent to '**The Gordon Beningfield Memorial Appeal**', **c/o The Countryside Restoration Trust, Barton, Cambs CB3 7AG.**

Foreword

It has been both a sadness, and celebration to help Betty Beningfield produce *Beningfield's Orchards*. This is almost certainly the final book showing the remarkable paintings of a remarkable man; Gordon Beningfield was the most outstanding countryside artist of his generation and *Orchards* is a fitting tribute to a husband, a father, a friend and a man who dedicated his life to fighting for the good things of the traditional British countryside.

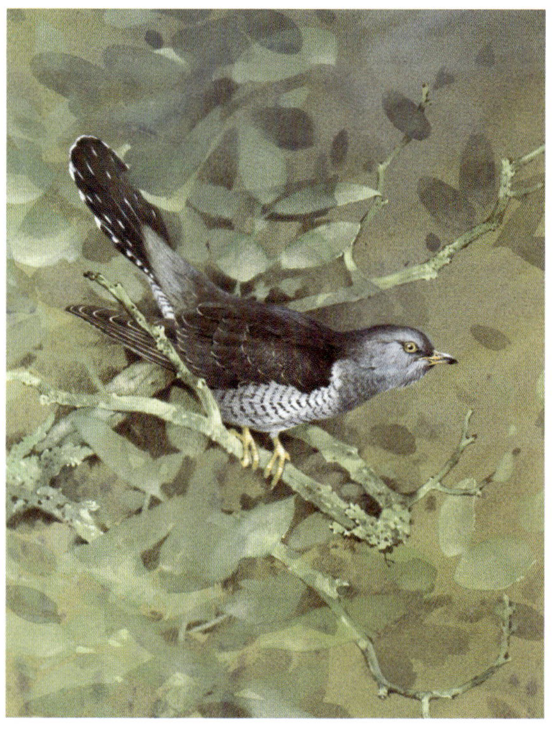

The cuckoo – the sound of spring – a declining sound.

Through inspiration, his art became conservation. What he saw and what he loved became his passion and his art. He loved beauty, he loved nature, and he loved the farm fields that made up his countryside. People too were part of his vision; the farmers, the tractor drivers and the shepherds who helped to create a living and a working countryside. The land was a place where nature and country people co-existed side by side; he saw it as a unique place of culture and of community life. Every day of the year was an adventure to him with new beginnings heralding the seasons and bringing fresh experiences and feelings. The arrival of the cuckoo; a woodcock flying silently through the trees; deer standing among bluebells and yes, the rattle of pips in an apple showing it was ready for eating – all these things gave him delight and gave him purpose. He grieved as he saw the countryside being ripped apart by modern industrialised agriculture; he was angered as he saw landscapes and wildlife taking second and third place to development and short-term economic gain and he could not understand how governments, through their policies, could actively break up rural communities and destroy the rural culture that delighted him so much. The demise of the British orchard was part of his concern and bewilderment – French, Dutch, South American and North American apples in the supermarkets during our own apple harvest. What was going on?

All these feelings were the feelings of a true countryman, but in total contradiction Gordon was born near the Pool of London on 31 October – Halloween – 1936 where his father worked as a lighterman. He was always proud of his London roots and he regarded it as a huge honour when he received the Freedom of the City of London in 1993. The importance of London to him is shown by his wonderful painting of Tower Bridge in the final book that he produced, *The Artist and his Work*. The launch of the book was in Tower Bridge itself and it remains one of my few regrets in life that I was unable to attend. There Gordon was among his friends and admirers, in a setting that linked him

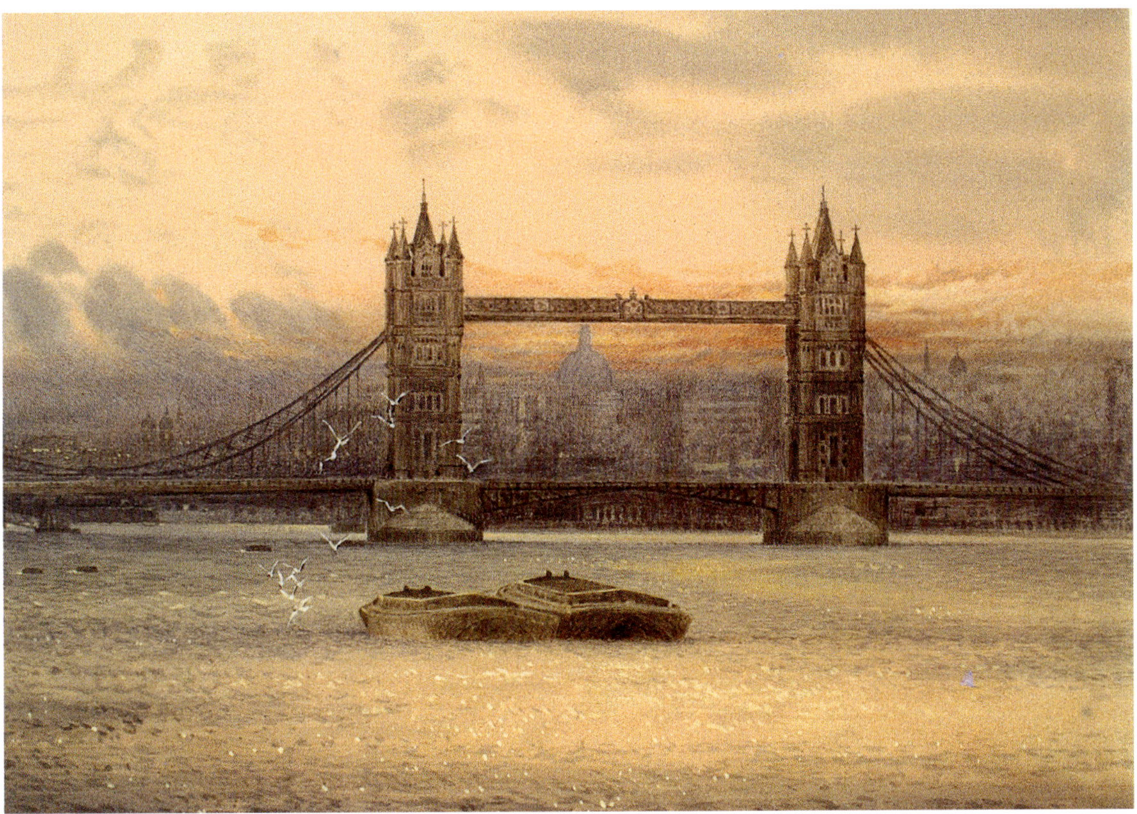

Gordon's home ground – London's Tower Bridge.

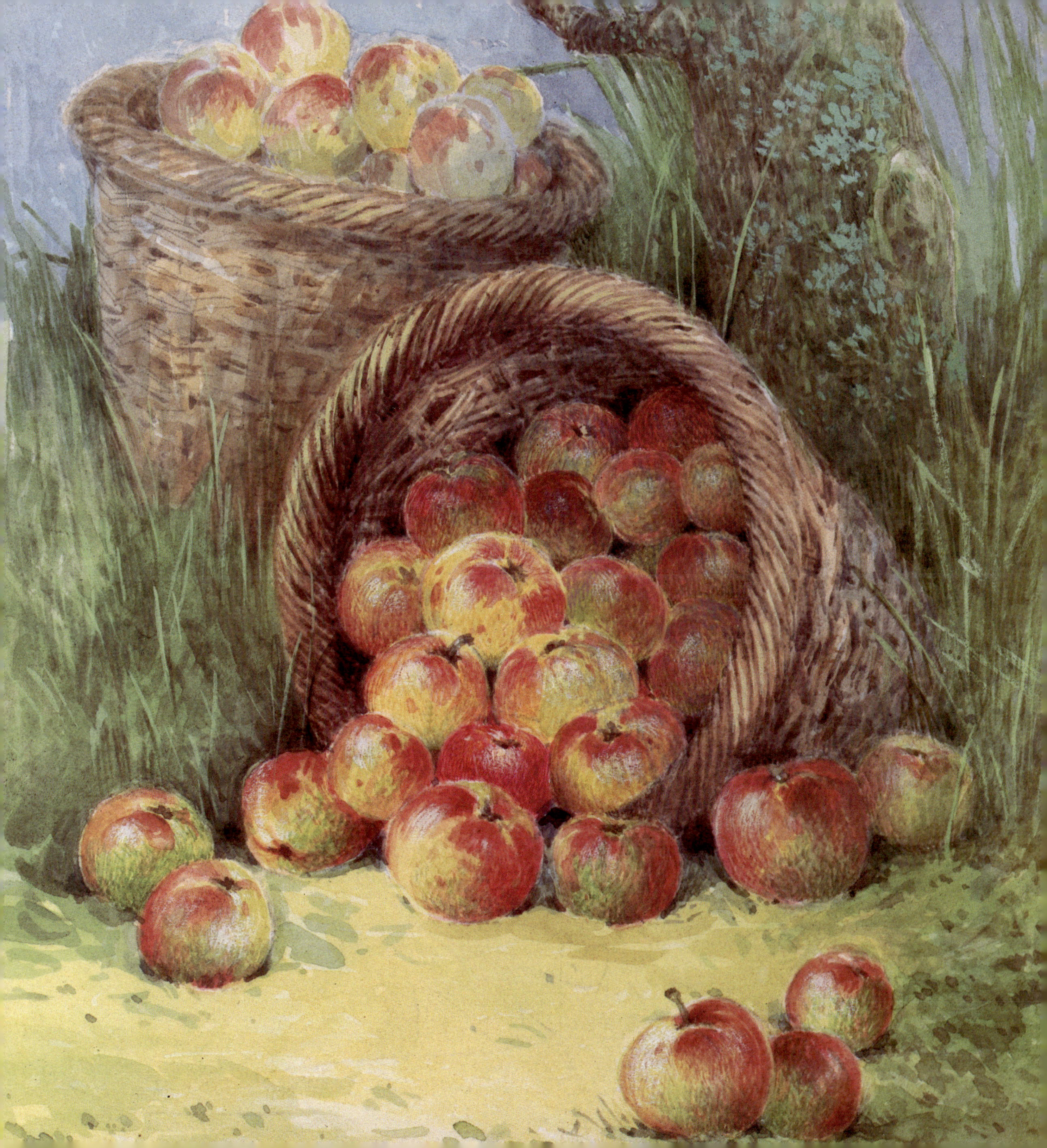

with his past, and a wonderful time was enjoyed by one and all. Unfortunately I missed it – I was filming *One Man and His Dog* somewhere in the north of England at the time, for the BBC – I write 'unfortunately' as that proved to be the last proper series of an exceptional programme before it was dumbed down by the BBC's urban establishment. Despite his love of London, Gordon became an 'Evacuee' during the Second World War and went to live in the country; later he came to see it as a release. His country life was a revelation and gave him a freedom and a pleasure that remained with him until the end of his life. Every day was an adventure and an exploration. In the early days he discovered for the first time hedgerows, blackberries, butterflies and birds and when Betty became his childhood sweetheart, it became a journey of discovery for both of them, a quest that continued with their daughters Sally and Sarah. This sense of adventure stayed with him right until his death on 4 May 1998. I would get phone calls saying, 'Have you heard the cuckoo? – I have' – 'I've seen my first brimstone butterfly today – have you?' – 'I've got long-tailed tits swinging on my nuts; I've never seen that before, isn't it incredible?' It was incredible, for a few days afterwards in the late 1990s I too had long-tailed tits swinging from my peanuts. 'Swinging on his nuts?' Gordon always had a sense of humour.

How the message circulated through the country's long-tailed tit population is unknown but after watching blue tits and great tits swing on peanuts, suddenly long-tailed tits decided to

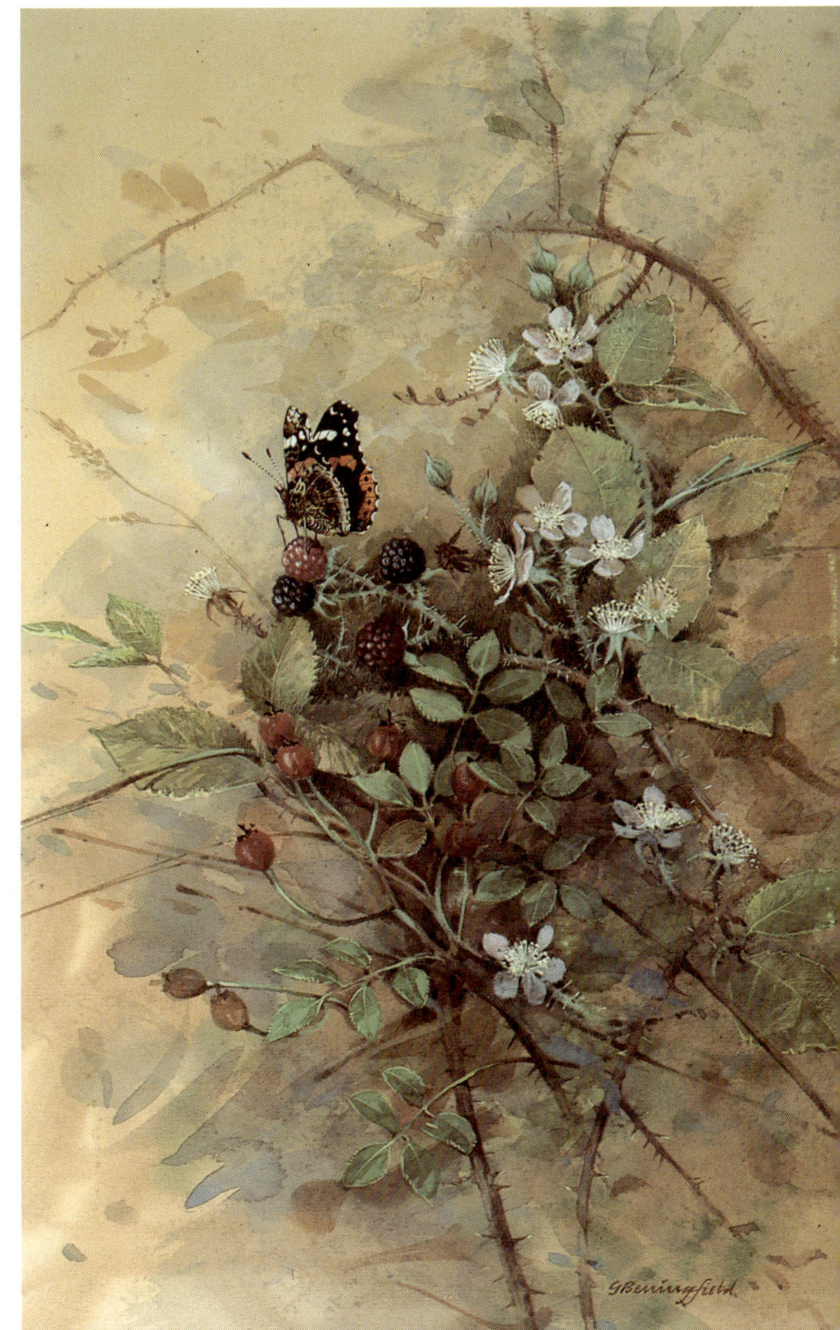

RIGHT: *A red admiral on blackberries.*

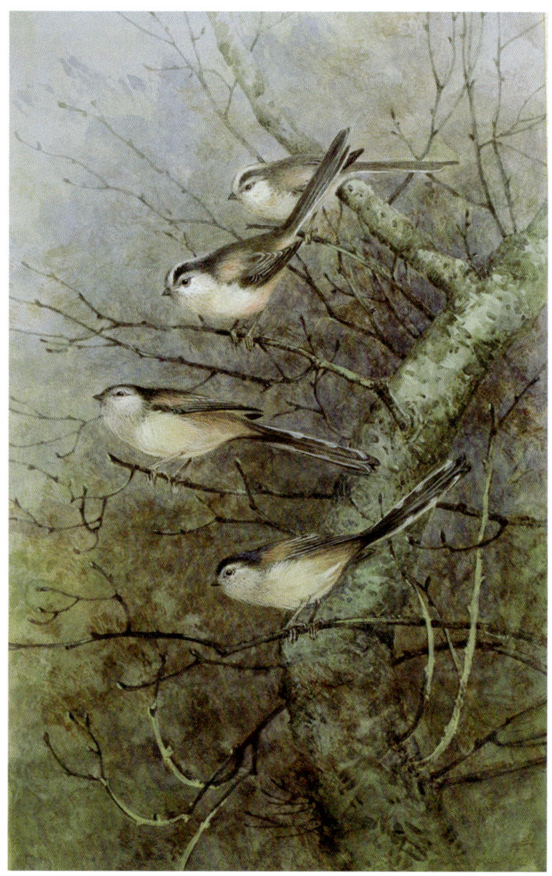

ABOVE: *Long-tailed tits.*

follow suit and the message of success and satisfaction seemed to spread rapidly through the entire long-tailed tit population. Interestingly since then the message has spread to goldfinches and as I write this, for the first time ever, I have a solitary robin, from a population of several in the neighbourhood, that swings and feeds from my peanuts.

Gordon's loss was one that all his family and friends still feel. It was a premature parting that left us grieving. But even in sorrow there were positive things to say and think about a good man. Gordon was vital in the formation of the Countryside Restoration Trust, which involved restoring and healing fields that had been damaged by over-intensive farming. Its first fields were in fact part of the flood plains of a tributary to the Cam; they were planted with the traditional hay meadow mixture of seventy grasses and wild flowers pioneered by the great Dame Miriam Rothschild. One of the flowers that her mixture brought back to my village and the CRT's Lark Rise Farm was the once common cowslip. By the time of Gordon's funeral, cowslips had returned in such large numbers that I picked a bucketful of them for his wreath. It summed up the life and work of Gordon Beningfield; how he loved, how he fought, how he appreciated the things of the traditional countryside and from the seeds of that wreath it is hoped that cowslips will grow on his grave for many generations to come.

Of the work that Gordon left behind was a collection of paintings and sketches about fruit, apples and orchards. It is this collection that has formed the basis for *Beningfield's Orchards*. After talking to Betty we decided that these pictures were far too valuable to simply allow to stay unseen in Gordon's studio or even to sell them off individually. So it was decided to track down as many other unpublished pictures that Gordon produced during his painting life, to create this one final book. Some of those found were a complete surprise, such as a beautiful mountain hare – then there were more butterflies, bluebells and a magnificent landscape of a river, water meadows and distant cattle. Not only is it a tribute to Gordon's great artistic talent but it also shows the message behind his art. Sadly, Britain has become a supermarket society forgetting its link

RIGHT: *A variety of Laxton desert apple bred by the famous Bedfordshire Laxton family.*

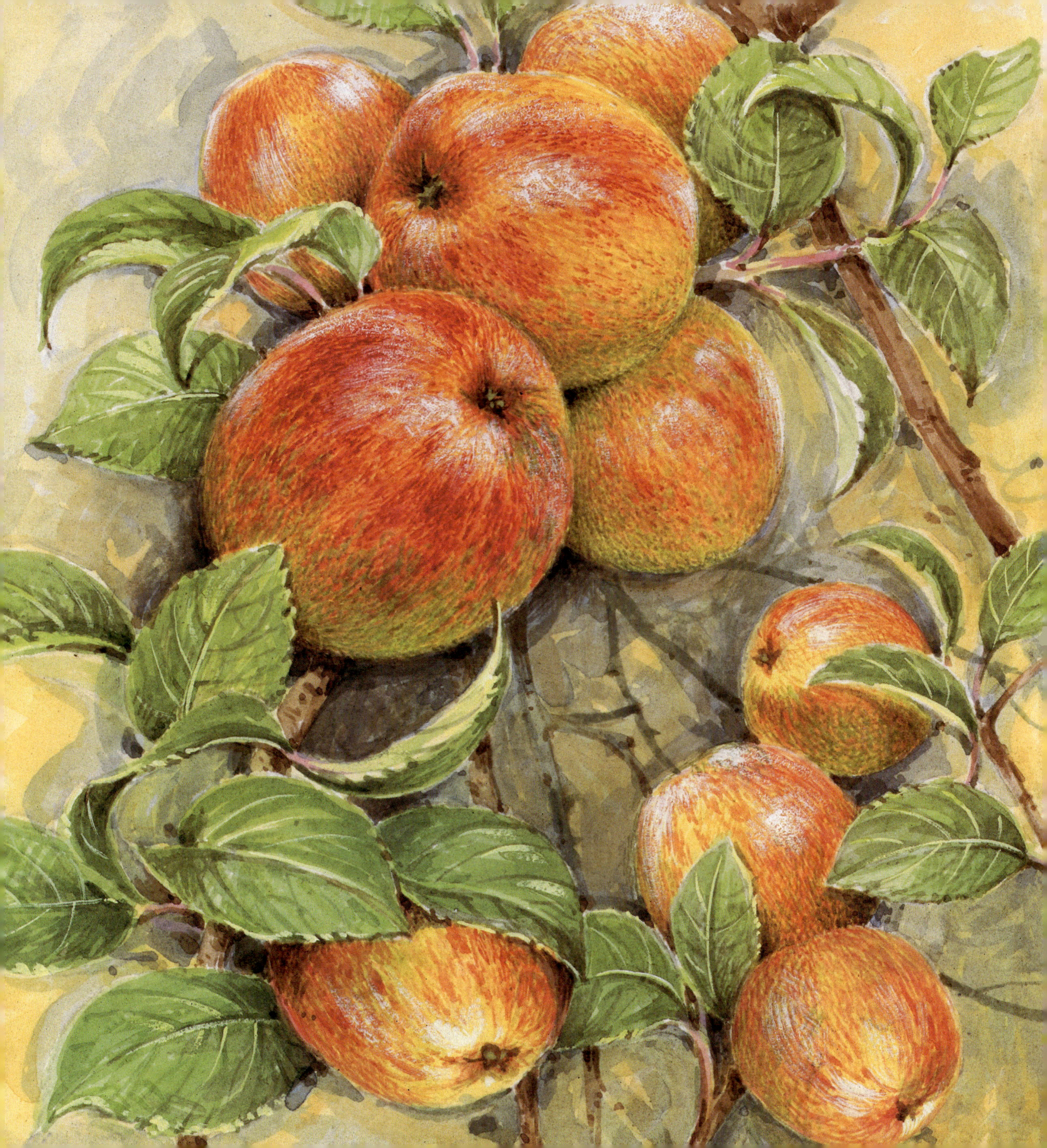

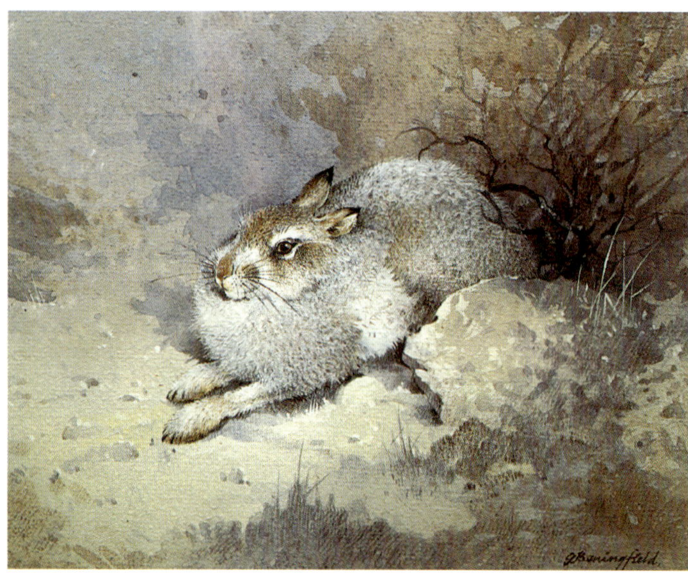

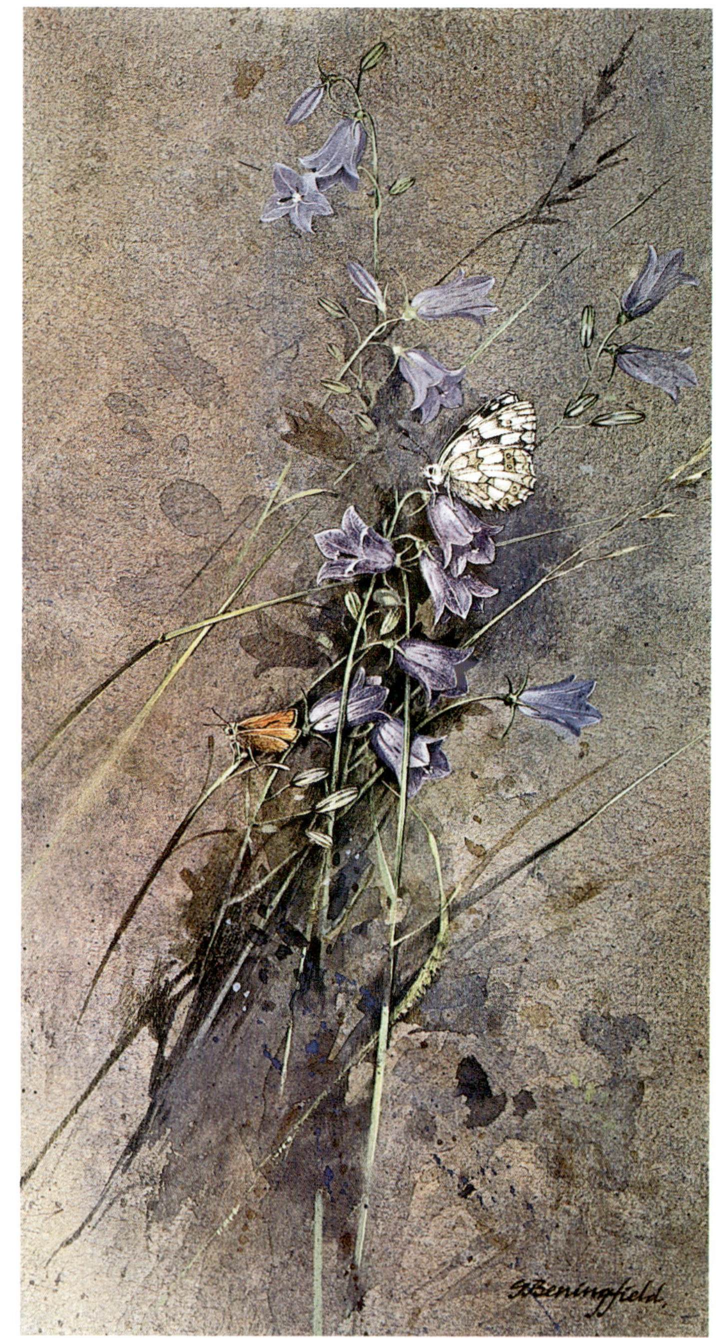

ABOVE: *A mountain hare.*
RIGHT: *Butterflies move from illustration to art.*

with real food and preferring cheap imported second rate produce – the message behind his apple art is simple – lose your apples – lose your countryside.

Gordon's own orchard gave him immense pleasure. He loved it as it provided the elements of wildlife that first made him famous. It produced wild flowers that others regarded as weeds, and it gave him butterflies which he saw almost as flying flowers – things of fragile beauty. Through his skill and his vision he turned butterfly illustration into art, and sketches into pictures of great beauty and delicacy. His own small orchard gave him a view of nature through the seasons, it gave him blossom, insects, birds, fruit, and winter fieldfares and redwings. It also gave him nettles and thistles,

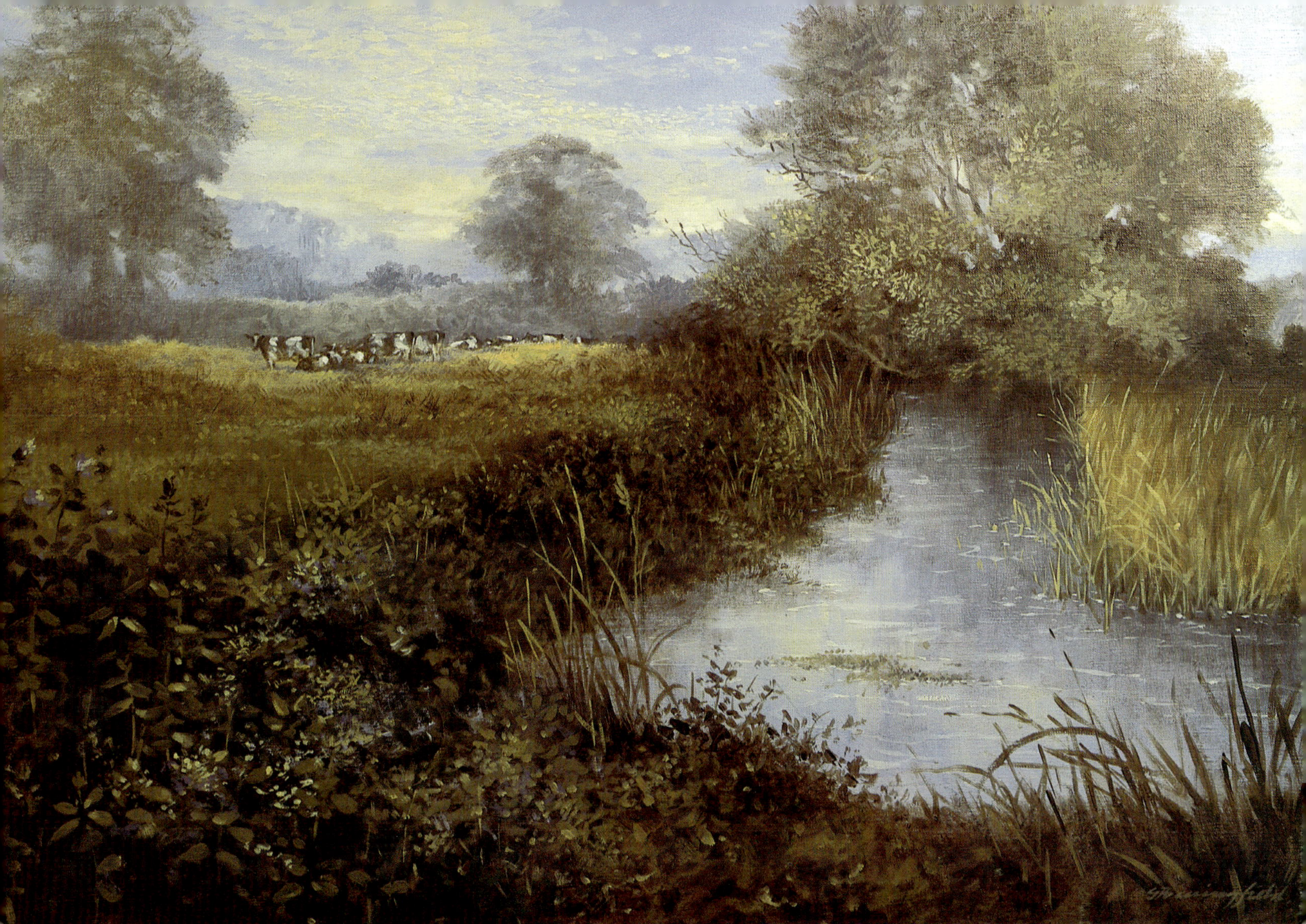

Grazing cattle and water meadows.

bindweed and twitch, all the plants that an orthodox gardener or farmer hates. In late summer he would have to wade waist deep through this stinging and pricking jungle to pick his fruit.

His art was remarkable. It developed from simple and almost self-conscious painting to the most delicate and intricate of work that to the ordinary eye simply defied belief. This transformation is shown clearly by some of the paintings here. The turnstones, redshank and ringed plovers (overleaf) were part of Gordon's earlier work and found by Betty in his study after we had completed *Beningfield's Vanishing Songbirds*, which was a pity; despite not being songbirds they would have added to the book, but that has been one of the problems. Gordon was an artist not a book-keeper

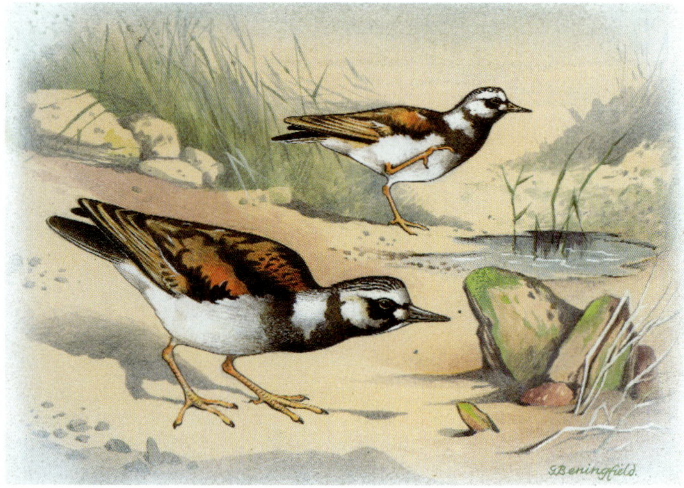

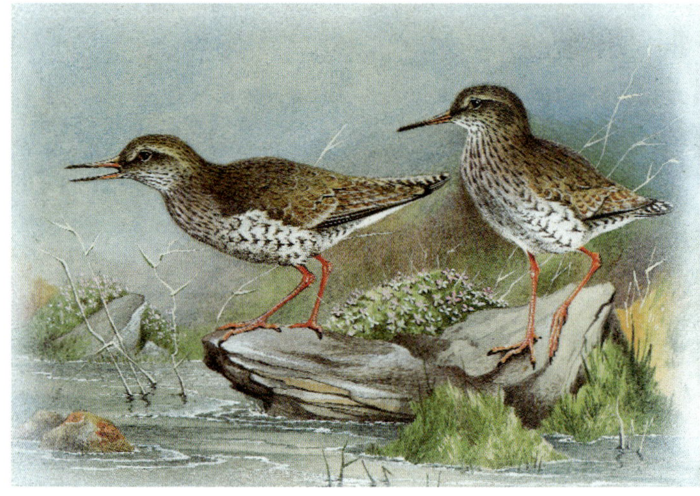

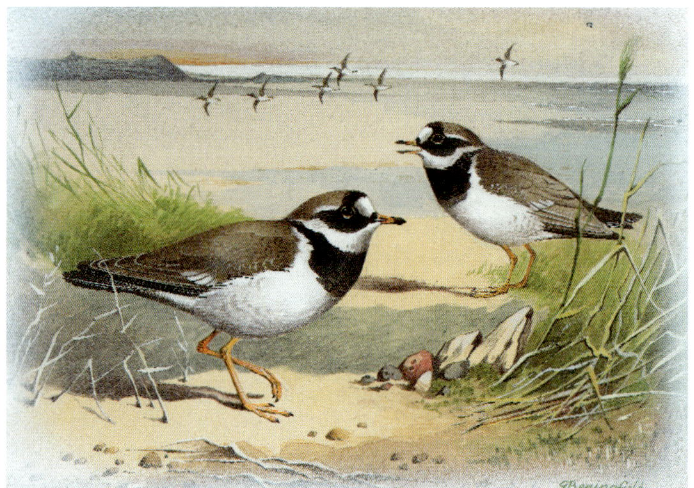

ABOVE LEFT: *Turnstones.*
ABOVE RIGHT: *Redshanks.*
LEFT: *Ringed plovers.*

and so he failed to keep accurate records of what he painted or where the paintings went. From these beautiful and stylised pictures his work developed incredibly as shown in his painting of bluebells and fallow deer. He loved woods and trees of all sorts and of course a wood around a farm, with fruit, is an orchard, and he loved them too. Woods with deer were a real part of his life and linked him strongly to Dorset. Because of this he became a self-taught expert on the works of Thomas Hardy and each year in spring and autumn he would look for deer in Powerstock Forest, often with his friend, the writer, Brian Jackman. It is fitting that the *Woodland Trust* now has a new wood in Dorset – Beningfield Wood.

All this was not bad for a boy who suffered from dyslexia and who left school at fifteen. Out of his love for Hertfordshire and Hardy country, much further south, came his love of farms and villages and his appreciation for farm animals, from the bull looking over a gate to sheep through all seasons of the year. Many of Hardy's characters were shepherds, or there were shepherds who led their flocks through his books, and Gordon became a collector of shepherds' crooks, lanterns, and bells, and he had a shepherd's hut in his garden. He painted them too with love and affection and the whole countryside, the whole culture, continually affected him and became part of his work.

Unlike so many conservationists, particularly those with a media image to maintain, Gordon would not sit on the fence; when he saw what he loved being damaged or threatened he fought, and as a result he spoke on platforms up and down the country. He criticised, he harangued, he showed the beauty under threat in his work and his audiences loved him for it.

RIGHT: *A rare Gloucester bull.*

BELOW: *Fallow deer in bluebells.*

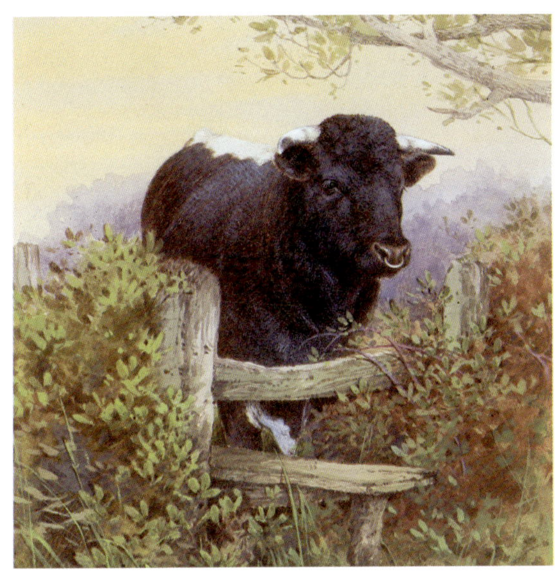

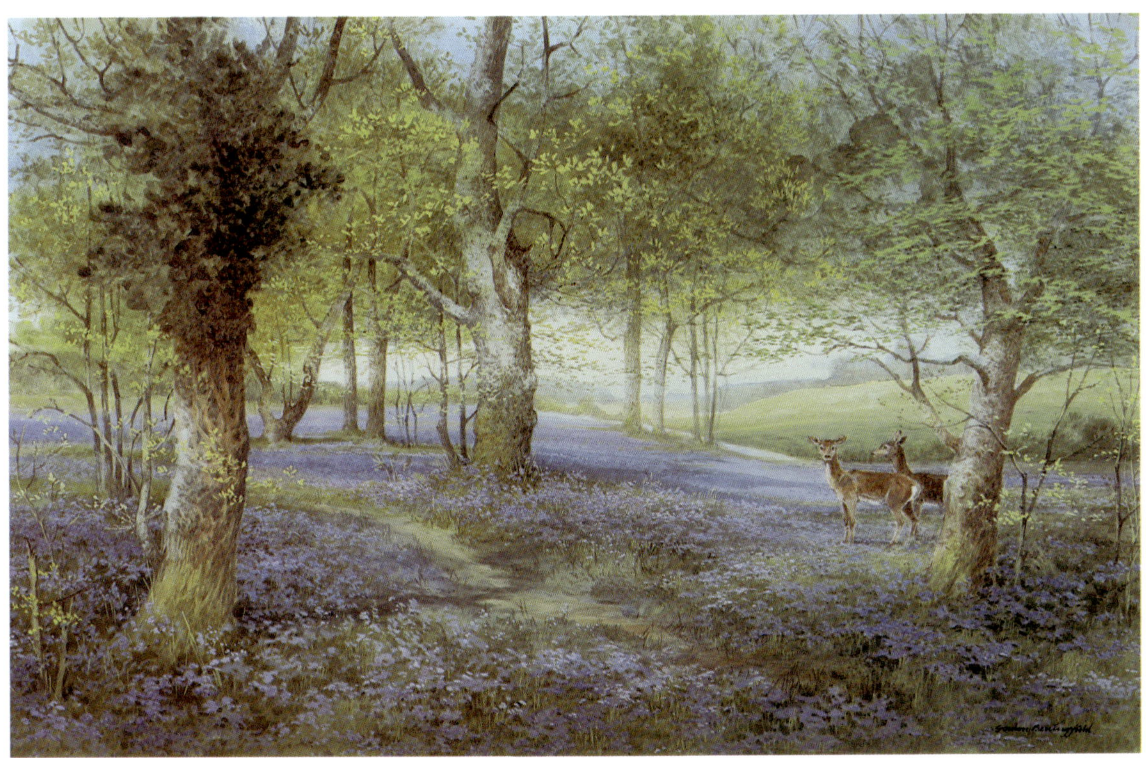

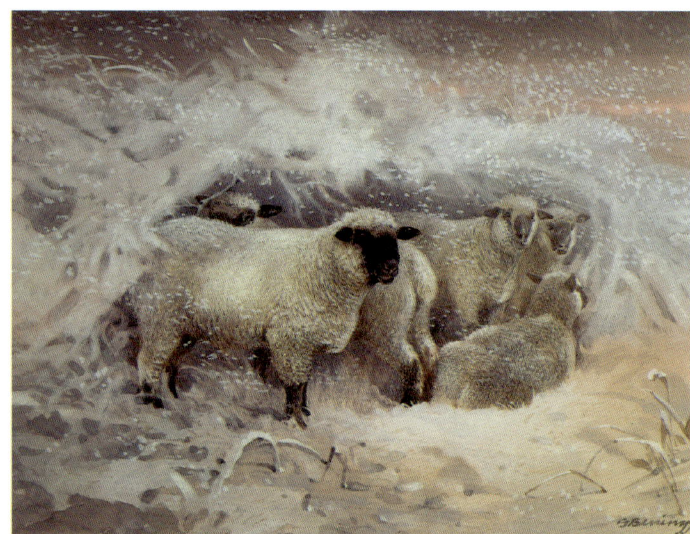

LEFT: *Sheep – a favourite Beningfield subject.*
BELOW: *The fox – an animal Gordon enjoyed painting and sketching.*

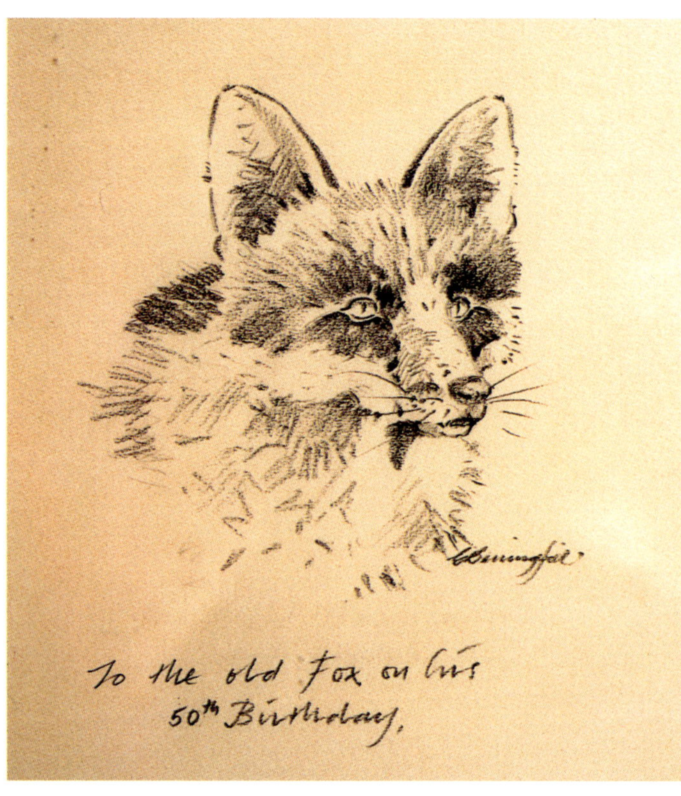

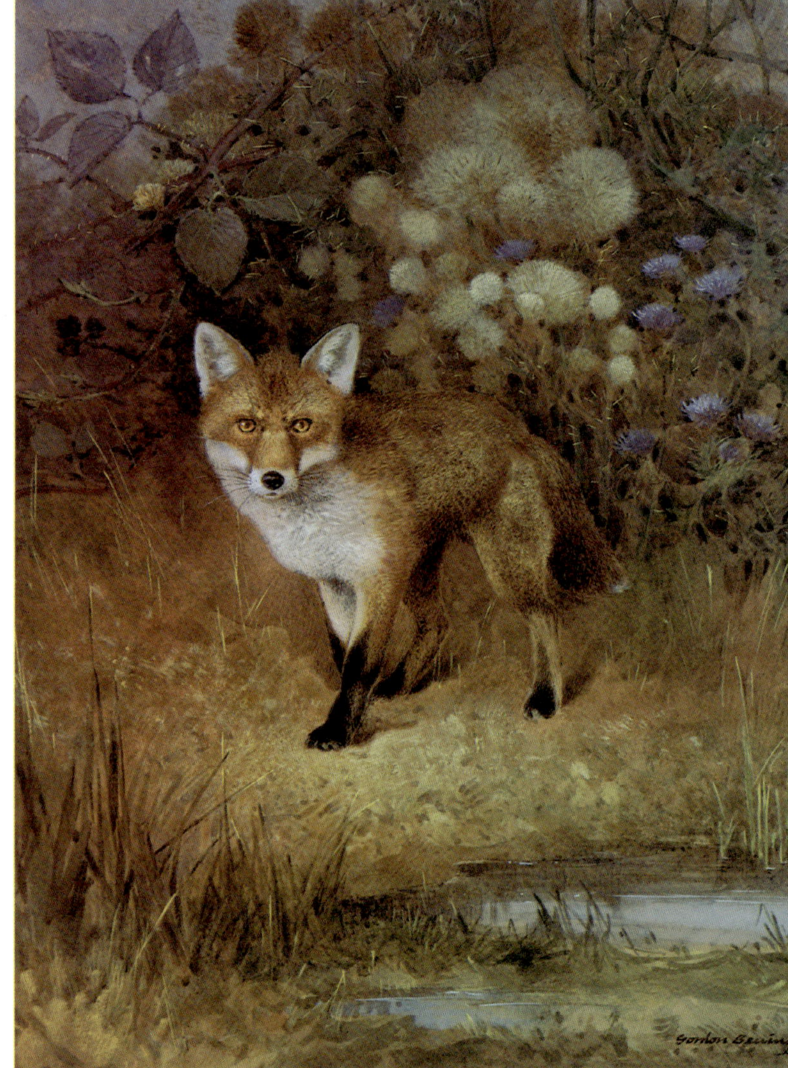

I had the privilege of sharing platforms with him on several occasions and they are memories that I cherish. It was an honour to speak with a man who I regarded as my closest friend and it was heart warming to see how ordinary people responded to him. At the end of a meeting he would be surrounded by those simply wanting to say, 'Hello, I agree with you – thankyou.'

Although conservation and the destruction of the countryside are serious and depressing subjects, Gordon was a very amusing and a happy man. I first met him when he wanted to interview me for a television programme, and film my tame vixen, Rusty. He loved foxes too and pictures and sketches of foxes featured regularly in his work. From the very first moment that I met him not only did I regard him as a serious conservationist but also as a very funny man and good company. Yes, times were serious; yes, there is cause for sadness – even despair – but he loved to laugh. He laughed, he talked, he joked, and the audiences laughed with him; he laughed at bureaucracy, at politicians, at madness and they laughed too; he painted beauty and poked fun at absurdity. His collection of photographs show his sense of fun – jiving with Betty. He loved parties, he loved music, he loved making a fool of himself, and he loved dressing up. He was a great fan of the music of the late Glenn Miller – whose plane went down in the war – and he struck up a long-

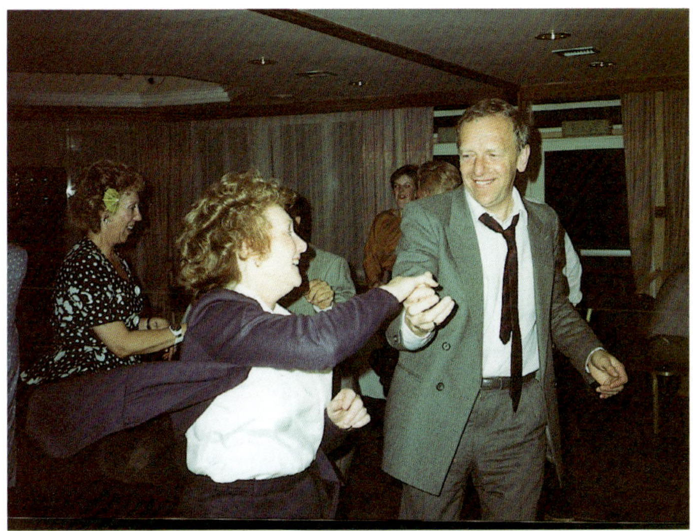

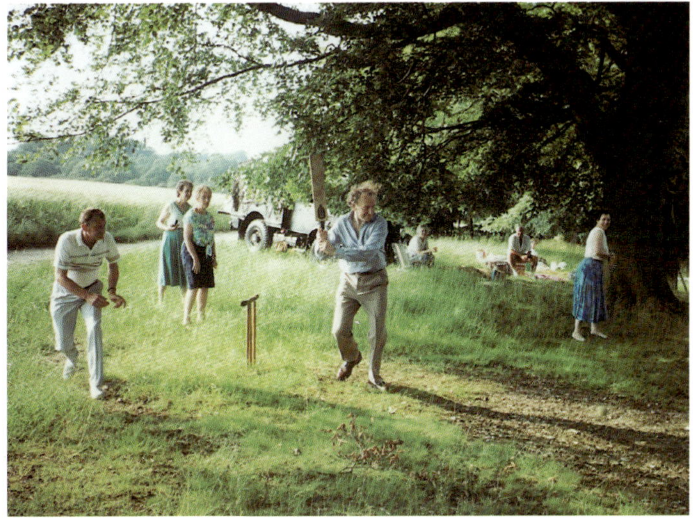

lasting friendship with Glenn Miller's brother, Herb. He enjoyed informal and spontaneous games of cricket with his friends and family, and he did all those things that most families do, but he laughed longer than most. He drove through the countryside in his two MGs, dressed up like a spitfire fighter pilot, with goggles, and nothing gave him greater pleasure than to visit the Duxford Imperial War Museum. There he admired those old planes that had once flown over the skies of London and still lingered on in his memories from boyhood.

Walking through the countryside with him was an education, looking, listening and laughing – what a combination. 'Is that a linnet?' 'Yes it's a linnet, innit' and so it went on right up to the end when he lost his hard fought battle with cancer. I hope that this book will continue his fight for the countryside, because our orchards, our farms, our way of life remain important and remain threatened. There continues to be a feeling of betrayal in the air for country people and I hope that his art helps to show that betrayal, and inspires people to resist it.

One of the great pleasures of producing this book has been to go back to Gordon's house at Water End and to look at his pictures with Betty and Sally, his elder daughter, and to think

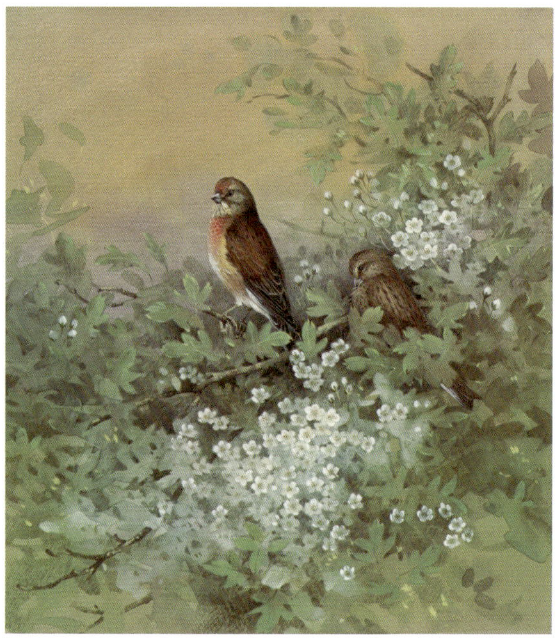

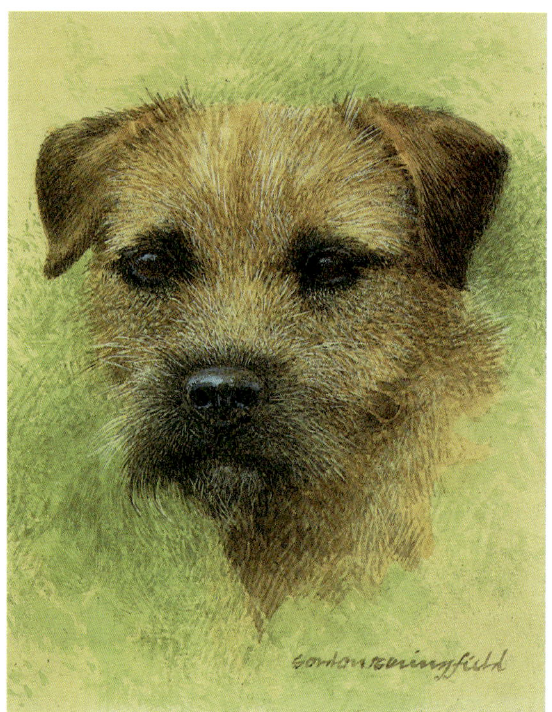

ABOVE: *A bush with a linnet in it.*
LEFT: *Not Gordon's Ted, but Sally's Rosey.*

how best to portray and display them. Betty too has a wonderful sense of humour and is a country woman through and through. There in the house is Ted, Gordon's little terrier that he loved so much. Now eight and still with a sense of puppy fun, plus the yapping bark of a true adult terrier. Gordon's sheep bells are in the corner and the smell of cooking from Betty's oven remains unchanged. What a wonderful country cook she is, and of course as we discussed orchards she fed me on apples – apple cake, apple pie and her wonderful apple and sausage casserole.

I hope many of those who read and enjoy *Beningfield's Orchards* will join those organisations mentioned at the back of the book; they are all still fighting hard to save the countryside that Gordon loved so much. I hope too that as they buy their food – their apples and plums – they will seek to buy them from British orchards and farms to help ensure their survival.

Being involved with the creation of *Beningfield's Orchards* has been an emotional experience as orchards have been an important part of my life from the time that I was a small child. Indeed apples were even important to me when I started writing for a living. At one point I lived as a tramp for a month, travelling under the name of James Grieve, a delicious variety of eating apple. I suppose that if I had been a woman I would have travelled as Granny Smith.

At one time nearly every lowland farm in Britain had a small orchard around its farmhouse and farmyard. We did, and remnants of

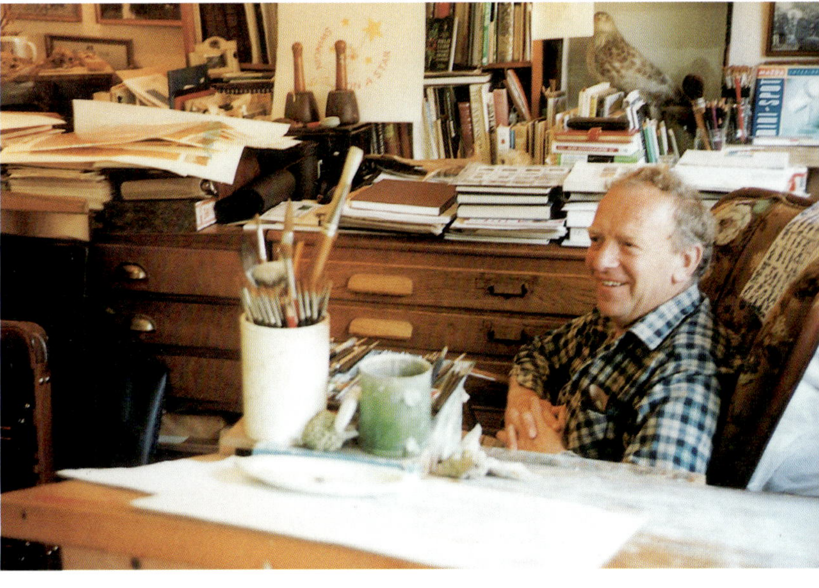

Gordon in his studio.

our old orchard can still be seen as well as a new one that I planted in the mid 1960s. My grandmother had a farm too and that was surrounded by old apple, pear and plum trees. In our farmhouse garden we had numerous fruit trees including a tree that grew the reddest and sourest of apples I have ever seen and virtually each apple always had its own maggot. One day I spent the whole day picking these maggot-filled apples and putting them in boxes which Father then took to the local market. I was disappointed when he brought back just sixpence for all those apples. The sadness today is that even with high quality, beautifully grown apples the producers in Britain get virtually nothing and so the acreage of orchards is falling and falling. At about the time when we went into the European Union – then called the European Economic Community – yes, we were lured in by political deception; Britain had about 153,500 acres of orchard. Today, thanks to cheap imports; the ignorance of supermarket buyers; the dominance of supermarkets distorting the market; the naiveté of consumers and the destructive influence of globalisation, the acreage of orchards in Britain today is only 53,500 acres representing a dramatic decrease of almost 66 per cent.

The memories of the orchard in my early years remain as clear as if they were yesterday; the white blossom of early spring as the plums burst into bloom, then the tinge of pink in May as apple blossom was the last blossom in the orchard; the wild crab apple blossom came too, scenting the hedgerows. It was when the blossom came that Father and Mother hoped there would not be a frost. 'We don't want the blossom to be cut'; they would say 'if we get a frost there will be no fruit'. To

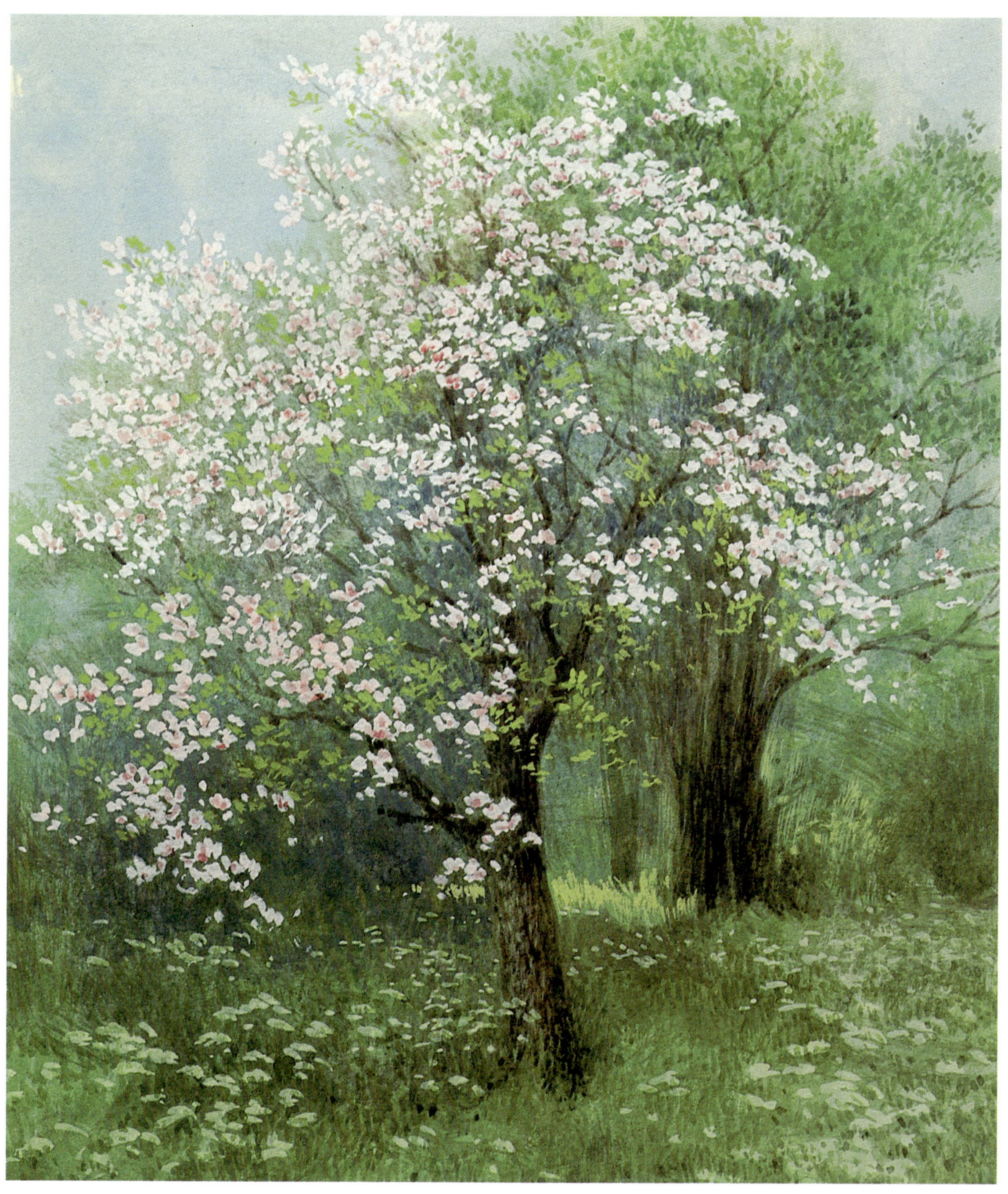

emphasise the point I had a great-uncle and aunt from the Fens who had a commercial orchard. They would tell us tales of how in the early days of their fruit farm, they had successive years when the frost cut their fruit and their debts grew and grew until they were on the verge of bankruptcy. Then war came with a season of abundant fruit and they were saved; they went on to farm for years at Gorefield just outside Wisbech in the Fens. In those early days too we had surplus fruit and Father would get us to help him pick it, put it in boxes and on our tractor and trailer we would take it to the railway station a mile down the road. Beautiful Early River plums with our fingerprints in their bloom were sent off to Liverpool by train, loaded up in the parish and sent off to all parts of England. That was before motorway madness arrived, when small quantities could still be sent to all four corners of Britain.

Now the Government's tax income from petrol and the obsession with size means that our roads are cluttered up with lorries and that large buyers will not take small quantities from small producers. It is a tragedy; as the politicians claim that our standard of living is rising, the quality of our lives is falling: as noise, size, pollution and speed all increase, so our awareness, sensitivity, and individuality all steadily decrease. The names of the fruit were as attractive as the plums, pears and apples themselves; there were Worcesters, Russets, Coxes, Blenheims; and of course the wonderful Bramley cooking apple. As well as these there were William pears, a pear so much tastier and juicier than the ubiquitous Conference. Then there were plums, in addition to the Early River there were Greengages, Monarchs, Victorias and Czars. Each one with a flavour and attraction of its own. Go into the supermarket today and the average shopper – sorry, they are now called 'consumers' – would be forgiven for thinking that temperate fruits were not grown in temperate Britain. Many of the countries from which the fruit comes are not temperate, but warm and the fruit lacks the taste of the British Cox, William pear or the Czar plum. There you have it; box after box, row after row of the inaccurately named French Golden Delicious – more like French Golden Disgusting; pears from Israel, large, plump and shining with an unnatural shine and a taste of mildly sugared water. Don't the customers know what real plums taste like and don't they know that plums are not highly polished but have an individual bloom? And then come the pears. There seems to be only one pear bought by the supermarkets – the Conference – a crisp Conference pear is a very acceptable fruit, but those from the continent have a much blander taste than those grown in English soils. The politicians tell us that the dominance of the supermarkets is not harmful – the consumer gets 'choice'. Yes, the consumer gets choice – it gets the choice of the supermarket. Those who want to eat English apples, plums and pears, have to eat instead, the foreign choices of the supermarkets, which is no choice at all.

And so it is a pleasure to have helped Betty Beningfield to produce not only a tribute to Gordon Beningfield, but a tribute to the British orchard, the British farm, and the British countryside. All these aspects of rural Britain need support. Support it by eating an English Cox or an Early River and enjoy them as much as I hope you will enjoy this book.

Robin Page – Apple Blossom Time – 2004

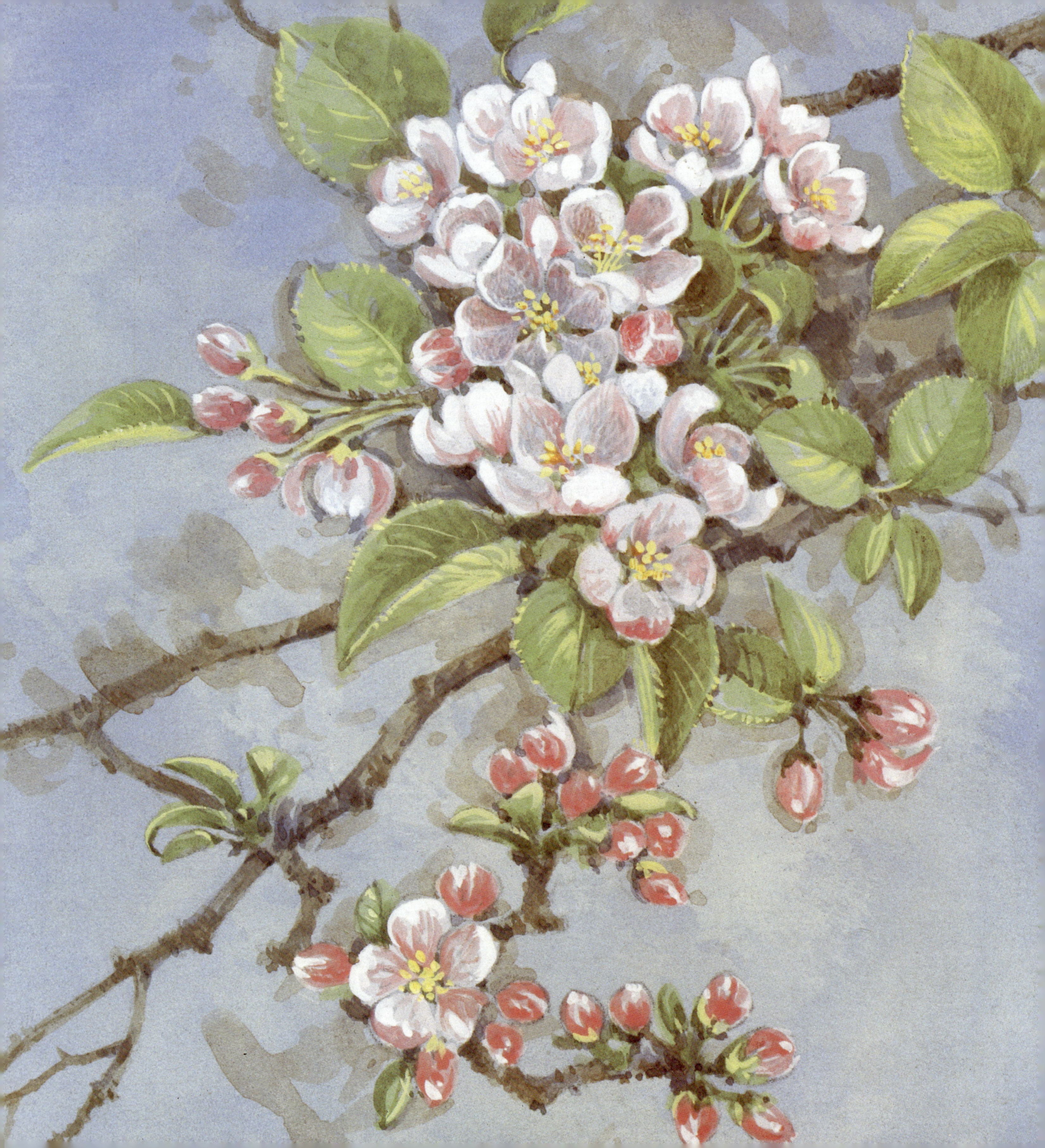

CHAPTER ONE

The Orchard

Gordon was always a great believer in tradition and one of the attractions to him about the English countryside was the place of orchards on farms and in country gardens. When he first moved into the countryside from London, nearly every farm and farmhouse was surrounded by a little orchard. Country houses, cottages and council houses also had their clumps of fruit trees at the bottom of the garden and self-sufficiency seemed to be the aim of all, from farmer to ferreter and from Duke to dustman. Consequently when we moved to Water End in 1974 Gordon was so pleased to have a little orchard, about half an acre in size; it was a total delight to him. Several of the old trees still remain and they are very old trees too. We have a huge ancient Bramley apple; in addition we have two other apple trees and they are so old and so unusual that we simply do not know what variety they are. I ought to have the varieties

RIGHT: *Bramley apples on an ancient tree – with hawthorn berries.*

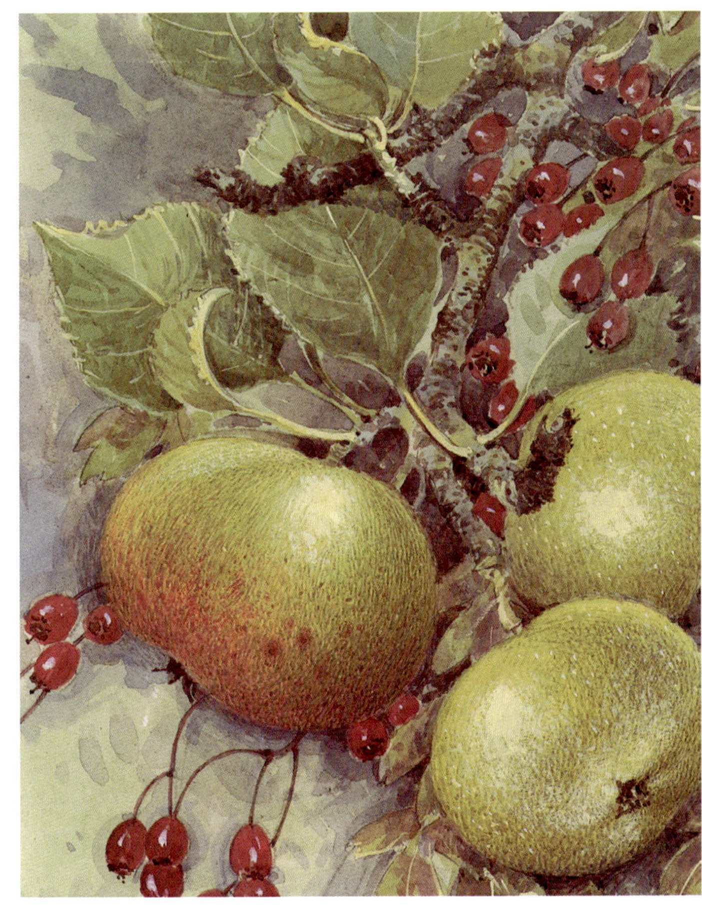

identified if possible. With the apples went plums, pears and hazel nuts, and so we have always had plenty of home grown fruit. Consequently the orchard year gave Gordon not only a harvest of fruit but also birds and butterflies; an abundance of wildlife to paint and to enjoy – it gave him pleasure.

The orchard year is a long one and does not simply spread from blossom until fruiting; an orchard is important for every month of the year and certainly ours is attractive from January to December. Whenever people came, Gordon would take them with pride to our beautiful wild orchard and it really was beautiful, and it really was wild. In the spring the succession of blossom was always a picture; plum, pear and then later on apple. Apple blossom is so delicate, fragile, white with a touch of pink and a very sweet smell. There are great varieties too in the shades of apple blossom from almost white to almost scarlet. In addition to this we also have what is considered by many to be the wild plum – bullace. It is a small yellow plum which when ripe is full of juice and ideal for making jam. That was yet another great attraction of

BELOW: *Snowdrops in the Beningfield wild orchard.*
RIGHT: *Orchard blossom.*

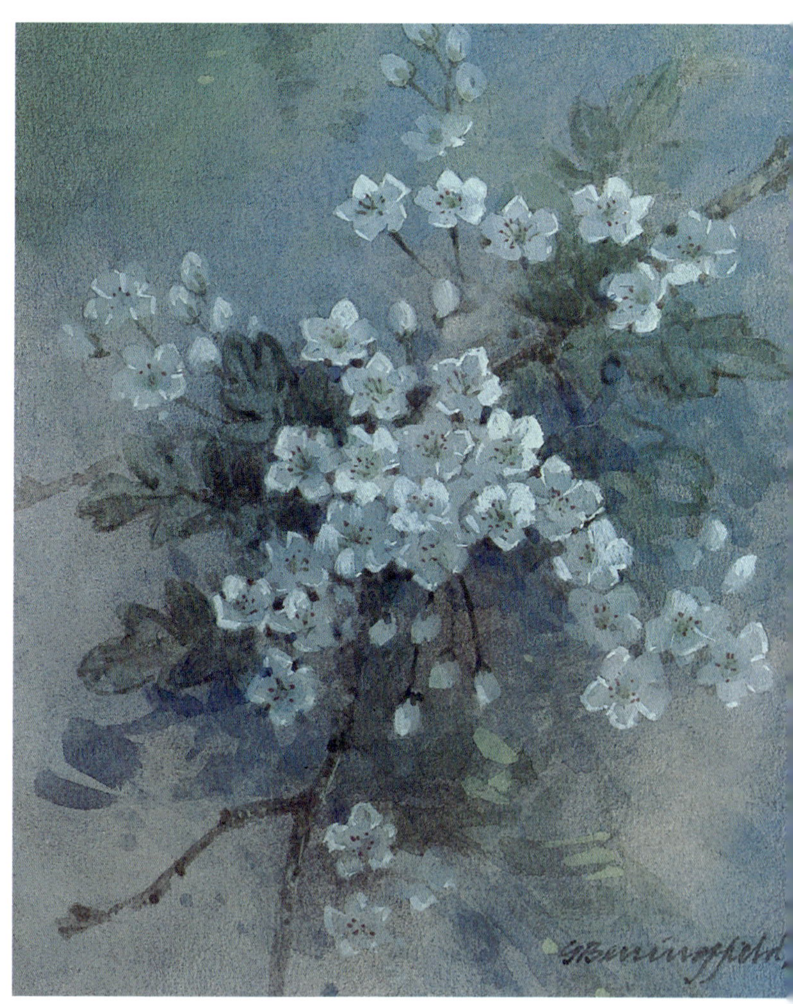

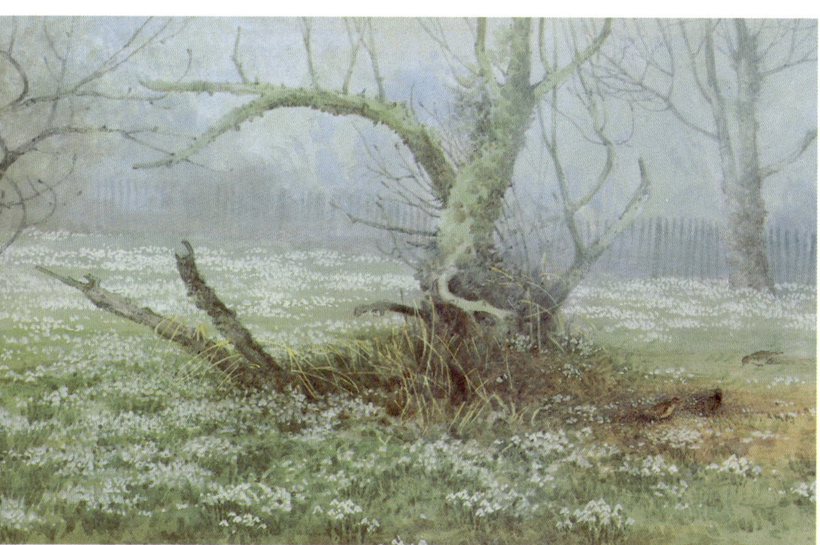

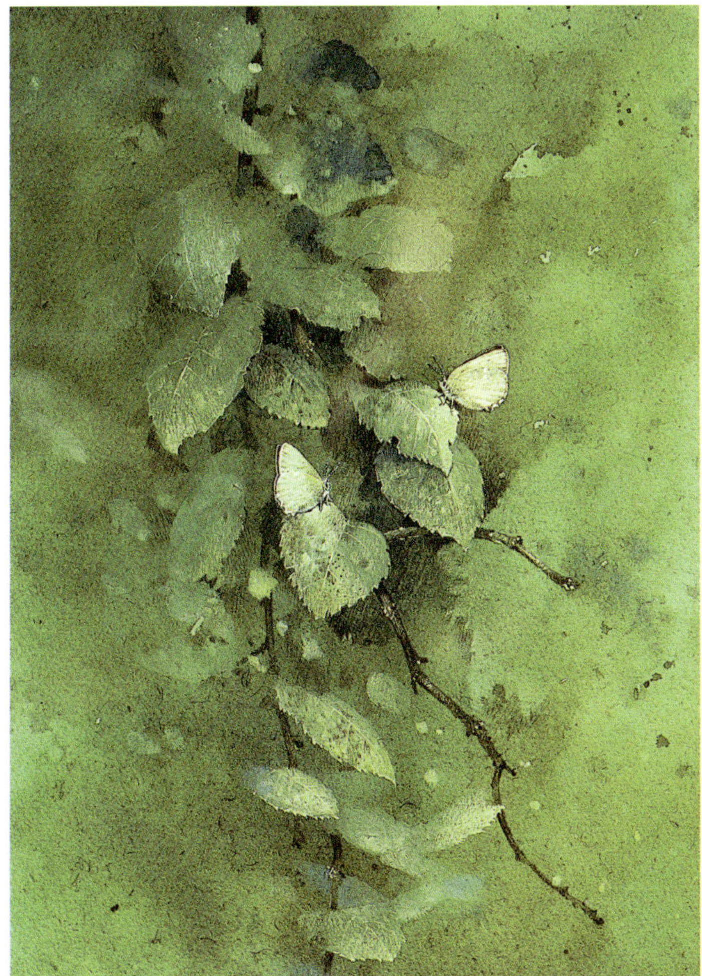

The green hairstreak.

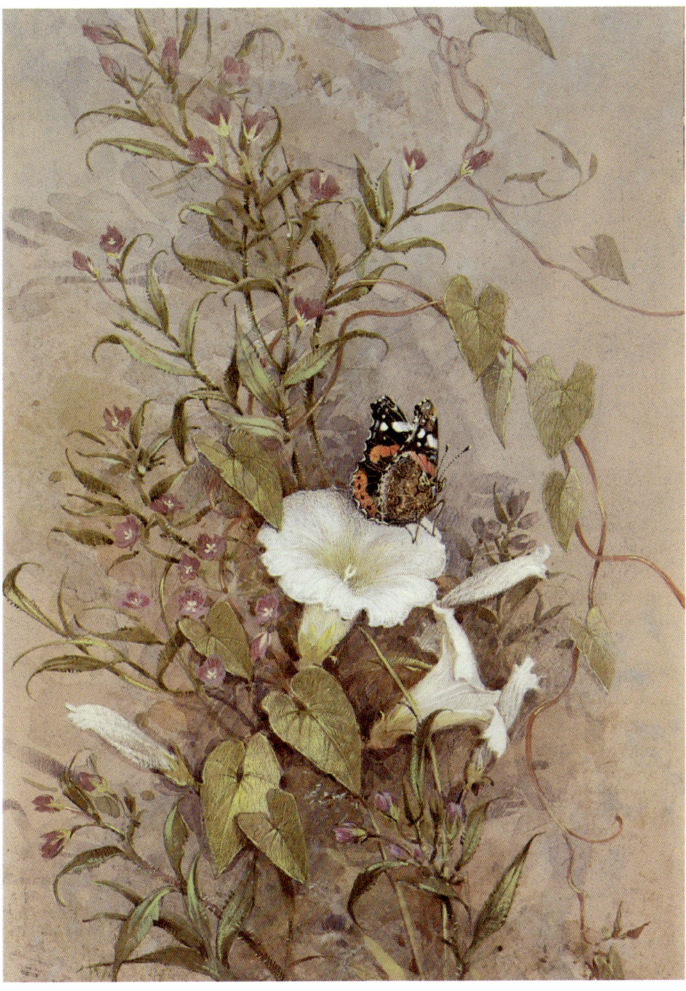

A red admiral on larger bindweed.

the orchard because I love cooking, so Gordon could eat the fruit or we could enjoy a variety of puddings and pies.

As Gordon's interest in butterflies developed so our little orchard became wilder and wilder. The flowering year in fact started before the blossom, it started with wild snowdrops, hundreds and hundreds of them, from their sheer numbers they must have been growing in this little orchard for very many generations. After the snowdrops come the daffodils and then yes, nettles and thistles as Gordon allowed these rampant thriving plants to grow beneath the trees to attract

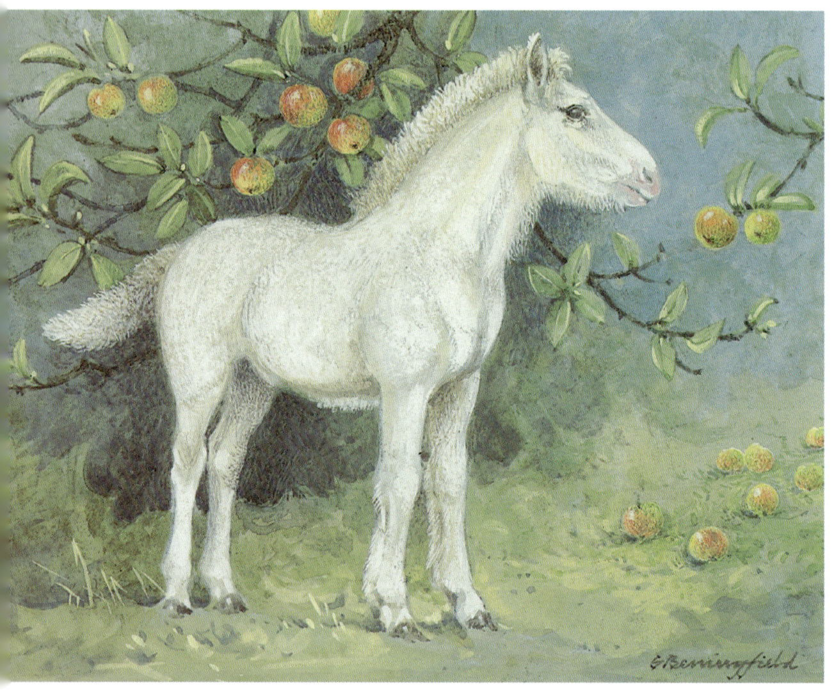

the butterflies and insects – and how the butterflies loved the orchard – all sorts of butterflies from the common red admiral, small tortoiseshell and peacock to the less common ones such as the visiting painted lady. It was always something of a mystery to Gordon why we never had one of his favourite little butterflies, the green hairstreak, in the orchard. All the necessary food plants for the caterpillar were there, including the buds of bramble and dogwood, and even the buds of runner beans. One of the most beautiful paintings that Gordon ever painted was the picture of the red admiral on the bellvine or bindweed flower. Like many country gardens our garden was full of bellvine which although it is troublesome in the flower garden or in the vegetable patch, in the orchard it can flower and look beautiful and the butterflies love it.

On one occasion we had a far bigger visitor in the orchard when our little pony, Rummy, found a way in and filled himself on fallen apples. It was a mistake, because if apples are left on the ground they begin to ferment, as of course fermenting apple juice in bottles becomes cider. This wild cider made our little pony quite tipsy, and he swayed and staggered about for some time until his hangover finally wore off.

Bumble bees like our wild orchard too and it is another of the great sadnesses of modern day life that all insect populations seem to be in steep decline and the various bumble bees are among them. However, if wild areas are left so that they can find nectar and pollen, as well as holes in which to breed, then bumble bees will flourish and they certainly flourish in our orchard. Bumble bees are among the earliest insects to fly in late winter and early spring and so they are very important in the pollination process. Because of this, good populations of bumble bees can also help produce good crops of apples, pears and plums. It is a tragedy that in many areas honey bees have become extremely scarce, particularly wild hives, as they have been attacked by the varoa mite. The mites eat the grubs of the bees and so the hives die out. It must be hoped that no similar parasite latches on to the bumble bee.

Birds too have always been a feature of our orchard; long-tailed tits, goldfinches, chaffinches, robins, jays, collared doves and we even have a rookery nearby and the rooks come in

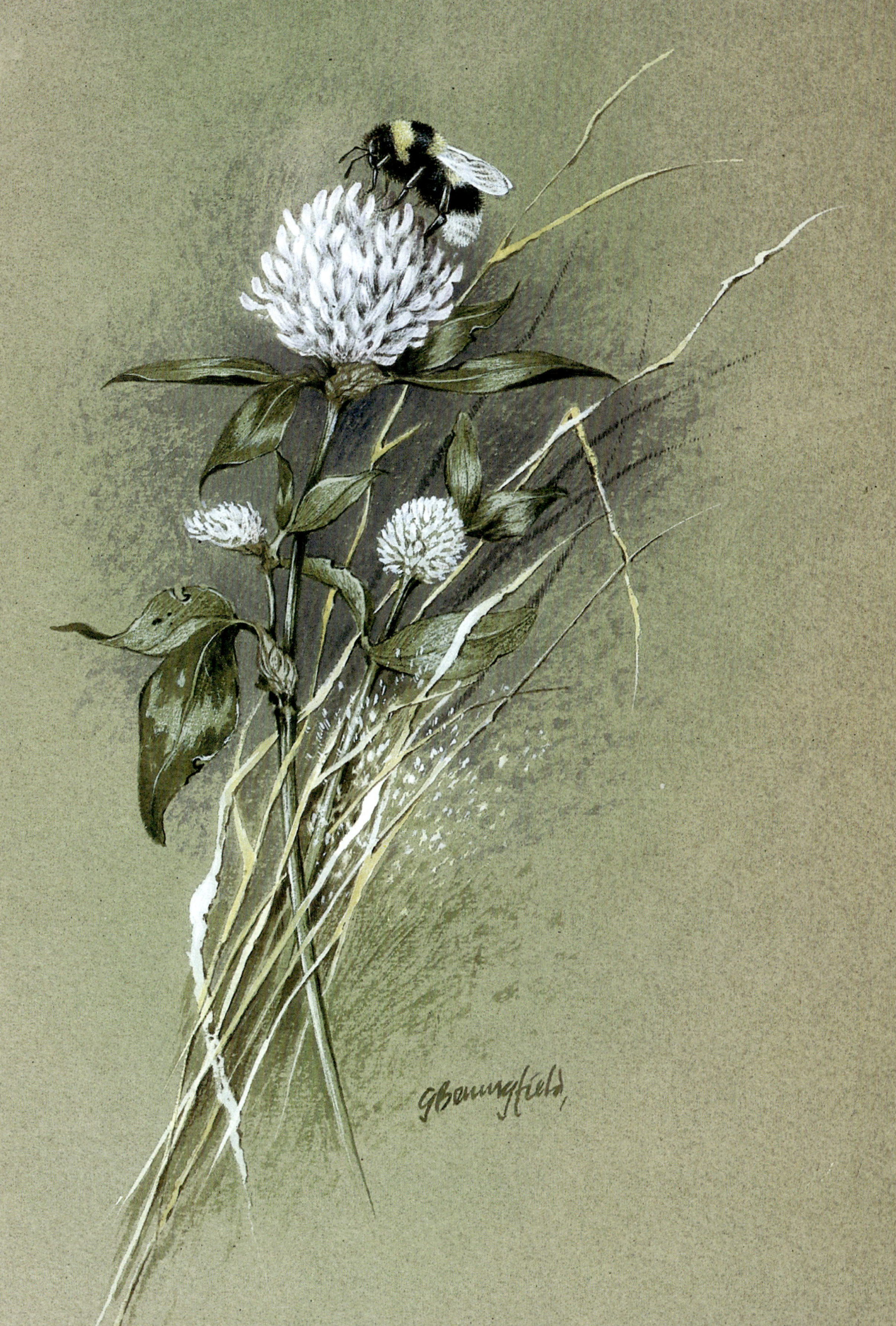

GBenningfield.

too. Most of the birds enjoy eating the fallen fruit and of course bullfinches, which are spectacularly beautiful birds are notorious for eating the buds of blossom. In some areas they are very unpopular with orchard owners. Blue tits and wrens are really attracted by our old trees and they also love the undergrowth which gives them plenty of shelter, and insects to eat. I am afraid that I don't leave the orchard quite as wild as Gordon left it, as I don't like getting stung by stinging nettles and scratched by thistles when I go to pick the fruit. The other bird that Gordon really loved to see in our big old apple trees was the

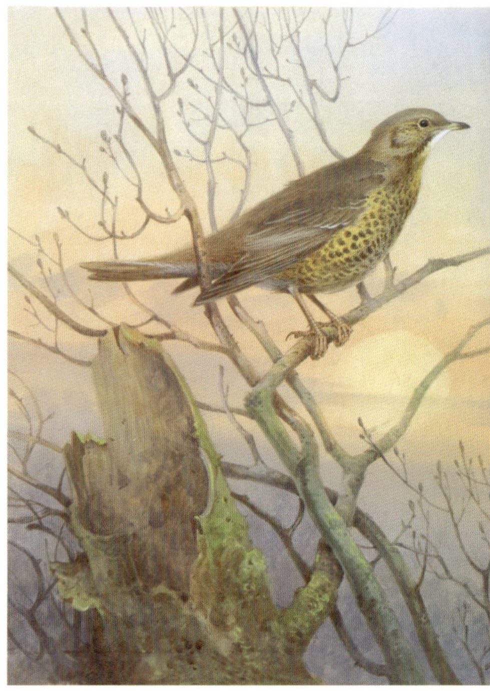

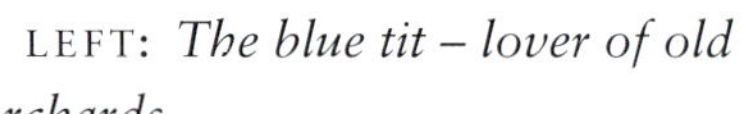

LEFT: *The blue tit – lover of old orchards.*
RIGHT: *The mistle thrush.*

mistle thrush. It was a favourite bird of his because the mistle thrush starts singing its song of spring before the leaves burst and he always used to point out the first songs that he heard because it indicated that spring was well on the way. Because of this mistle thrushes also rear their young much earlier than most other birds, and it is not unusual for the fledglings to be out of the nest at the time the apple blossom is in full bloom.

Animals too, apart from our pony enjoy the fruit and we have always been very lucky to have dormice. They are such agile and beautiful little animals it was always a great pleasure if not a privilege to have these very

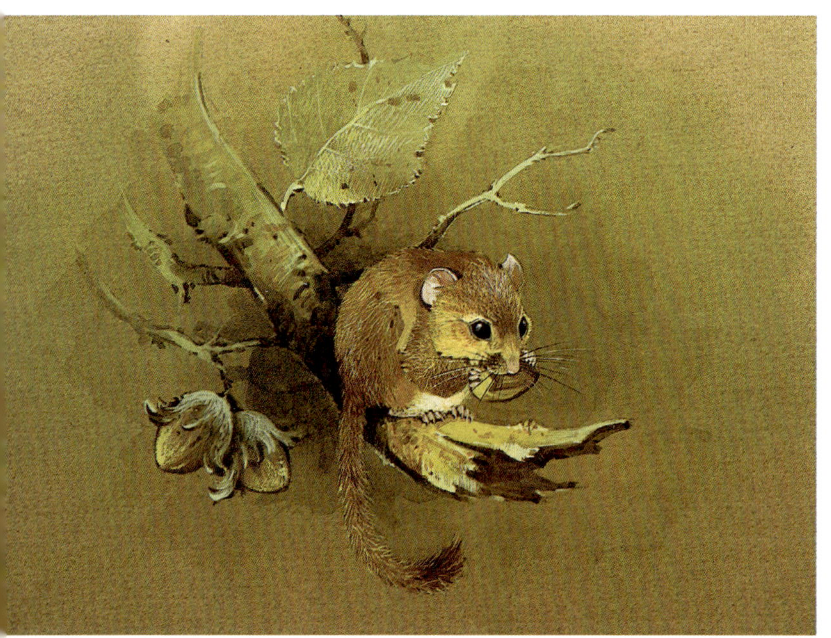

A dormouse with hazel nuts.

attractive visitors. Their diet is very wide – as long as it is fruit, flowers or nuts – and so they have a great selection of flowers and blossom, nuts and fruit in our garden. We have hazel nuts nearby and so our little wilderness has always been something to admire if you are a dormouse.

Unusually too the River Gade flows by the border of the orchard and so not only can we have woodpeckers, long-tailed tits and mistle thrushes to watch, but at the very edge we can even see kingfishers and herons. On special days Gordon has even seen teal on the Gade, a 'spring' of teal. It is an apt name as these attractive little ducks seem to leap out of the water into flight and they are one of the most striking wildfowl to be found in Britain. Tufted ducks too can occasionally be seen on the Gade, and so we are very fortunate to have such a wide range of wildlife within viewing distance of our little orchard.

Of course, in the general countryside not only was it traditional to have a small orchard but it was normal to have a small pond to allow farm animals to drink, and so many farms had pond wildlife to be seen from their orchard edge as well. It added to the attractiveness of the countryside and also to the variety of wildlife that could be seen, without having to go to a nature reserve or a site of special scientific interest. I suppose modern day ecologists would say that the old, traditional farms had greater 'biodiversity'.

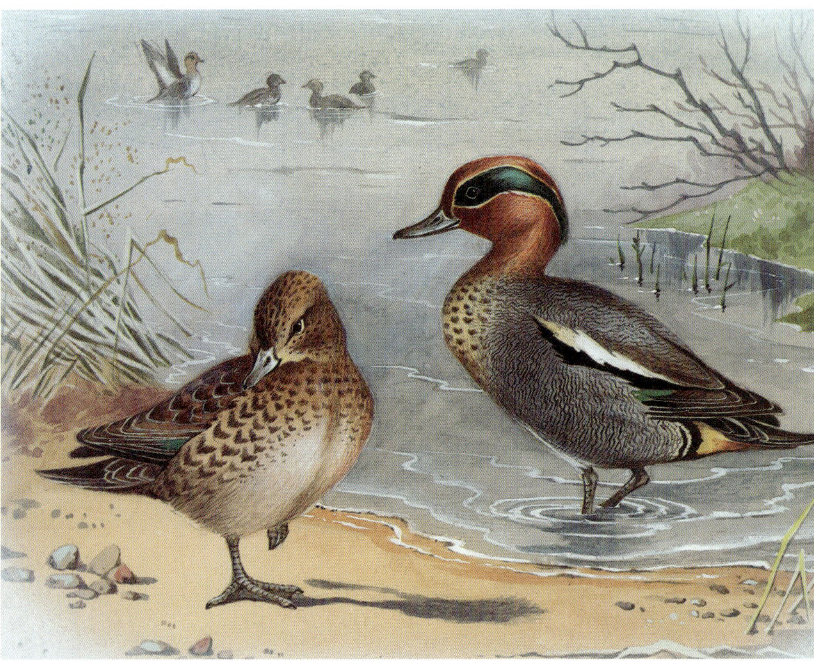

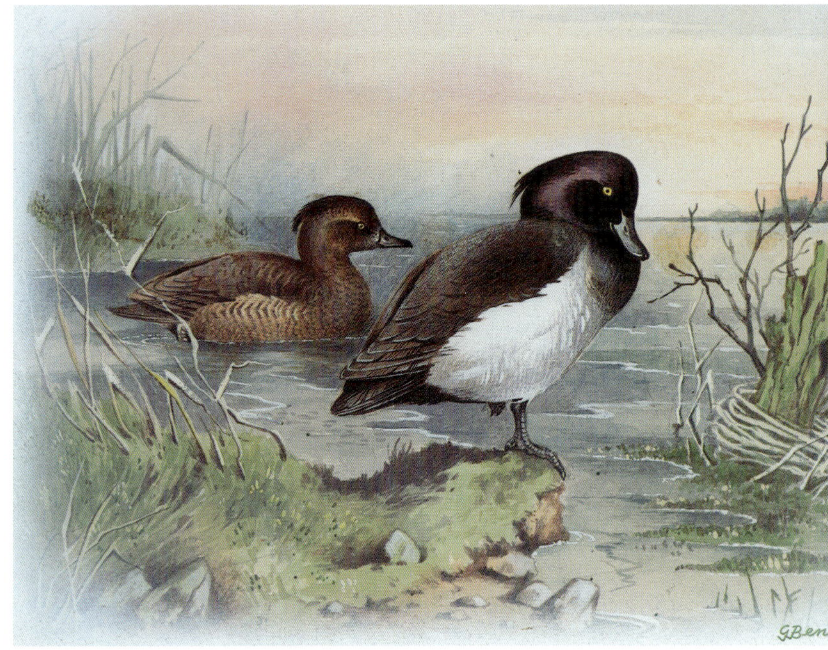

TOP RIGHT: *Teal.*
RIGHT: *Tufted duck.*

But then comes the autumn and the fruit itself; how Gordon loved traditional British apples, the Cox, the Blenheim and the Worcester. My favourite apple has always been the Cox and I think the Bramley is a cooking apple which has no rival. It is a good quality apple with a fine tart taste and when it is cooked it can make a wide variety of absolutely delicious dishes. It can even be eaten raw and it is overflowing with juice that has a bitter edge – being not too tart but certainly not too sweet. I suppose the attractiveness of the fruit was yet another element of the orchard which appealed to Gordon immensely, as orchards have always been a feature of many childhoods. Seeing attractive fruit in somebody's garden or in a farmyard turned most schoolboys of Gordon's generation into 'scrumpers'; and Gordon almost certainly went scrumping from time to time. Stolen apples, making the pockets bulge, became almost a badge of pride for school children making their way home at the end of the day. Part and parcel of this too, were the shouts of angry farmers or old ladies waving sticks to drive the children from their gardens and away from their fruit trees.

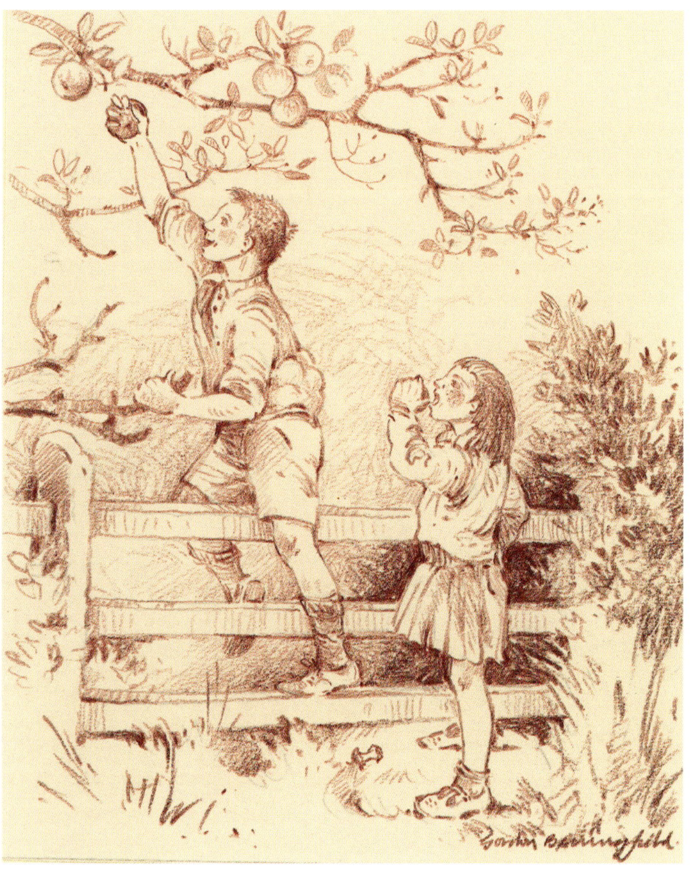

It was at the back end of the summer when fruit was plentiful that butterflies were also important in the orchard. Red admirals in particular love fallen and bruised fruit; at that time of the year too, many late plants are flowering as others are seeding, and so it is both an unusual and a very attractive time of the year.

But even after the fruit has been picked and the leaves fall there is still much to be gained from the orchard, as fallen branches or fallen trees of plum, pear or apple all make excellent logs. They burn well and the smoke has a very pleasant smell. To go into a room on a cold winter's day where apple logs are burning is a complete pleasure; the warmth hits you and so does the very attractive smell of the smoke. Nothing could be better than sitting in an armchair in front of an apple log fire with the other great gift of the apple at your side, a mug of top quality cider – or a swig of Somerset apple brandy.

LEFT: *Scrumping – a sport of childhood.*
RIGHT: *Comma butterflies on wild blackberries.*

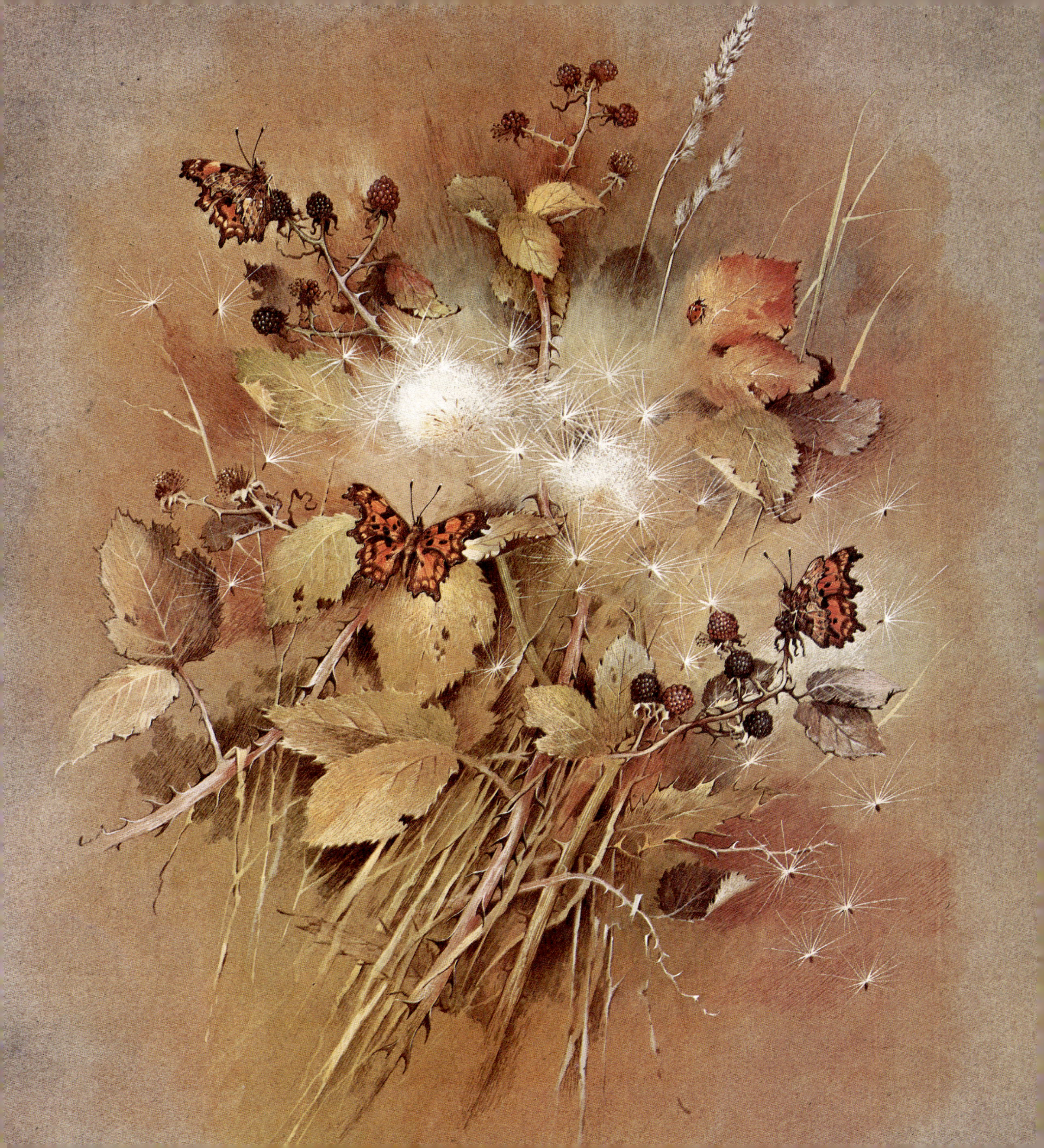

One of Gordon's favourite paintings was of a little cottage he found in Gloucestershire. The washing was out, the bullaces, or wild plums, were just coming into blossom and wood smoke was coming from the chimney. That one picture says so much about the quality of country life, of homeliness, hard work and comfort all shown in the house, the garden and the still, cold sky.

Logs and fires – Robert Louis Stevenson summed them up well in his poem *Winter*:

In rigorous hours, when down the iron lane
The redbreast looks in vain
For hips and haws,
Lo, shining flowers upon my window-pane
The silver pencil of the winter draws.

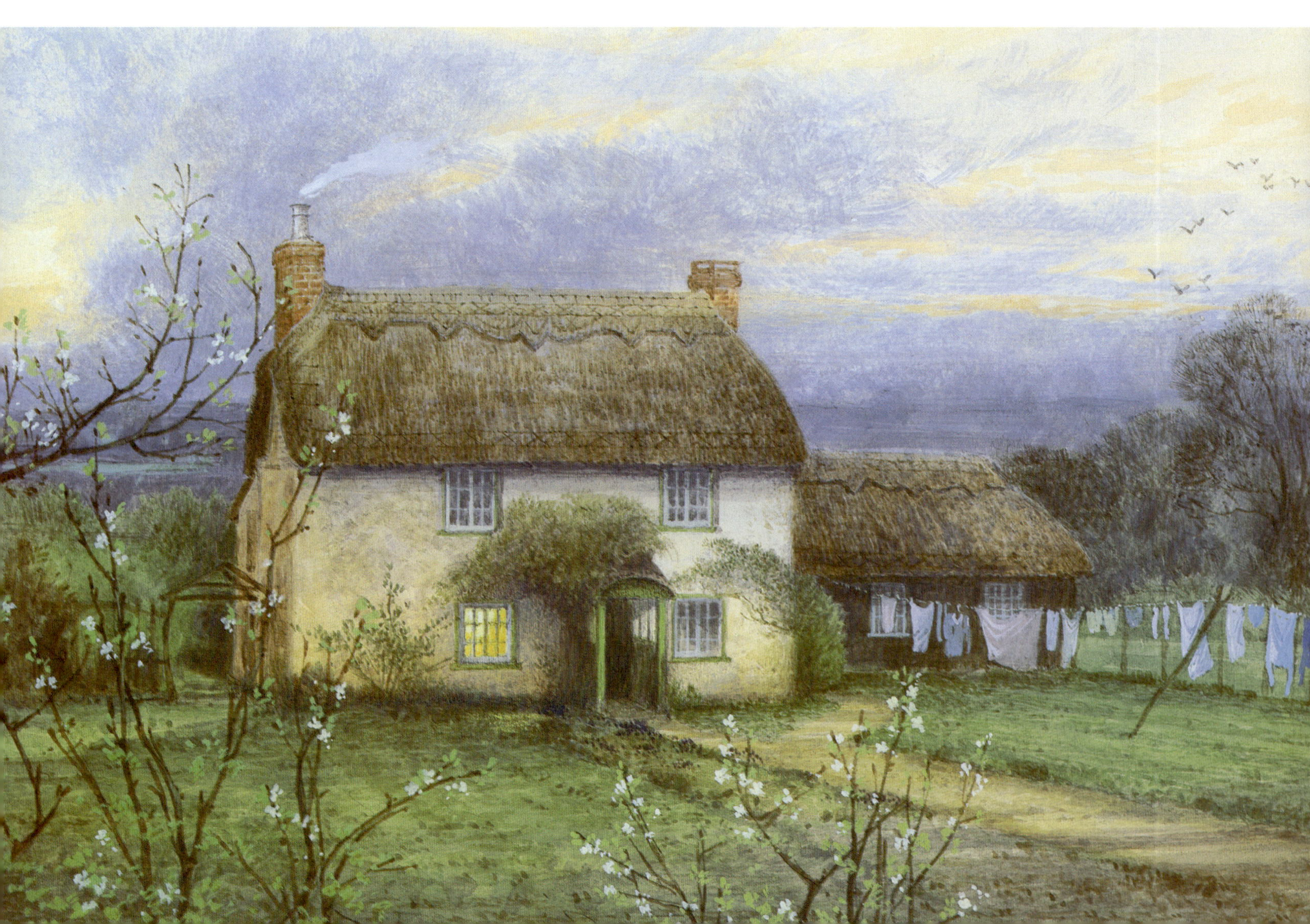

The Orchard

When all the snowy hill
And the bare woods are still;
When snipes are silent in the frozen bogs,
And all the garden garth is whelmed in mire,
Lo, by the hearth, the laughter of the logs-
More fair than roses, lo, the flowers of fire!

I hope those people who have still got fruit trees in their garden will be encouraged to keep them. I also hope that those people who have not yet enjoyed picking their own fruit for eating or for cooking will be encouraged to plant their little orchards too, even if it is only three or four trees at the bottom of the garden. The rewards will be tremendous both in terms of fruit, wildlife and simply the joy of looking at the spring-time blossom.

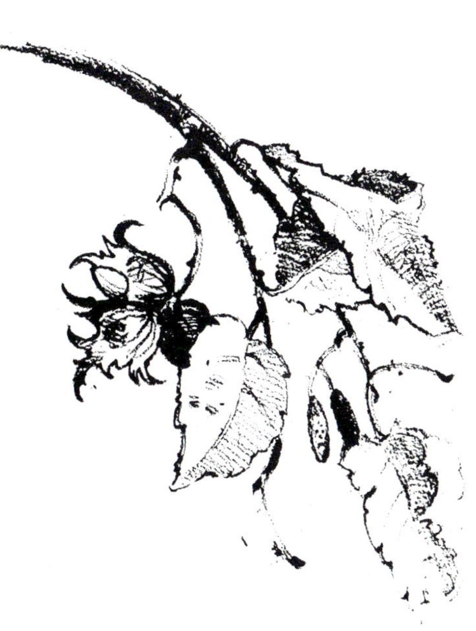

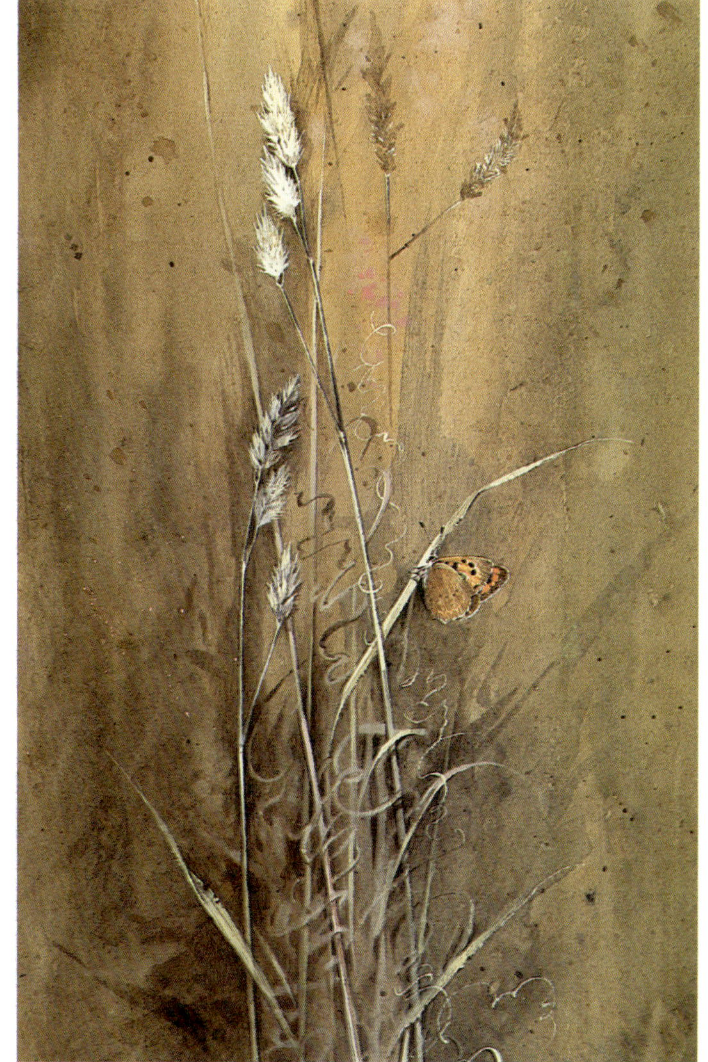

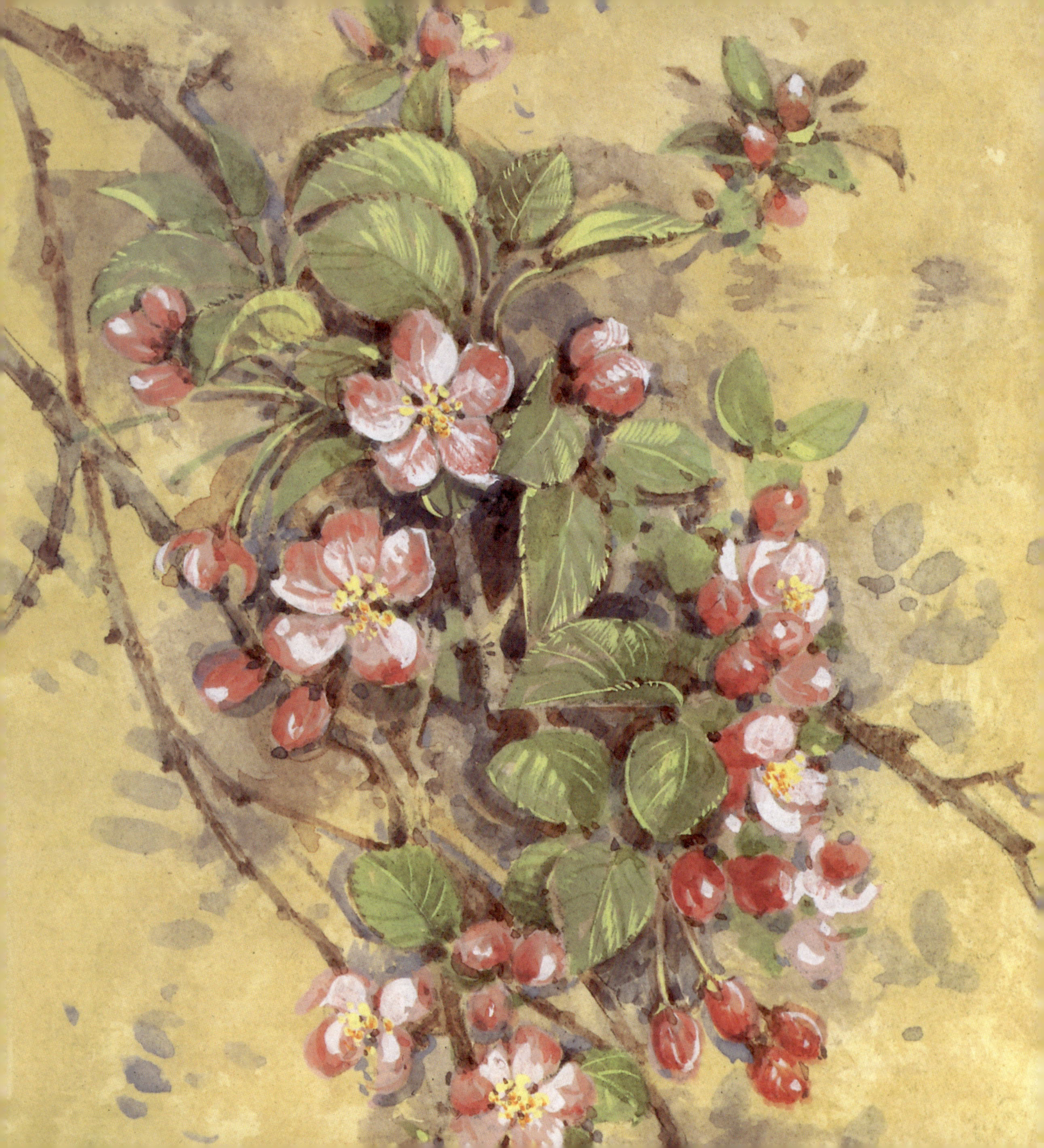

CHAPTER TWO

Blossom and Bloom

To every thing there is season, and a time to every purpose under the heaven:
A time to be born, and a time to die: a time to plant, and a time to pluck up that
*   which is planted;*
A time to kill, and a time to heal; a time to break down, and a time to build up;
A time to weep, and a time to laugh; a time to mourn, and a time to dance;
A time to cast away stones, and a time to gather stones together; a time to
*   embrace, and time to refrain from embracing;*
A time to get, and a time to lose; a time to keep, and a time to cast away;
A time to rend, and a time to sew; a time to keep silence, and a time to speak;
A time to love, and a time to hate; a time of war, and a time of peace.
Ecclesiastes Chapter 3, verses 1–8

Thinking of blossom and bloom made me think of seasons and so I thought that these wonderful lines from The Old Testament – Ecclesiastes were for me, an important way of starting this chapter. Blossom sets off another season in the year – spring. It is an important time in the year for the countryman and for the person who just loves the countryside. The spring starts with wild blossom and goes on well into May with the wild crab apple and the ordinary cultivated apples. The first blossom is the white wild blossom to be seen in the hedgerows. Many people believe it to be blackthorn (sloe), but it is not – it is a relation of the blackthorn, it is the cherry-plum, which was introduced into Britain as long ago as Roman times; in some places it has become wild and in others it has been planted as a hedgerow tree. It is early and beautiful and it hints of the changing season, from winter to spring and coincides with the beautiful haunting song

Apple blossom in the spring.

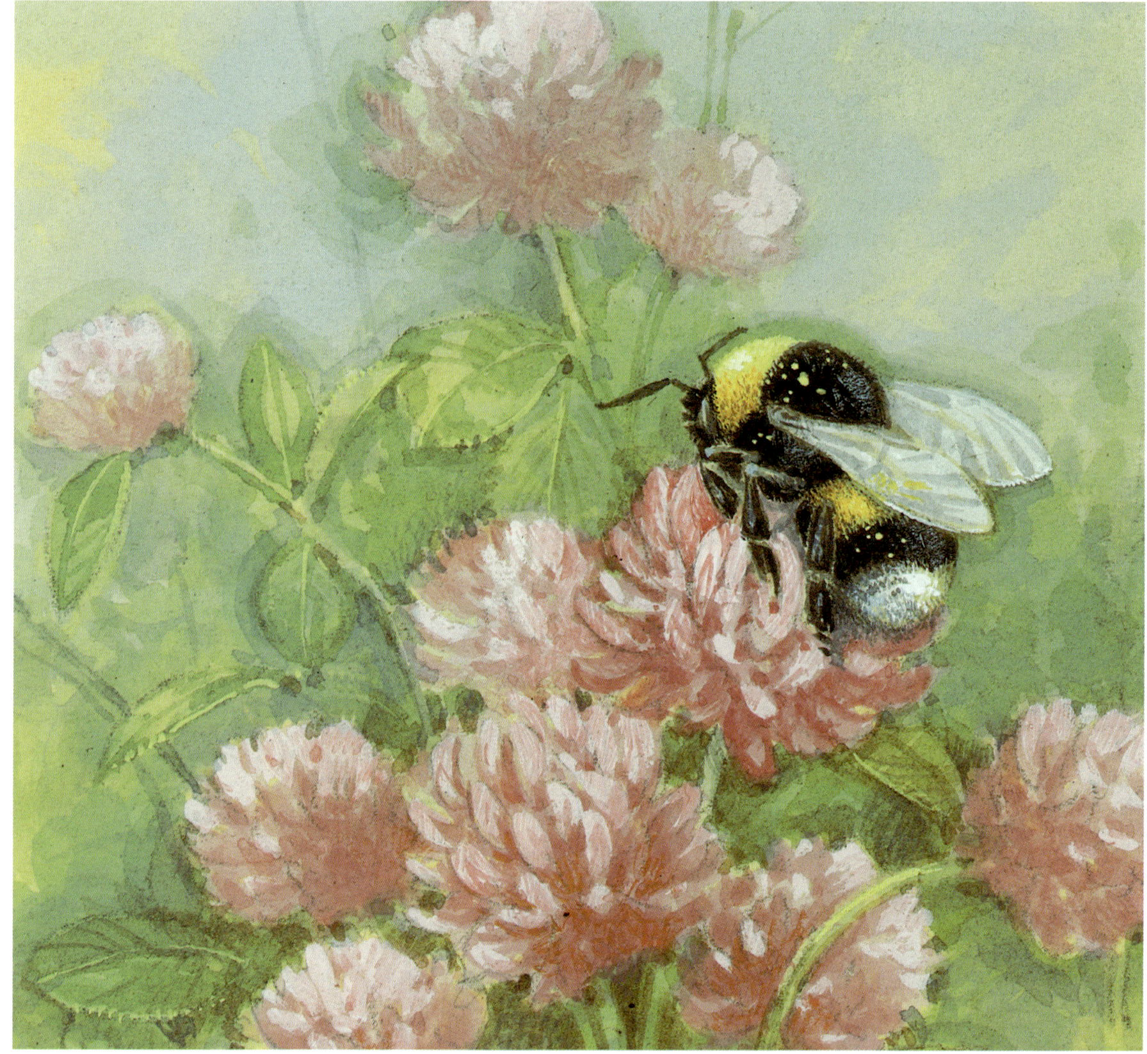

ABOVE: *The bumble bee – an important part of the pollination process.*
RIGHT: *Carter's Blue apples and a small tortoiseshell butterfly.*

of the mistle thrush. After the wild plum, comes the white blossom of the greengage and the garden plum. On a cold morning it can look as white as snow but it does mean that sap is rising and as the day warms, bees and insects will start their task of pollination. It is shame that we have to rely so much on the bumble bee. At one time it was the honey bee that arrived in large numbers

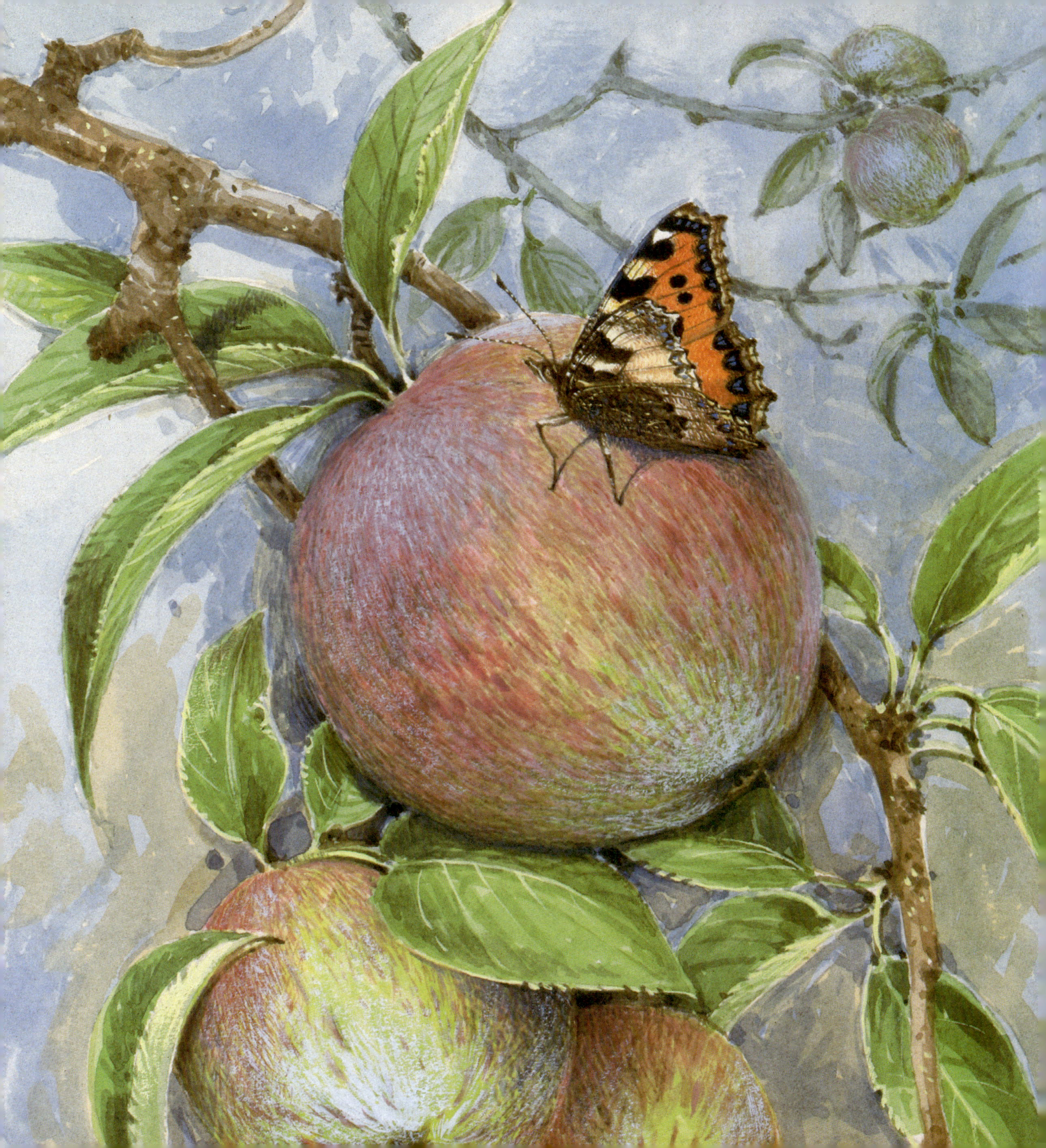

on the blossom and it is only those lucky enough to have a bee-keeper near at hand these days who can have honey bees visiting their trees. Now over large tracts of Britain, honey bee hives are only kept alive with the use of chemicals to kill the varoa mite. Indeed those small areas where the hives are still healthy are extremely fortunate. The honey bee is a truly remarkable insect, and in *Henry V*, Shakespeare outlines the structure of the hive which he believes is remarkably like the structure of human society:

> *For so work the honey bees;*
> *Creatures that, by rule in nature, teach*
> *The act of order to a peopled kingdom.*
> *They have a king, and officers of sorts:*
> *Where some, like magistrates, correct at home;*
> *Others, like merchants, venture trade abroad;*
> *Others, like soldiers, armed in their stings,*
> *Make boot upon the summer's velvet buds;*
> *Which pillage they with merry march bring home*
> *To the tent-royal of their emperor:*
> *Who, busied in his majesty, surveys*
> *The singing masons building roofs of gold;*
> *The civil citizens kneading up the honey;*
> *The poor mechanic porters crowding in*
> *Their heavy burdens at his narrow gate;*
> *The sad-ey'd justice, with his surly hum,*
> *Delivering o'er to executors pale*
> *The lazy yawning drone.*

Sadly if you own a garden with an orchard there is no time to become a 'lazy, yawning drone'; there is simply too much work to do.

After the plum blossom comes the pear – again white – but as the pear tree can be far taller than the plum, its appearance is often far more striking. On into May comes the apple blossom scenting the air and it is truly one of the remarkable transformations of nature, how a fragile blossom becomes a beautiful apple. Blossom and blooming is a time of happiness when the sun's warmth gains and we can really feel the change of season.

I think Gordon would love me to quote Thomas Hardy here about the weather, but sadly Hardy is always Hardy, and after a wonderful first verse he brings us back to earth with a jolt in the second.

This is the weather the cuckoo likes,
    And so do I;
When showers betumble the chestnut spikes
    And nestlings fly:
And the little brown nightingale bills his best,
And they sit outside at 'The Travellers' Rest',
And maids come forth sprig-muslin drest,
And citizens dream of the south and west,
    And so do I.

This is the weather the shepherd shuns,
    And so do I;
When beeches drip in browns and duns
And thresh and ply;
And hill-hid tides throb, throe on throe,
And meadow rivulets overflow,
And drops on gate-bars hang in a row,
And rooks in families homeward go,
    And so do I.

At this time of year, if it is not raining, the scented buds can be joined by what WH Davies described as *Flying Blossoms*:

These Butterflies, in two and threes,
That flit about in wind and sun –
See how they add their flowers to flowers,
And blossom where a plant has none!

The tortoiseshell and peacock butterflies were pictures Gordon painted as two of his first stamps, and he captured their beauty completely. I think the pictures (overleaf) also show his great love and feeling for butterflies. But the season of blossom and bloom is added to by other butterflies that will sometimes fly

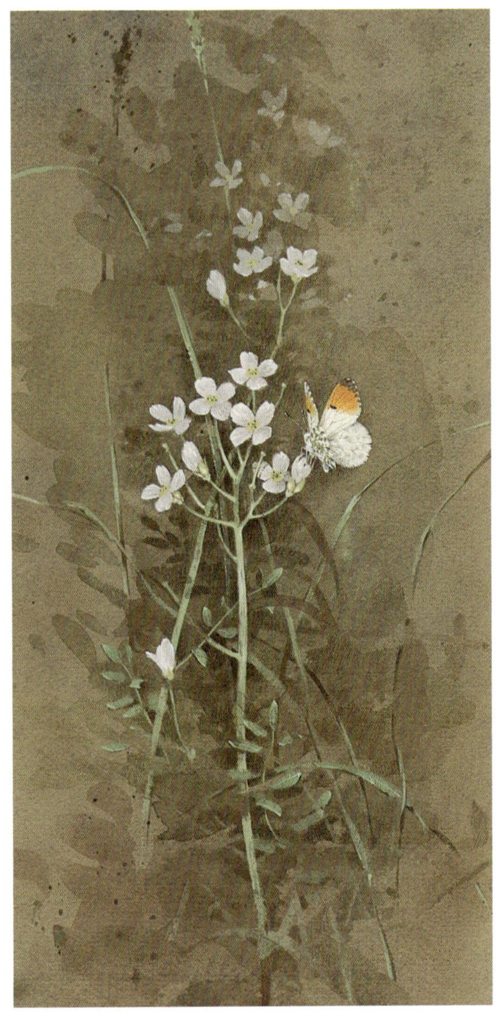

One of Gordon's favourite butterflies, the orange tip sitting on a cuckoo flower.

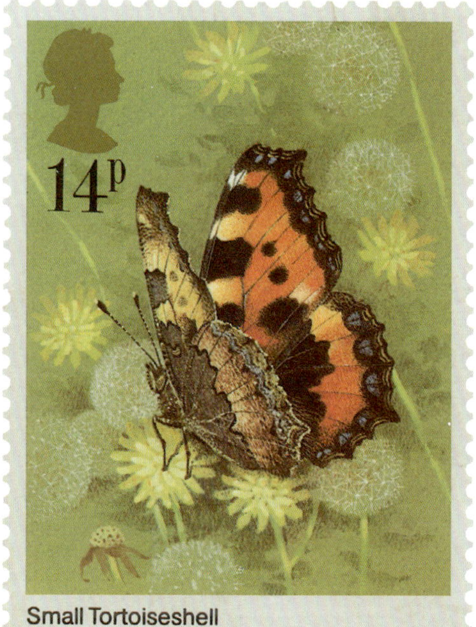

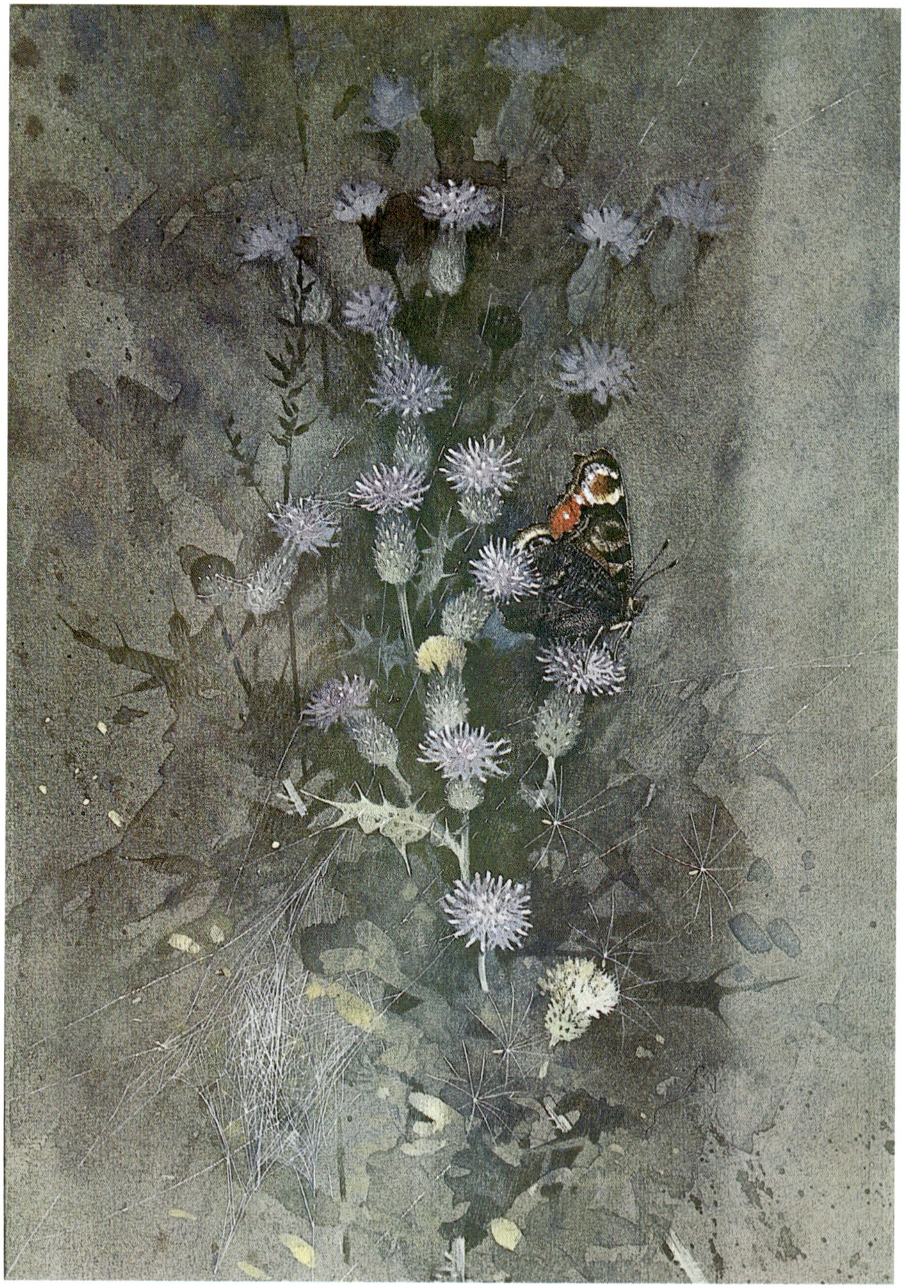

Small Tortoiseshell

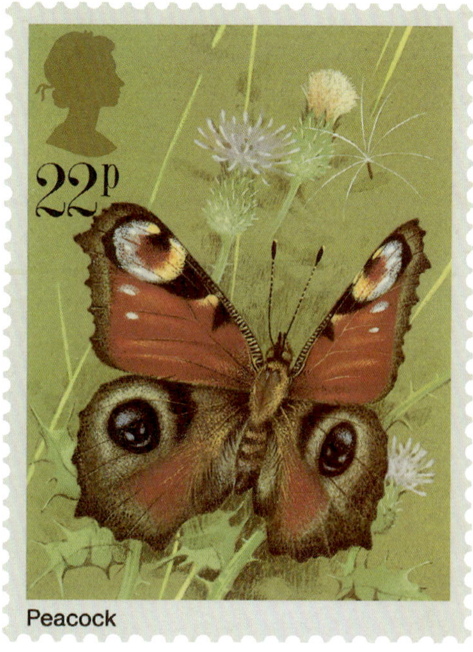

Peacock

ABOVE: *Peacock on thistle.*

through the garden or up into the boughs at this time of year, the holly blue, the speckled wood, the cabbage white (large white), the brimstone and, of course, the orange tip. The orange tip was one of Gordon's favourite butterflies. It lays its eggs on Jack-by-the-Hedge and cuckoo flower, and this too is the season of the cuckoo – or at least it should be. It is yet another one of our rural tragedies that in many areas the call of the cuckoo is falling silent as fewer and fewer of these remarkable birds return for their British summer.

Below the early blossom, snowdrops flower and so there is pure white above and pure white below. Slowly the white is added to with yellow; the lesser celendine, a beautiful flower of early spring and then the primrose, whose season again spreads on into May with the blossom of the apple. It is a great pity that John Clare is considered by some to be a 'minor poet'. In my opinion he catches the mood of the countryside so clearly and accurately that he ought to be mentioned as a 'major poet', and he too recognised the importance and beauty of the primrose.

BELOW: *Snowdrops in Gordon's orchard.*

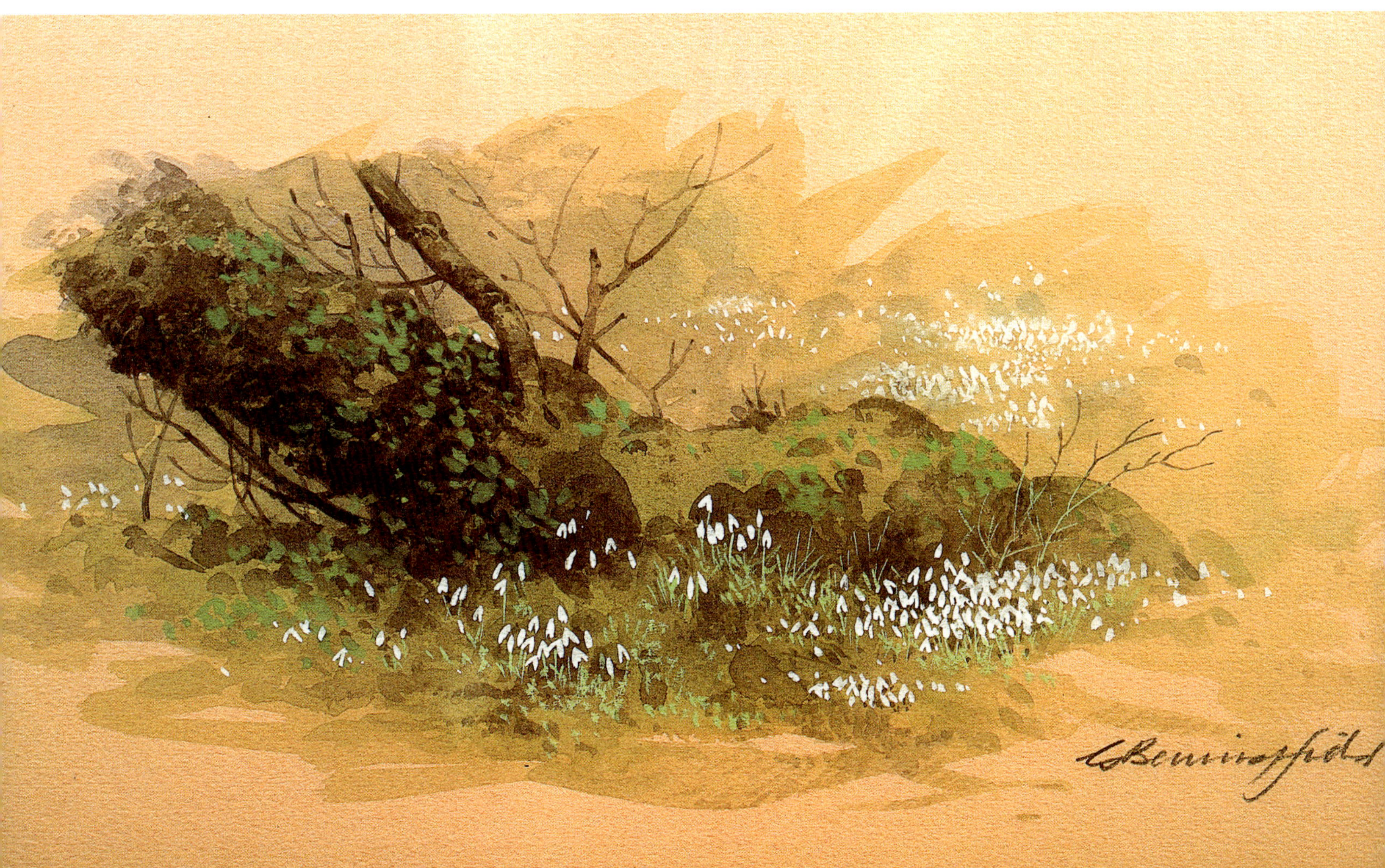

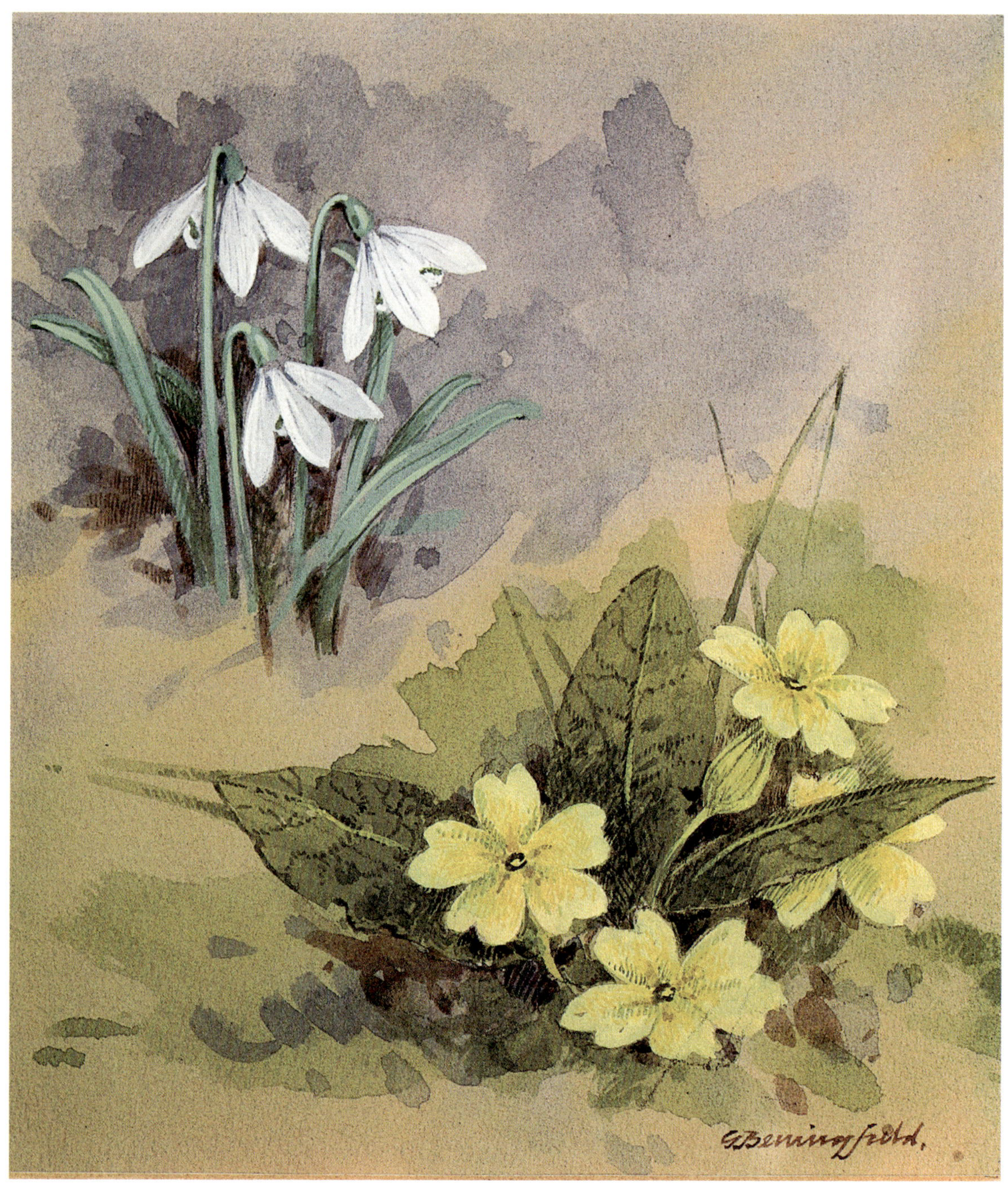

To a Primrose

Welcome pale Primrose! starting up between
Dead matted leaves of ash and oak, that strew
The sunny lawn, the wood, and coppice through
'Mid creeping moss and ivy's darker green;
How much thy presence beautifies the ground!
How sweet thy modest, unaffected pride –
Glows on the sunny bank, and wood's warm side!

LEFT: *Early signs of spring – snowdrops and primroses.*
BELOW: *The wheatear.*

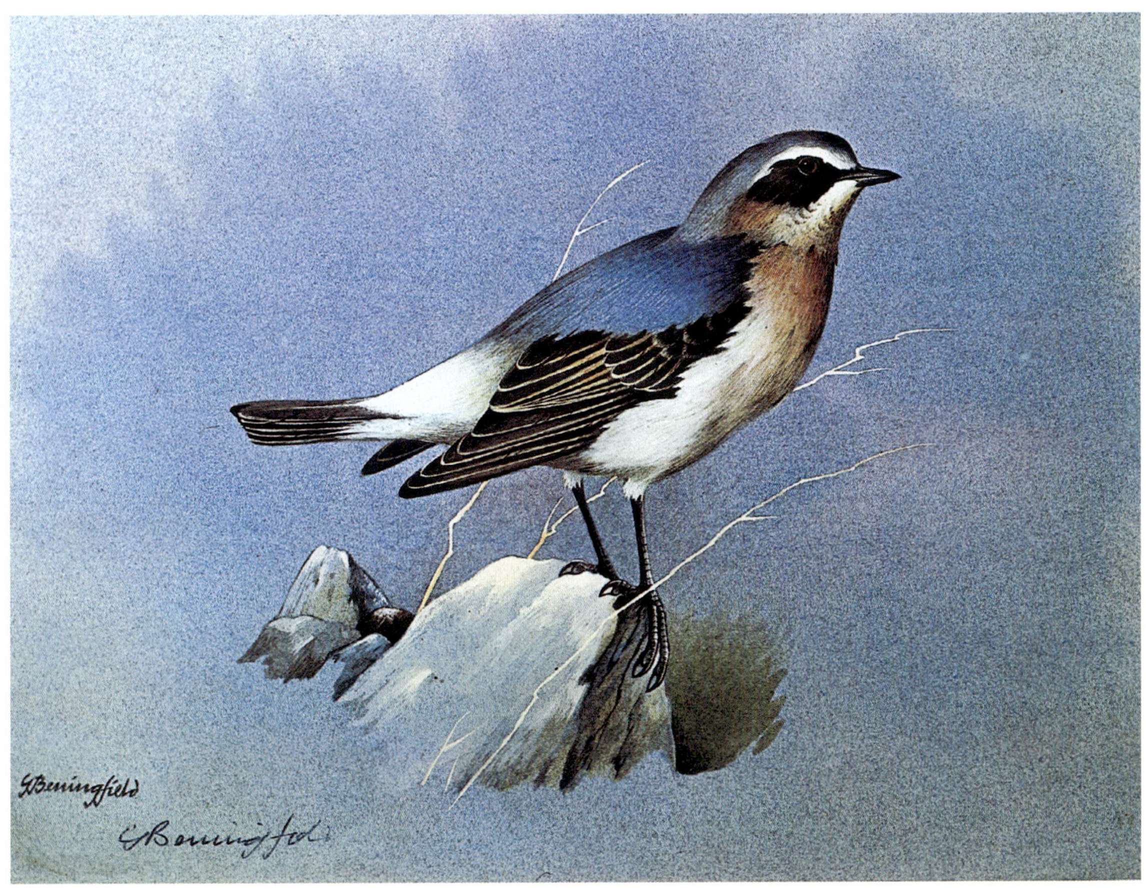

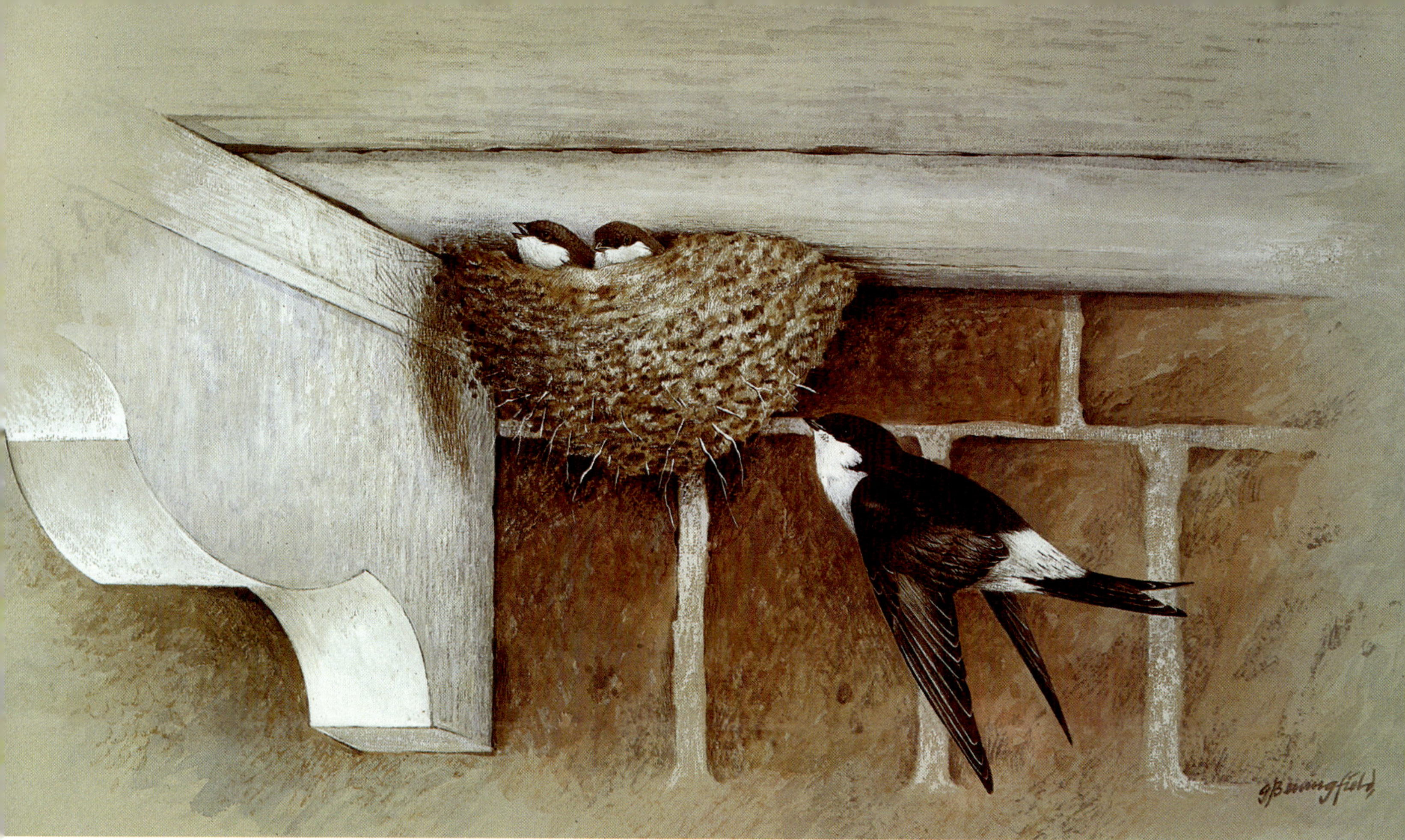

A house martin with young in the nest.

> *And where thy fairy flowers in groups are found,*
> *The schoolboy roams enchantedly along,*
> *Plucking the fairest with a rude delight.*
> *While the meek shepherd stops his simple song,*
> *To gaze a moment on the pleasing sight;*
> *O'erjoyed to see the flowers that truly bring*
> *The welcome news of sweet returning Spring.*

It is in blossom time that the attractive wheatear arrives. In Hertfordshire it simply passes through; it is a beautiful little bird and travels on to different parts of the country, preferring areas of moorland and rough lowland areas of gorse and heath. At one time it loved fallow land, in the days when old methods of agriculture left many fields fallow; as a result in Northamptonshire its country name was 'clodhopper', as it perched and flew from clod to clod. In Norfolk it has an interesting name too, it is called 'Coney Chuck'. Although it has a very attractive song in which the beginning is rather similar to the skylark, it also contains numerous 'chocks' and 'chucks'. In areas of sandy Norfolk, with hard-grazed grass from rabbits (coneys) its country name becomes 'Coney Chuck'. The wheatear picture we found locally as a print owned by one of Gordon's oldest friends.

The other birds that arrive at blossom time are always welcome, the swallow, house martin, sand martin, and swift. What a time to arrive. It was always the highlight of Gordon's day when he saw the first swallow of spring and we loved to have them nesting nearby. House martins too are wonderful birds making nests under the eaves of houses out of mud. It was always a great disappointment to Gordon that we never did have house martins nest here, but elsewhere along the River Gade there are houses in villages with house martins and of course the river, plus the boggy areas and puddles around it, give them a ready supply of mud at nest-building time. Their journey is

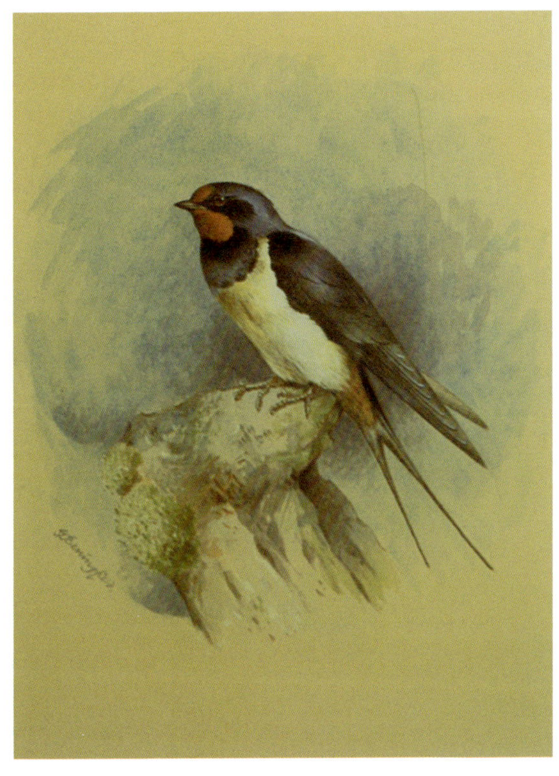

The swallow – a very important part of a traditional summer.

also a remarkable one – to fly from Africa to get here for apple blossom time. Sadly we are getting too neat and tidy for the swallows and house martins as they do need mud and puddles from which to build their nests and they also need old sheds and buildings where they can nest happily. Being flying hunters, they feed on insects and need a good supply of food; with the decline in farm animals in southern England it has inevitably led to a decline in the insect population and so a decline in these two remarkable birds.

So yes, the season of blossom and bloom is always one that I welcome but its welcome extends far beyond the flowers that seem to overflow from the branches in the orchard, for with every blossom comes the promise of future fruit.

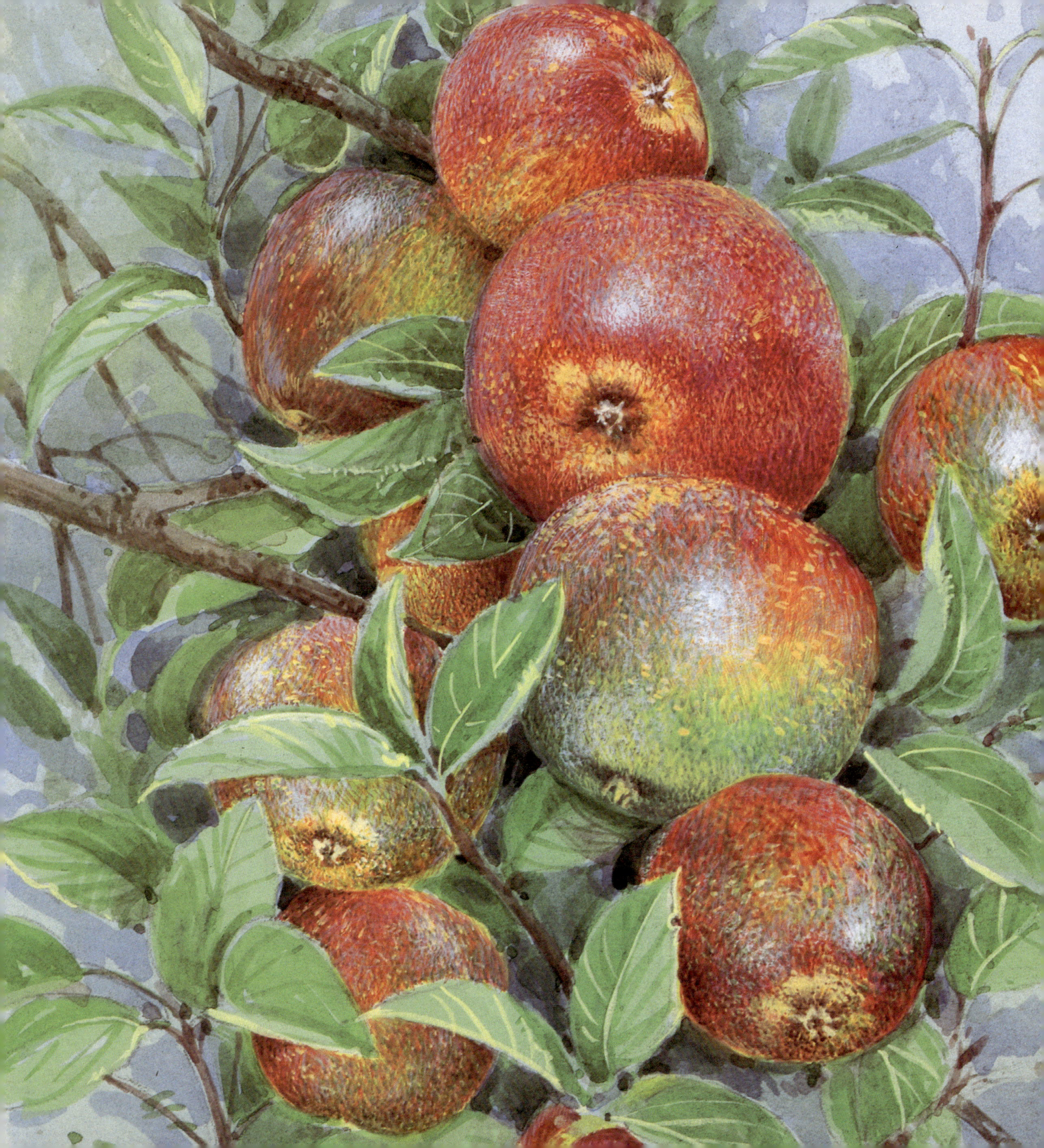

CHAPTER THREE

Fruit of the Bloom

The whole purpose for having an orchard is simple, to supply the home with good fresh fruit, or if it is a commercial orchard, to provide the owner and those who pick the fruit with a living, or seasonal additions to their pockets. The perfect orchard would contain even more than plums, pears and apples, it could also contain cherry, damson, and the ancient fruits of medlar, quince and nuts – hazel, cob and walnut. It is astonishing how in today's economic and social climate most people considering orchards think only of 'apple', but until comparatively recently pears and plums were an important part of every orchard and fruit harvest. In addition most fruit stall holders at markets up and down the country would stock English pears and plums. *Tree Fruit Growing* volume 2, by the appropriately named Raymond Bush and published in 1943 gives details of the plums and pears that could be grown as well as apples. He recalls that a famous nurseryman from 'Somersetshire' named John Scott, had a collection of 1800 different types of pear for both eating and cooking around 1870. But by the time the book was published in 1943 John Scott's list of pear varieties had fallen to just 36.

Again, many shoppers today have forgotten, or do not know, that there are desert and cooking types of pear and both can be absolutely delicious in their proper place. Among the cooking pears are Williams Bon Chretien – which is the pear loved by American canners and made famous under the name of Bartlett. In addition to this there are Pitt, Maston Duchess, Vicar of Winkfield, and several more. Similarly there are numerous delicious desert pears as well as the ubiquitous Conference. There is Clapp's Favourite, Winter Nelis, Dr Jules Juyot and Laxton's Superb – showing that Thomas Laxton, and later his sons, were interested in far more than the apples which have taken their name around the whole world. In fact in the early days the family was known not only for breeding fruit, but also for breeding peas and strawberries. It has to be said that although

The world's most popular apple – Cox's Orange Pippin.

the common Conference, is a very tasty and crisp pear, and is the one favoured by commercial growers, and also the supermarkets, some of the less well known varieties are even tastier and more 'succulent'; indeed they are so juicy that the word should be spelt 'suckulent'.

Similarly there are very many varieties of plum. The Czar is one of the best producers in Britain, often cropping well despite frost and bad weather. A good all-round plum is the Pershore, or Yellow Egg, which is a very good plum for eating, jamming, bottling and cooking; at one time it was even more popular than the Victoria which now seems to have taken over from it. In addition to this there are many other really good plums and do not forget the Greengage, which is extremely sweet and tasty but an unreliable fruiter. The Monarch, is a big reliable plum and ripens at the very end of September; the Warwickshire Drooper, the Early Laxton and Rivers' Early Prolific, which is now normally called the Early River are all excellent varieties. The Early River is an absolutely delicious plum and was developed by Thomas Rivers who was a famous nineteenth century nurseryman from Sawbridgeworth in Hertfordshire.

Over the years an astonishing four thousand varieties of apples have been developed by cross breeding and there are now still over two thousand types in existence. The history of the apple goes back into antiquity to the time of Adam and Eve. To have lured Adam with the forbidden fruit, it must have been a very tasty apple – probably the forerunner of the Cox's Orange Pippin.

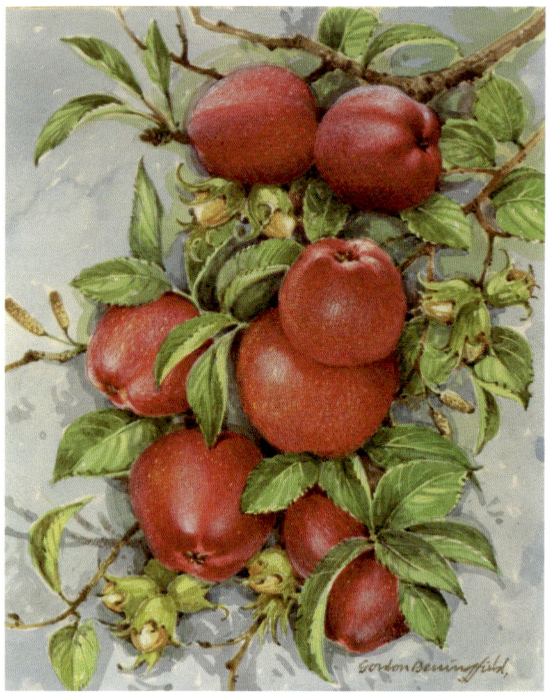

Although Adam obviously thought the apple was excellent and worth throwing away 'Paradise' for, in fact all apples have been developed from the crab apple which grows wild throughout Britain and the temperate zones of Europe and South East Asia. There are even related species in the United States although it is not quite clear how the apple migrated to North America in the first place.

British apples have always been so varied and tasty for eating raw and cooked that when Britain was going through its period of exploration and expansion settlers took their apple pips and seedlings with them to the four corners of the earth. Apples were grown in Australia, South Africa, New Zealand and North America, and it is ironic that the

LEFT: *Star Crimson Delicious.*

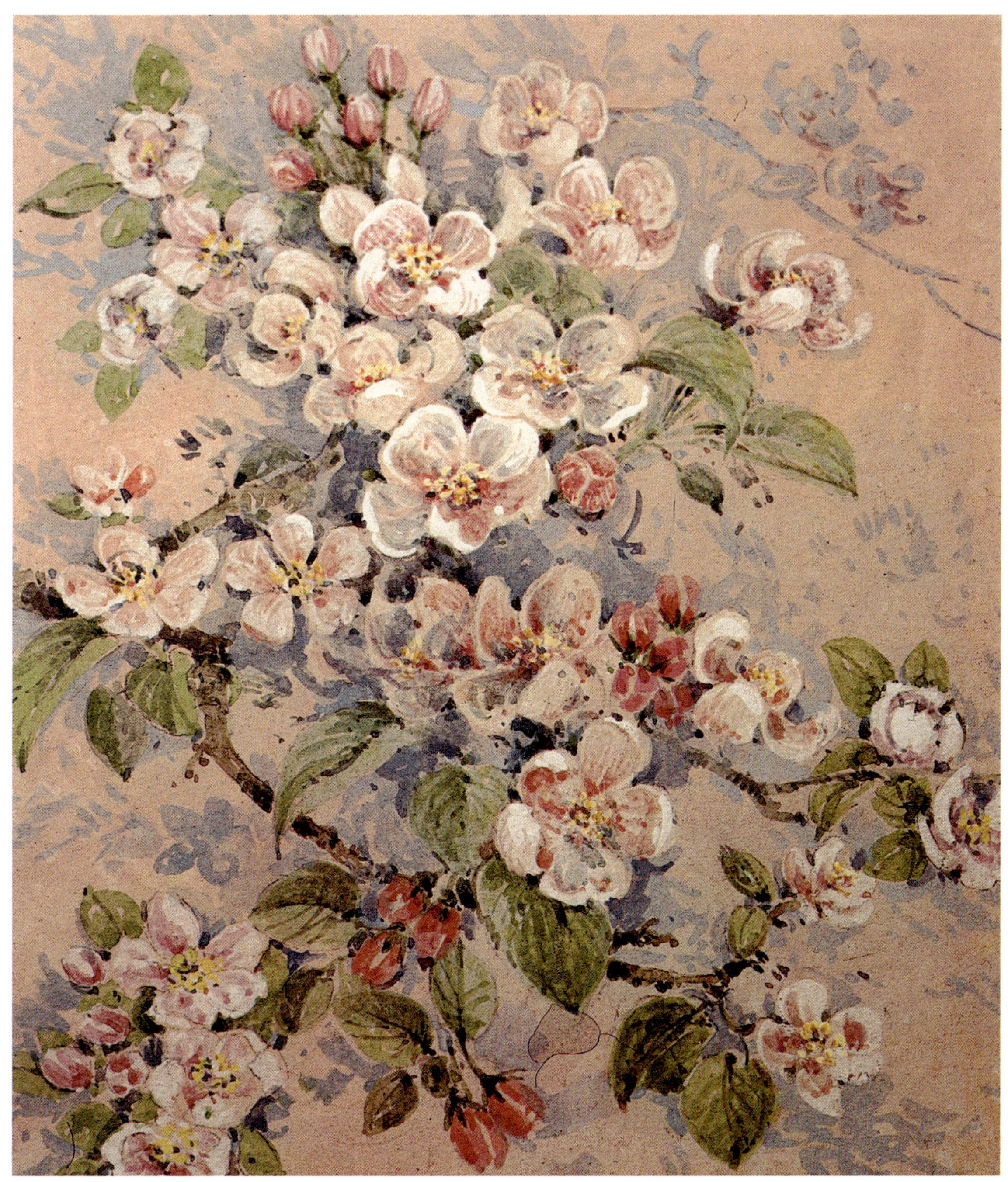

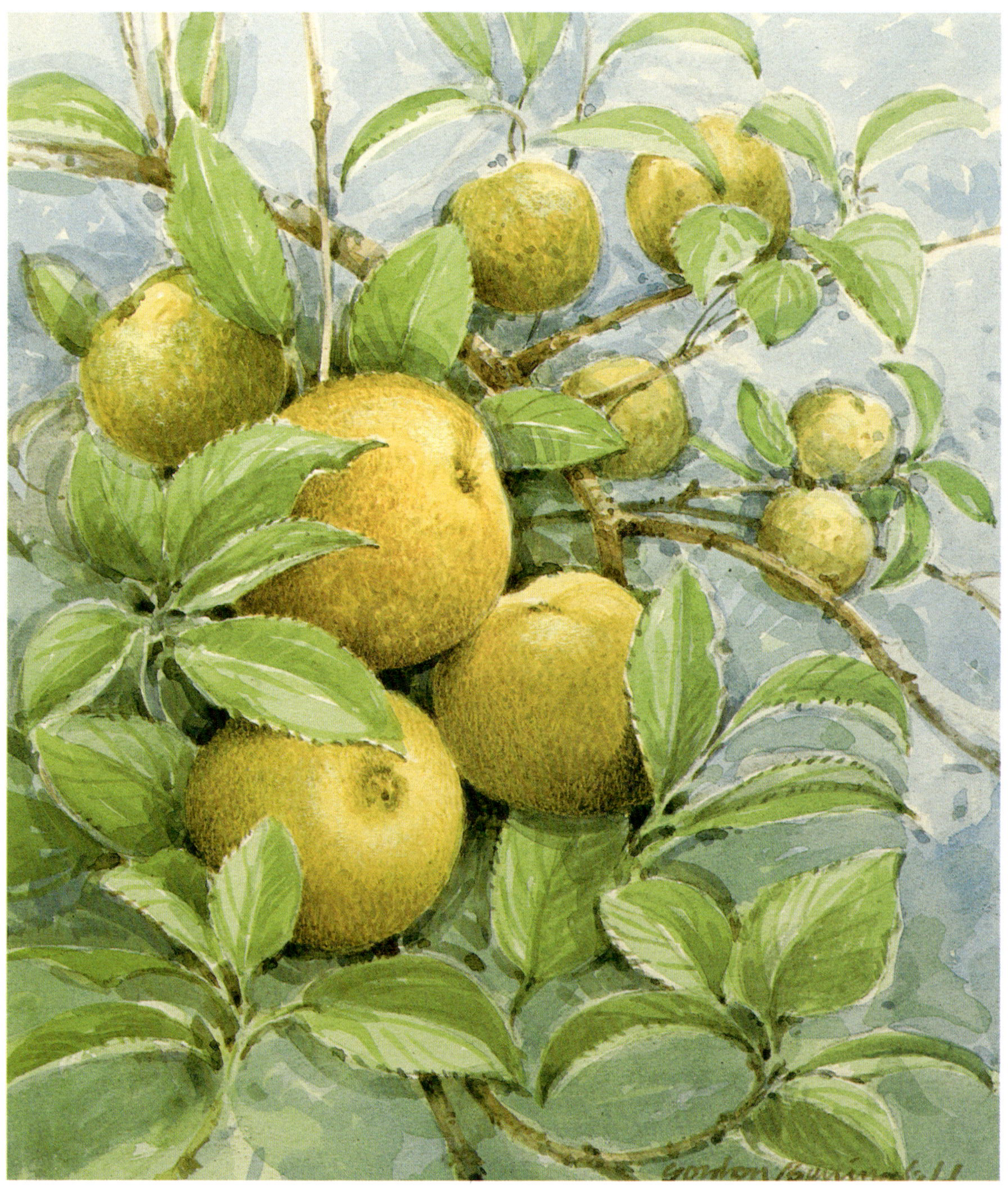

nurserymen of the new world developed such good varieties that they then exported both the apples and the seedlings back to Britain.

One of the main advocates of American apples was that great rural writer and fighter, William Cobbett, who loved many of the North American varieties. It is quite an education for some people to realise that the Golden Delicious – and indeed all the 'Delicious' types of apple were developed in the USA. Australia too has areas which are ideal for apples and the famous Granny Smith is of 'Oz' origin; it is named after the memory of Mrs Maria Ann (Granny) Smith who grew the first one in 1868.

More recently other apples have been developed and among the most famous is the Braeburn from New Zealand which has been grown commercially since 1952. It is believed to have been grown originally from a seedling of 'Lady Hamilton'; sadly, in England, because of our indifferent weather it often fails to mature.

Despite this Britain still has many areas where wonderful apples are grown and the famous apple-growing regions are Kent, Bedfordshire, Cambridgeshire, Worcestershire and Suffolk, with Devon, Herefordshire and Somerset being particularly famous for cider apples and 'Scrumpy'. Among our great varieties of apple are the Cox's Orange Pippin, the Worcester Pearmain, and the good old juicy James Grieve must not be forgotten; then there are the two famous cookers, the Bramley and the Newton. In addition there are various Blenheims and Russets that can be cooked or eaten raw, and an assortment of rare apples all with unique texture and taste.

Gordon was particularly fond of our Blenheim tree and we also have one exceptionally large Bramley. Russets were another of his favourites and he also enjoyed Cox's and Worcester's. Considering apples are 84 per cent water and 13 per cent sugar it is amazing that such a fruit should be so attractive and delicious.

The history of some of the old apples is fascinating. The famous Bramley cooking apple, which if stored properly will keep from September until March, is quite remarkable. It was first raised between 1809 and 1813, by Miss Mary Anne Brailesford and planted in a garden in Southwell in Nottinghamshire. It did so well that it was admired by nurseryman Mr Henry Merryweather, in the middle of the 1800s, when the tree was in the garden of the local butcher, a Mr Bramley. Consequently the apple is not named after the person who planted it, or indeed after the person who spread its reputation, but after the local butcher, who by chance happened to have this first wonderful fruiting apple.

The Newton Wonder is even more remarkable. It was found by an Inn Keeper, Mr Taylor, growing in the thatch of 'The Harding Arms' at Kings Newton in Derbyshire. He transplanted it into his garden where it survived until the 1940s. In the late 1890s it was recognised as a

The Leathercoat Russet – excellent for winter eating.

potentially valuable apple and it has been regarded as an excellent cooking apple ever since. Like the Bramley it will keep well into March and it is highly prized as an apple to be kept and used throughout the winter.

The Worcester Pearmain was quite naturally developed at St John's near Worcester, by a Mr Hale and the James Grieve was developed by James Grieve in Edinburgh, from a Cox or a Pott's seedling, and recorded in 1893. Although we tend to think of 'English apples'; in fact varieties of apple are to be found from all parts of Britain. In addition to the James Grieve, Scotland also has the Beauty of Moray, Galloway Pippin, Tower of Glamis, Bloody Ploughman and many more. From Wales there is Monmouthshire Beauty, St Cecelia, and even one called Sissy. From Ireland comes Gibby's Apple – I suppose the name 'apple' was a guide to the Irish for the type of fruit they were eating. They must have had great problems when eating another variety of apple called Irish Peach. Then, still from Ireland, there is the White Russet, Reid's Seedling, Greasy Pippin, Widow's Friend, and various others. In England virtually every region and every county can trace several local varieties.

Of Gordon's paintings the Star Crimson 'Delicious' is one of those that was bred abroad from old British stock, and then came back to Britain as a new variety. The original Golden 'Delicious' was developed in West Virginia and various other types of Delicious were then crossed from the Golden Delicious. Nearly all the 'Delicious' apples really do deserve the extravagant claim in their title, except those supermarket French 'Golden Delicious' which are usually picked too early and sold before they are ripe. Captain Kidd is also known as Kidd's Orange Red, and is of New Zealand origin. It is a cross between a Cox's Orange Pippin and a Delicious and was introduced into Britain in 1932. Captain Kidd was a fruit farmer and an amateur breeder whose aim was to combine the quality of the best English varieties with the colour of the American apples, hence both the taste and the colour of Captain Kidd.

The Carter's apple too from Chapter 2, where the small tortoiseshell is resting on a large apple, is yet another variety that has come to us from America. It is thought that it was bred as long ago as the 1840s by Colonel Carter in Alabama; it then virtually disappeared but was rediscovered by American enthusiasts and is now grown again both in the United States and in Britain. It is a large apple with a very attractive blue bloom and it has a sweet fragrant flavour.

But the most famous and the tastiest apple of them all is the Cox's Orange Pippin. It was developed in about 1825 by Richard Cox a retired brewer at Colnbrook Lawn, Slough. It must be the most famous thing to have come from Slough, even more famous than John Betjeman's poem *Come lovely bombs and fall on Slough*. After it had been developed by Richard Cox it was grown commercially, probably by about 1862, by Thomas Rivers in Hertfordshire and from there it was

The Captain Kidd, named after the New Zealander who first grew it.

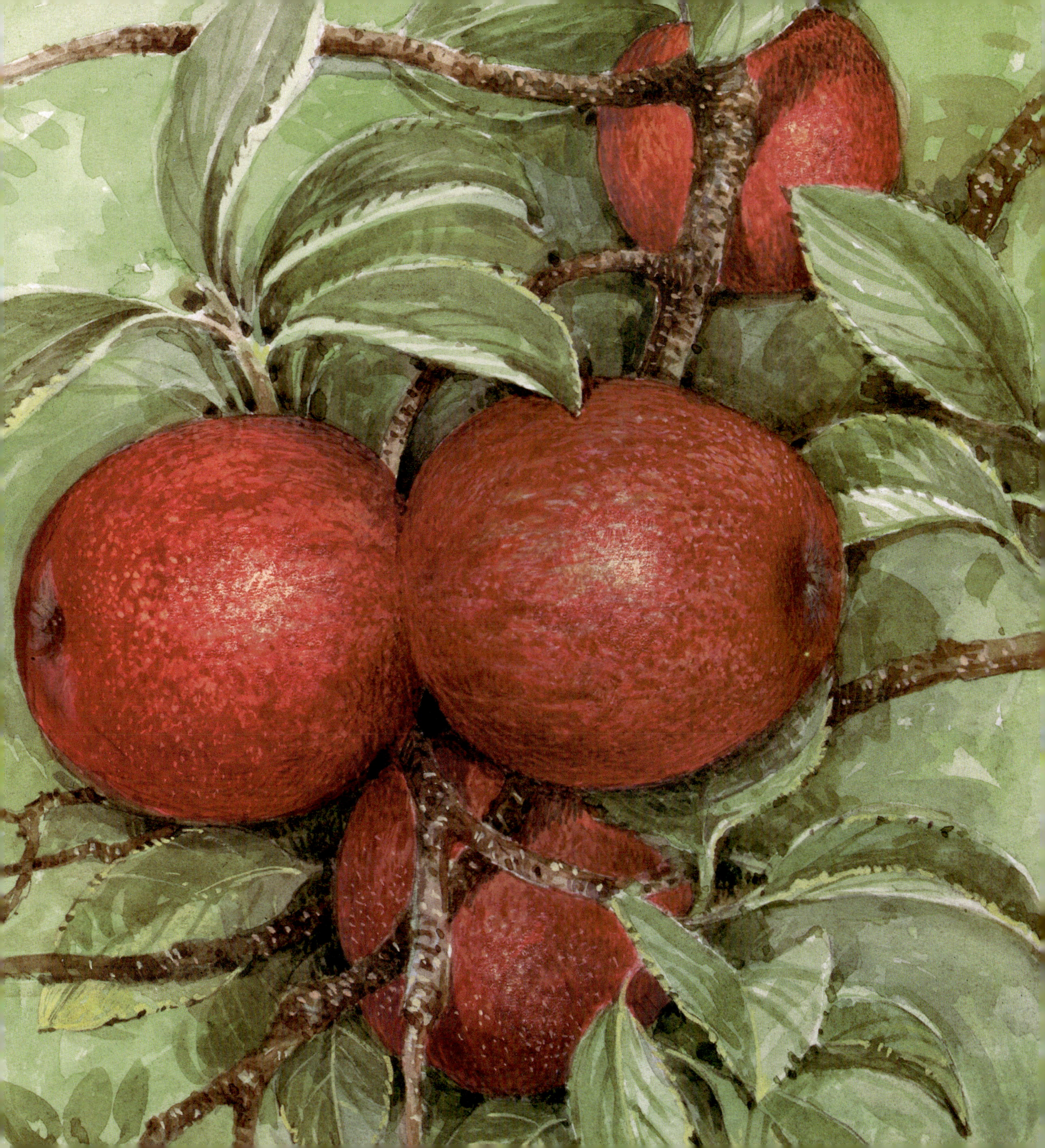

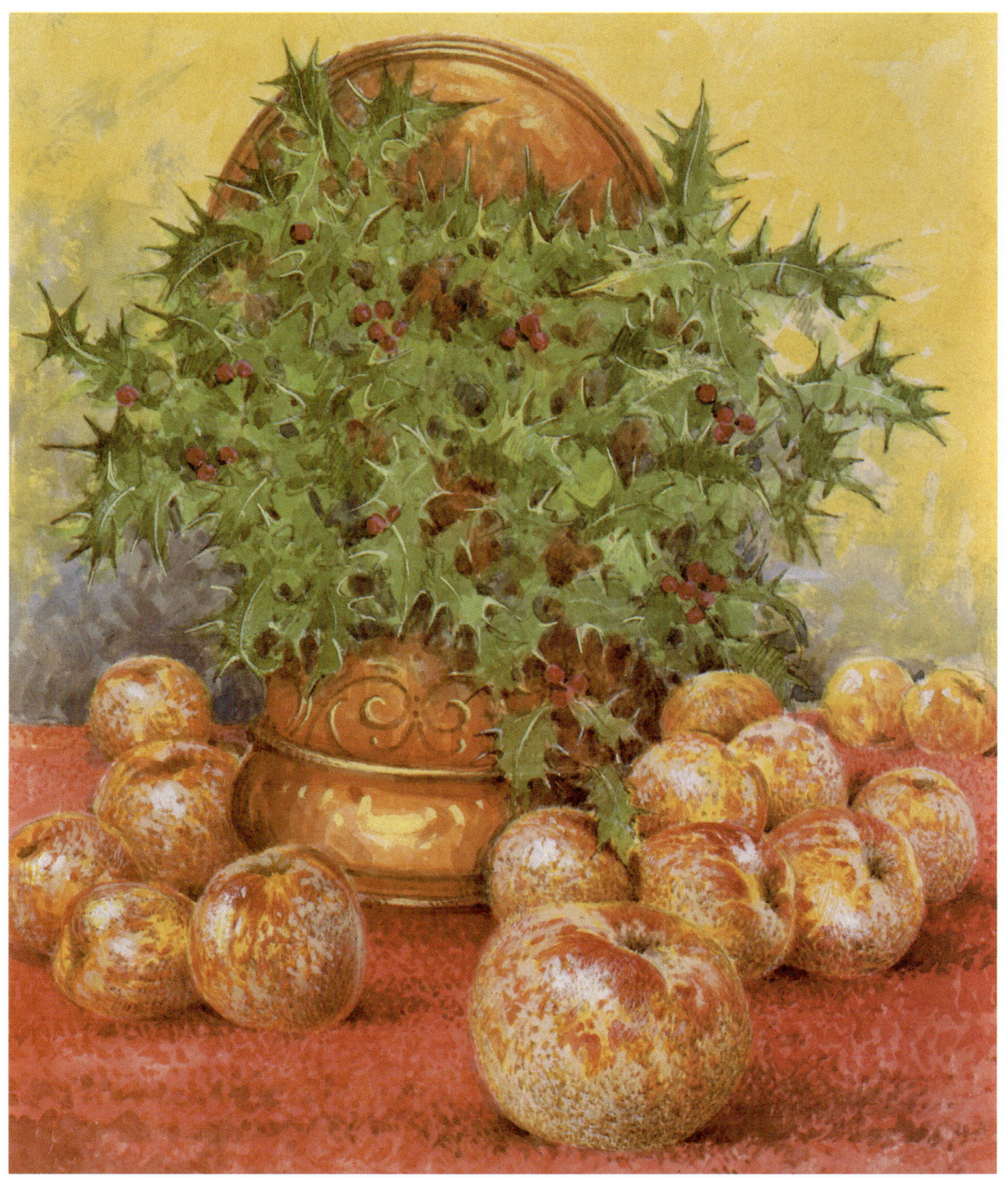

eagerly planted by market gardeners in London, the Vale of Evesham and Kent. From this beginning it has spread all over the world and is universally accepted as the world's most delicious apple.

Other apples are of course extremely tasty; the various Russets have a very crisp and unique flavour and can keep well if stored properly and the Blenheim is another excellent tasting apple which can last well into winter. It was originally found way back in the 1700s when a local cobbler, or tailor, found it growing against the boundary wall of Blenheim Park. After he moved it into his garden the fruit was so popular that others wanted to grow this very distinctive and tasty apple and so with the approval of the Duke of Marlborough, who lives at Blenheim Palace, it was renamed the Blenheim Orange.

In times gone by, with the then population being spared the great wonders of electronic entertainment, gardening, particularly growing fruit and vegetables was far more important than it is today. Consequently many ordinary people were very keen gardeners and enthusiastically planted new varieties to see what the taste would be; they also hoped that their fruit would contribute to the larder and so substantially reduce the cost of living. Because of this even in children's books there were pages and chapters about gardening and planting; in one old book called *Poems That Every Child Should Know* there is a long poem by William Cullen Bryant, called *The Planting of the Apple Tree*:

The Planting of the Apple-Tree has become a favourite for 'Arbour Day' exercises. The planting of trees as against their destruction is a vital point in our political and national welfare.

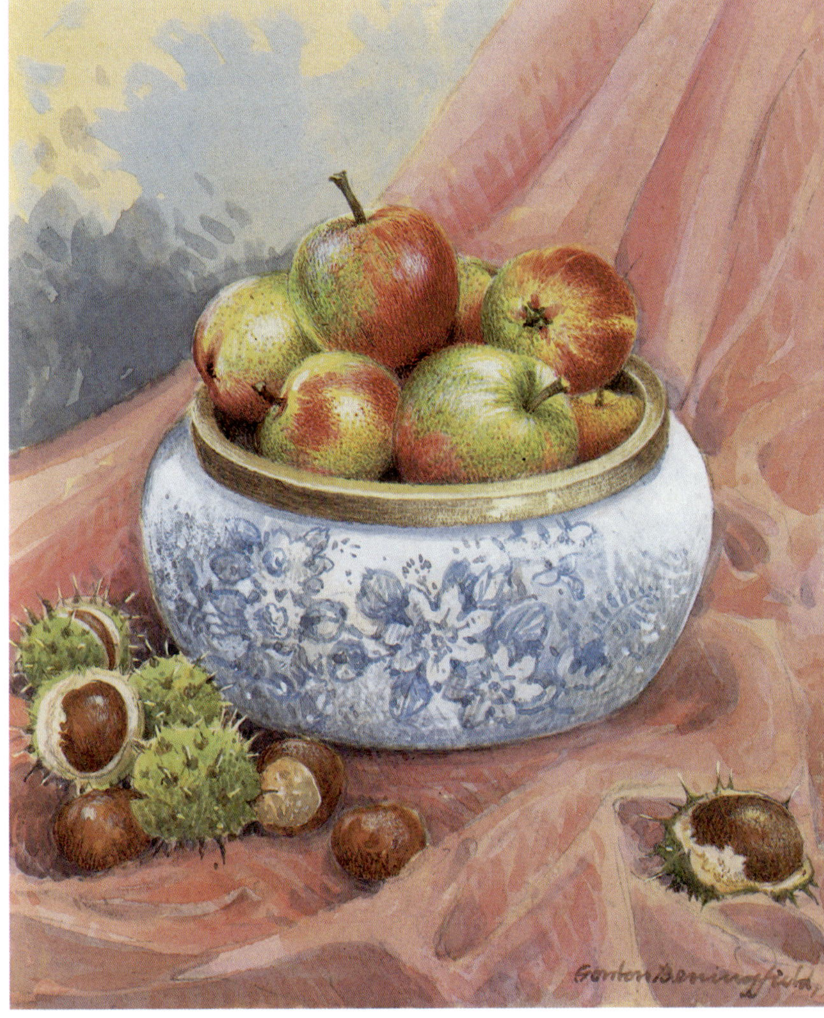

Come, let us plant the apple-tree.
Cleave the tough greensward with the spade;
Wide let its hollow bed be made;
There gently lay the roots, and there
Sift the dark mould with kindly care,
And press it o'er them tenderly,
As round the sleeping infant's feet
We softly fold the cradle sheet;
So plant we the apple-tree.

What plant we in this apple-tree?
Buds, which the breath of summer days
Shall lengthen into leafy sprays;
Boughs where the thrush, with crimson breast,
Shall haunt, and sing, and hide her nest;
We plant, upon the sunny lea,
A shadow for the noontide hour,
A shelter from the summer shower,
When we plant the apple-tree.

What plant we in the apple-tree?
Sweets for a hundred flowery springs,
To load the May wind's restless wings,
When, from the orchard row, he pours
Its fragrance through our open doors;
A world of blossoms for the bee,
Flowers for the sick girl's silent room,
For the glad infant sprigs of bloom,
We plant with the apple-tree.

And loosen, when the frost-clouds lower,
The crisp brown leaves in thicker shower.
The years shall come and pass, but we
Shall hear no longer, where we lie,
The summer's songs, the autumn's sigh,
In the boughs of the apple-tree.

And time shall waste this apple-tree.
Oh, when its aged branches throw
Thin shadows on the ground below,
Shall fraud and force and iron will
Oppress the weak and helpless still?
What shall the tasks of mercy be,
Amid the toils, the strifes, the tears
Of those who live when length of years
Is wasting this apple-tree?

'Who planted this old apple-tree?'
The children of that distant day
Thus to some aged man shall say;
And, gazing on its mossy stem,
The gray-haired man shall answer them:
'A poet of the land was he,
Born in the rude but good old times;
'Tis said he made some quaint old rhymes
On planting the apple-tree.'

Because of the love of apple trees there is much lore connected with apples and gardens. Using country lore the first important day is definitely Christmas Day and if the sun shines through the apple trees on that day then a good crop of apples is forecast later in the year. The problem is that either those early countrymen had bad memories, or there were three different old countrymen each with a different little rhyme.

One says:

If the sun shines through the apple trees on Christmas Day
when autumn comes they will a load of fruit display.

While another who must think that his use of language is far greater said:

If would Christmas Day be fair and bright
you'd have apples to your heart's delight.

While the final rustic poet proclaimed:

Sun through the apple trees on Christmas Day
means a fine crop is on the way.

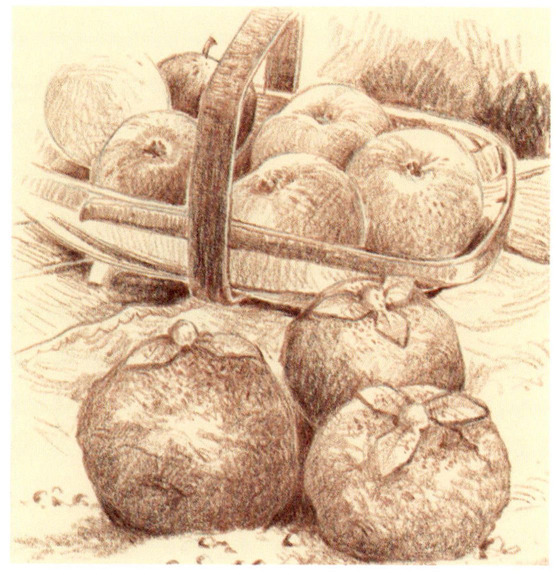

January is a very busy time for apples, as from Twelfth Night the apple trees have to be 'Wassailed'. The idea was to Wassail the orchard – charm the trees into a good harvest. Sometimes this was done with a fire as well, so it was a great big celebration with a bonfire and singing. To make the whole thing even better a large bowl full of cider – that miracle of the apple which turns juice into alcohol – was drunk, as well as a concoction of roasted apple, sugar, ginger, nutmeg, cinnamon with wine or beer. The drink was carried into the orchard to toast the trees. What was left was then poured over the trunks to shouts, or even the firing of guns, to let the sleeping trees know how much the people were hoping for a good apple harvest later in the year. So the drink was carried into the orchard and no doubt many individuals were carried out of the orchard back home with very bad heads. It was also a custom in some places to eat 'Twelfth Cake', a magnificent baked cake and inside a bean and pea were surreptitiously placed – whoever got the slice with the bean was then proclaimed 'King of the Bean', for the evening, presumably; for the sake of decency the girl who got the pea was only called 'The Queen'.

Into March fruit lore gets very serious; there is a warning of early blossom for it may be too early:

If apples bloom in March, for fruit you may search.

From Herefordshire there is also a concern over a dry March:

March dust on an apple leaf
Brings all kinds of fruit to grief.

Early warmth is then followed by the 'blackthorn winter'. When the blackthorn is on flower – the wild sloe – it is often accompanied by frost. That is really dangerous for its relative the domestic plum, as well as to any fruit which is flowering at the time, as the blossom may well be cut and then no fruit will follow.

Next comes June:

A dripping June, sets all in tune.

July creates an interesting situation when the ordinary farmer wants a dry 15 July which is St Swithin's Day as it says:

St Swithin's Day, if thou dost rain,
For forty days it will remain;
St Swithin's Day if thou be fair,
For forty days 'twill rain nae mair.

Consequently on St Swithin's Day all cereal farmers are looking to the sky hoping it will remain blue and clear, and all the fruit farmers are looking up hoping for rain as St Swithin's Day is the day when nature will 'Christen the Apples'; if it rains on St Swithin's Day then a good crop of fruit will follow. By the time the corn is growing well and a good harvest is promised, it will also be clear what the plum crop will be like:

A good wheat year, is a fine plum year.

But beware, fruit-picking time can be a dangerous time; if the apple actually has blossom at the same time that it has fruit then it foretells of an imminent death:

A bloom on the tree when the apple is ripe
Is a sure sign to the end of somebody's life.

A line which is more obvious says:

There can be no autumn fruit without spring blossoms.

It then becomes very important to pick the fruit properly and to store it correctly as Barnaby Googe wrote:

The apple declareth his ripenes by the blacknes of his kernels. They are gathered after
the 14th of September, or there about, according to their kinde, and not before the
Moone be seventeene daies old, in faire weather, and in the afternoone: Those that fall

from the tree must be laid by themselves. It is better to pull them, than to shake them, least they be bruised in their falling. They are kept in faire lofts, vaults, or cold places, with windows opening toward the North, which in faire weather must be set open.

For many people, until quite recently, it was normal to store both apples and potatoes in separate clamps; the way to make a clamp was, and is, simple. Cover the ground with a bed of straw and then heap the apples on it; cover them with thick straw with all the straw sloping downwards to drain the water and then cover the straw with soil to hold everything in place. If the clamp is made in a sheltered position then the apples will remain in good condition until they are used right up to early spring. The only problem with a good apple clamp is how to keep other apple-lovers out – so make sure that rats and badgers are kept away. When storing the fruit it is also sensible to take note of a number of other little pieces of lore:

> *A rotten apple spoils its neighbour.*
> *Gather apples for storing during the sinking of the moon.*
> *Seek not every beautiful apple to be good.*
> *A goodly looking apple can be rotten at the heart.*

It is also interesting to note that:

> *A windy year is an apple year*

and to all countrymen past, present and future:

> *The fairest apple hangs on the highest branch;*

and: *The sweetest pear hangs on the highest branch.*

It is a fact that the best fruit, even including wild blackberries, always seem to be at the highest point where they cannot be reached.

Eating apples is also reckoned to be a way of keeping good health, hence:

> *An apple a day keeps the Doctor away*

RIGHT: *The Prince Charles – alas not named after H.R.H. Prince Charles who is a great advocate of British apples and the traditional orchard.*

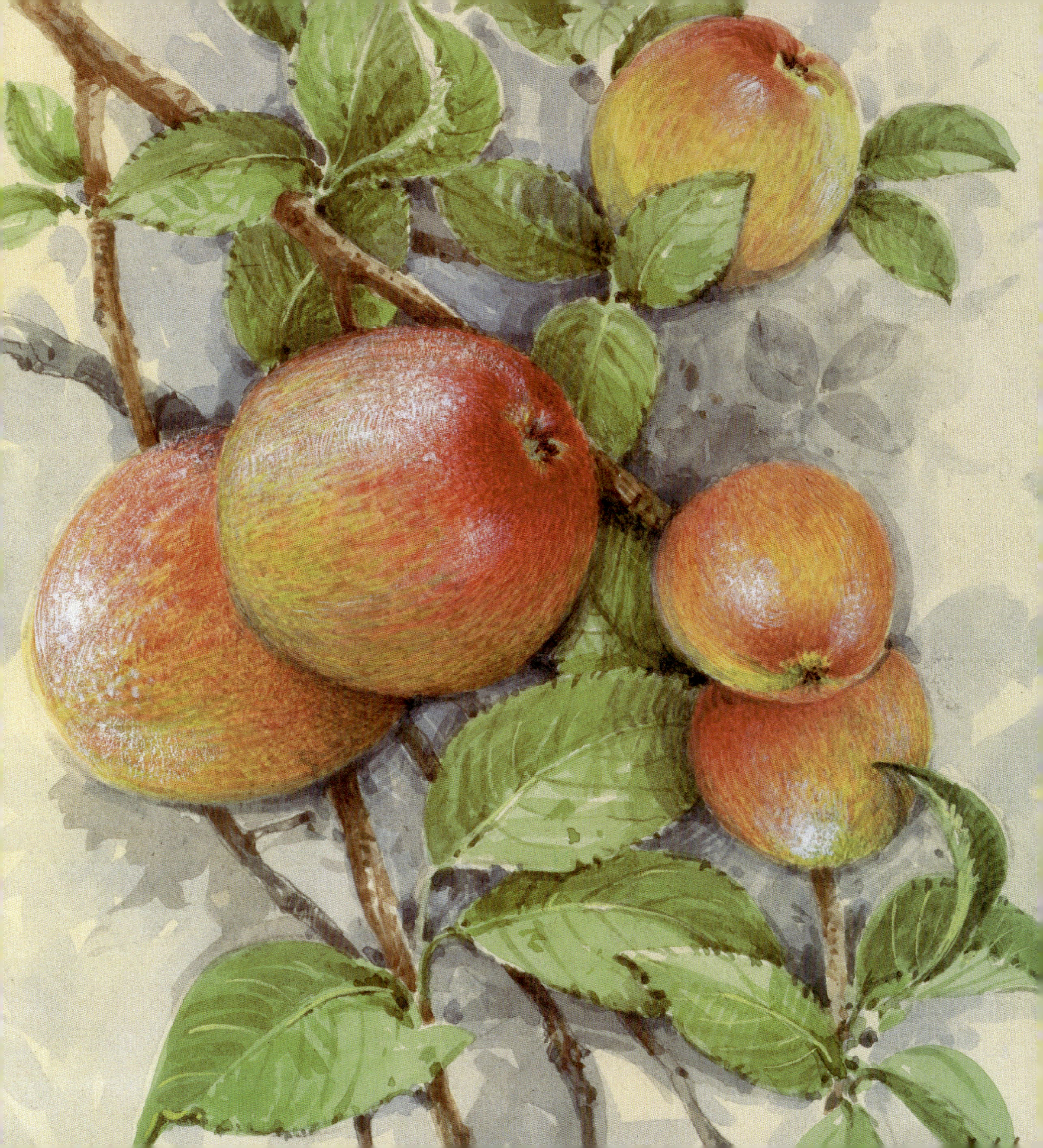

and   *Eat an apple going to bed, and make the Doctor beg his bread.*

Apples can also be used in a number of traditional remedies:

> *Rotten apples or mouldy ones were often wiped on awkward sties in the eye and rotten*
> *apples were also applied to chilblains to try and control the burning and the itching.*

Worse still, in the days of small pox, it was considered that if an apple was placed in a sick person's room, when it went mouldy the small pox was believed to have left the patient and gone into the apple. In addition the scent of apple wood was reckoned to be very good for health in general.
    Apples are also featured in love both requited and unrequited:

> *I will give my love an apple without e'er a core,*
> *I will give my love a house without e'er a door,*
> *I will give my love a palace wherein she may be*
> *And she may unlock it without e'er a key.*

> *My head is the apple without e'er a core*
> *My mind is the house without e'er a door,*
> *My heart is the palace wherein she may be*
> *And she may unlock it without e'er a key.*

Other efforts of predicting love take place on Halloween, 31 October. Apple pips have to be stuck onto cheeks, each pip having been given the name of a potential lover; the last pip to fall off represents the most suitable partner. If sticking pips to cheeks is too messy, they can be placed on the bars of the fire for:

> *If you love me bounce and fly*
> *if you hate me lie and die.*

Whole apples could also be used and unmarried young people should fasten an apple to a piece of string and then twirl them round in front of a hot fire; the one whose apple falls off first will marry first; the last one will die unmarried.
    Halloween was also Gordon's birthday and we would often play apple-bobbing at his party – trying to pick a floating apple out of a bowl of water with your teeth. Another variation was to try to eat an apple suspended from a beam.

St Thomas' night, 21 December, is another busy night for would-be lovers with apples. A single apple should be cut in half; if the number of pips in each half is equal a marriage will soon take place, but if one of the seeds is cut the course of true love will not run smoothly. Two damaged pips indicate that there will be a widowhood.

More simply a girl wanting to obtain a glimpse of her future lover should take a Golden Pippin apple and walk backwards to bed, speaking to nobody on the way; she should then place it underneath her pillow and St Thomas is said to grant a vision of the future lover to the sleeping girl. The other sure way of finding out the lover-to-be, either in desperation, adoration or complete fantasy is to peel an apple, making the rind as long as possible; then throw the peel over the shoulder and on landing it will spell the initials of the lover. If anybody believes all this then it is quite clear that they have been with apples in liquid form for far too long, and it must be alcohol speaking.

So fruit in the orchard, fruit on the tree, fruit in the bottle and fruit in folklore are all important and all contribute to a green thought – similar to *A Green Thought* written by Andrew Marvell.

What wondrous life is this I lead!
Ripe apples drop about my head;
The luscious clusters of the vine
Upon my mouth do crush their wine;
The nectarine and curious peach
Into my hands themselves do reach;
Stumbling on melons, as I pass,
Ensnared with flowers, I fall on grass.

Meanwhile the mind, from pleasure less,
Withdraws into its happiness;
The mind, that ocean where each kind
Does straight its own resemblance find;
Yet it creates, transcending these,
Far other worlds, and other seas;
Annihilating all that's made
To a green thought in a green shade.

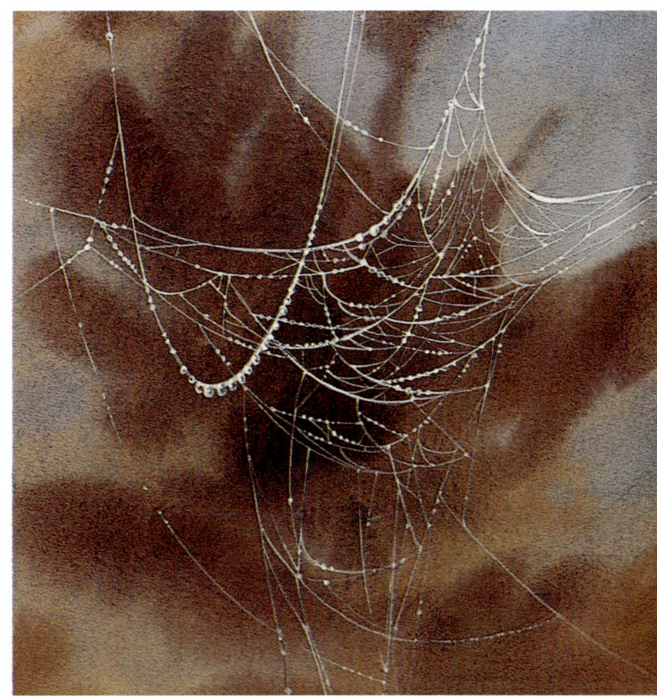

Spider's web and dew – a familiar sight at the time of the apple harvest.

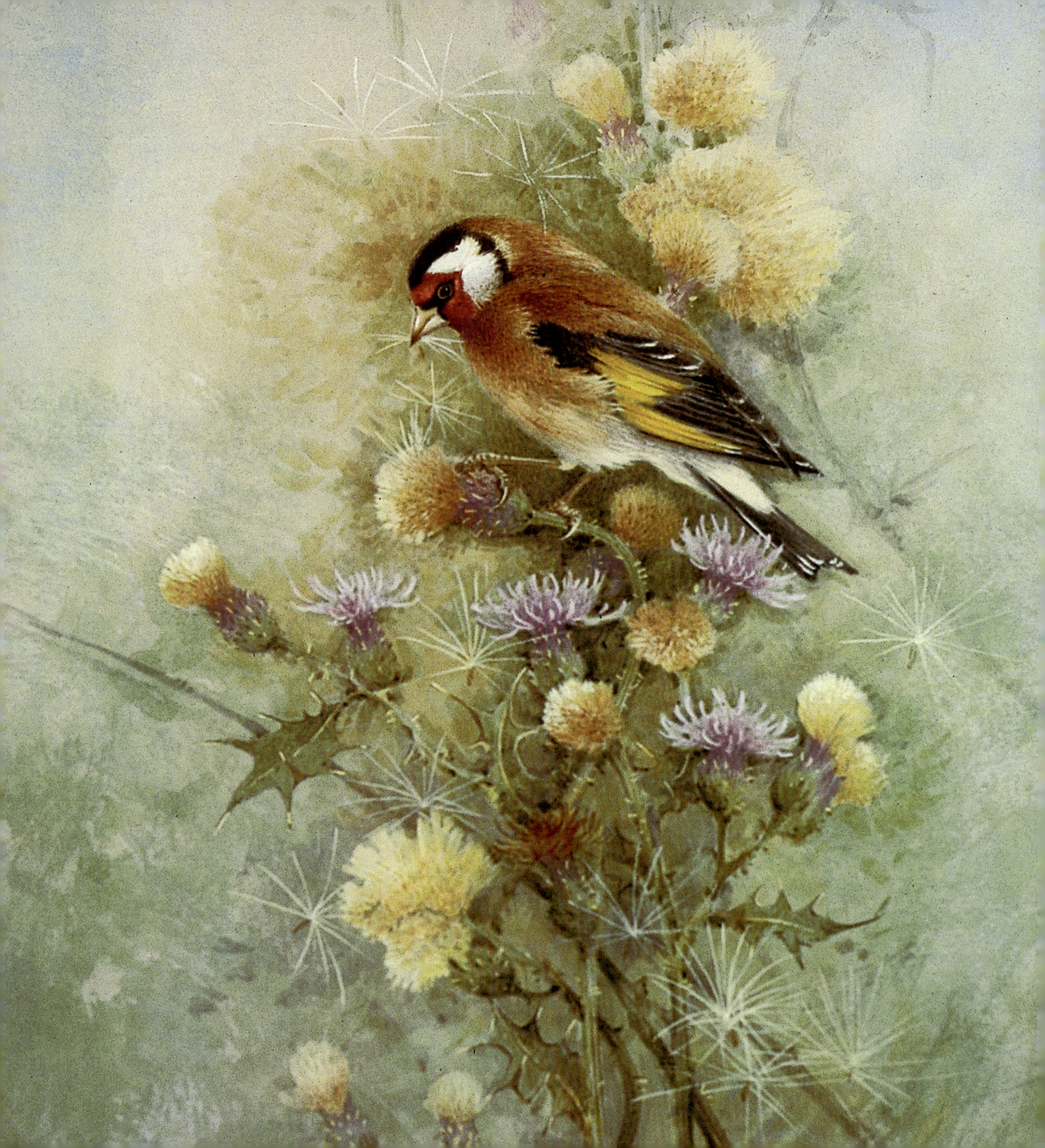

CHAPTER FOUR

Birds, Bees and Butterflies

Not only is the orchard the obvious place to find fruit, but it also attracts much wildlife; this is true of both the bottom of the garden orchard, and the large commercial orchard. Birds, butterflies and bees are among the creatures that really feel at home among fruit trees – the older the better. It is the same for all trees, the older the tree, then the better it is for wildlife. The cracks, the severed limbs and the old peeling bark provide wonderful places for insects, and this brings in the birds looking for grubs, bugs and eggs from the smallest tit to all three types of woodpecker. Indeed it is the demise of the really old orchard that has had a devastating effect on that wonderful and peculiar bird – the wryneck, which is now thought to be extinct as a breeding bird in Britain.

Nearly all the birds that we regard as common and welcome garden birds are also very fond of orchards. The finches love them, goldfinches, greenfinches and chaffinches are regular visitors to orchards and the

LEFT: *The goldfinch, a real lover of orchards.*
RIGHT: *The great-spotted woodpecker.*

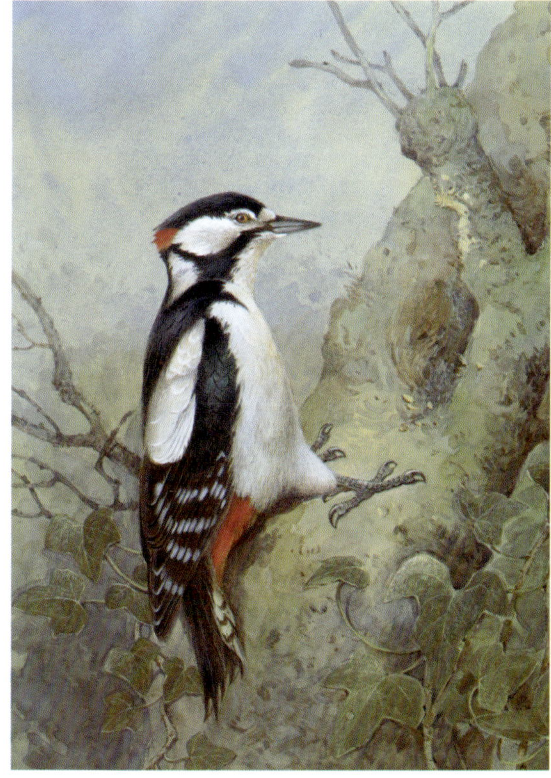

beautiful bullfinch visits them too often, particularly in the early spring when it feasts on the buds of blossom; as a result bullfinches were extremely unwelcome in the days of widespread commercial orchards. Since then the population of the bullfinch has plummeted and in the last twenty-five years the overall population has declined by well over 60 per cent. From Betty Hughes' charming poem it is clear that some fruit tree owners forgave the bullfinch.

I saw upon a winter's day
A bullfinch on a hedgerow spray;
He piped one note.
And since the countryside was mute,
As pure as rain I heard the flute
Of that small throat.

He picked a rotting willow-seed;
He whistled, in his joy to feed,
A whole sweet stave.
His sloe-black head, how shining sleek,
How strong his blunted sooty beak,
His eye, how brave!

Then boldly down he came to drink
Out of a roadside puddle's brink,
Half ice, half mud;
So coral-breasted, sturdy, merry,
That I forgave him plum and cherry
Nipped in the bud.

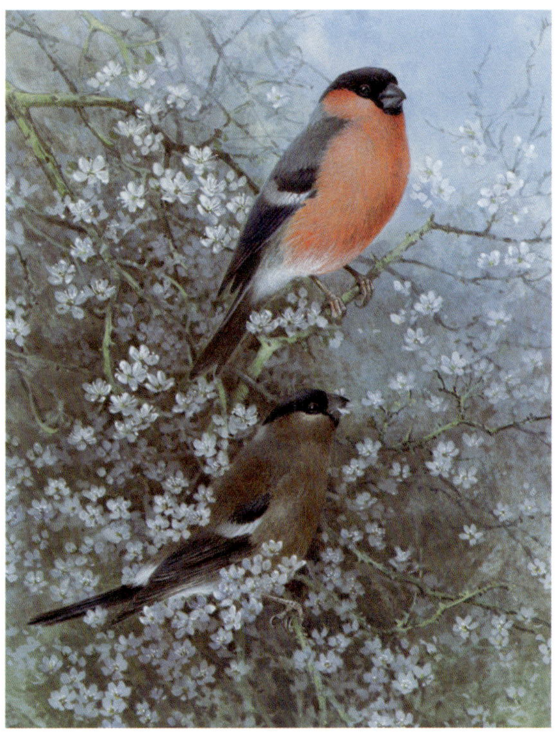

The bullfinch – the fruit growers least favourite bird.

Greenfinches, chaffinches and goldfinches also do very well in orchards with plenty of food and good places in which to build their nests. Goldfinches seem to prefer apple trees to fit their beautiful little nests into the forks of branches. The first hint that a nest is there is when the young are on the wing and the family group can really be called 'a charm'. All the 'finch' nests slightly differ. Of course at one time when Gordon was a boy, egg-collecting was still common and people got to appreciate the beauty of nests. Now that egg-collecting is illegal – quite rightly – one of the unfortunate aspects is that people no longer appreciate the astonishing skill that all birds show in the construction of their nests. One great egg collector and writer on British birds' eggs was a Yorkshire man called Henry Seebohm; in the 1896 edition of his book *Coloured Figures of the Eggs of British Birds*, is a Memoir: *'Henry Seebohm was born at Bradford, in Yorkshire. In July, 1832, and at the time of his death was but 63 years of age, still full of energy and the elaboration of schemes for the production of even greater works than he had hitherto attempted. An attack of influenza, in the early part of 1895, rendered him so weak that nothing but absolute rest could have restored him to health, and this the activity of his brain prevented him from achieving, so that the malignant anaemia to which he secummed, had full play, and he expired on the 26th November, 1895.'* Fortunately before the great man expired he described the nests of the finches; of the goldfinch he wrote; *'the nest is a charming piece of bird-architecture. It is much smaller than that of the chaffinch, but is to a certain extent made on the same model. It usually measures from 1½ to 2 inches in inside diameter and is about 1 inch deep. It is often made of*

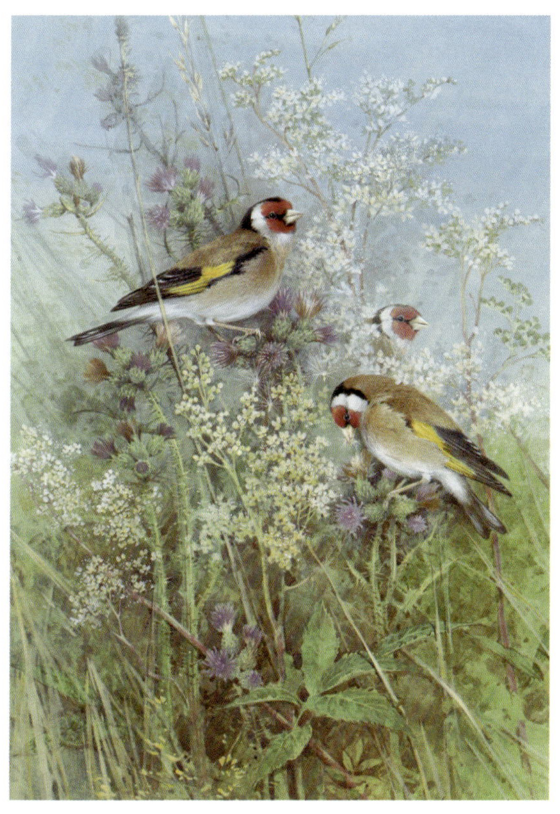

Goldfinches often nest in apple trees.

moss, lichens, vegetable down and a few long hairs.' We have found goldfinch nests in our apple trees and they are beautifully lined often with horse hair or cow hair.

Of the chaffinch he says: *'The nest of the Chaffinch, being so elaborate and highly finished, naturally takes some little time in its construction; indeed, with the exception of the Long-tailed Titmouse, the female Chaffinch probably takes more time to build her charming little nest than any other British bird.'* He likes the work of the greenfinch too: *'Few nests are prettier than that of a Greenfinch. It is not so neat as the nest of a Goldfinch or Chaffinch; but its very slovenliness is the secret of its beauty. The outside is made of moss, dry grass and wool.'*

He clearly appreciates the bullfinch too: *'The Bullfinch is found commonly, although more or less locally, in all the wooded portions of Great Britain. It breeds throughout Western Europe, from Germany westwards, and south to the Mediterranean. The nest of the Bullfinch can readily be told from that of almost every other British bird. It is a very beautiful construction, the frame-*

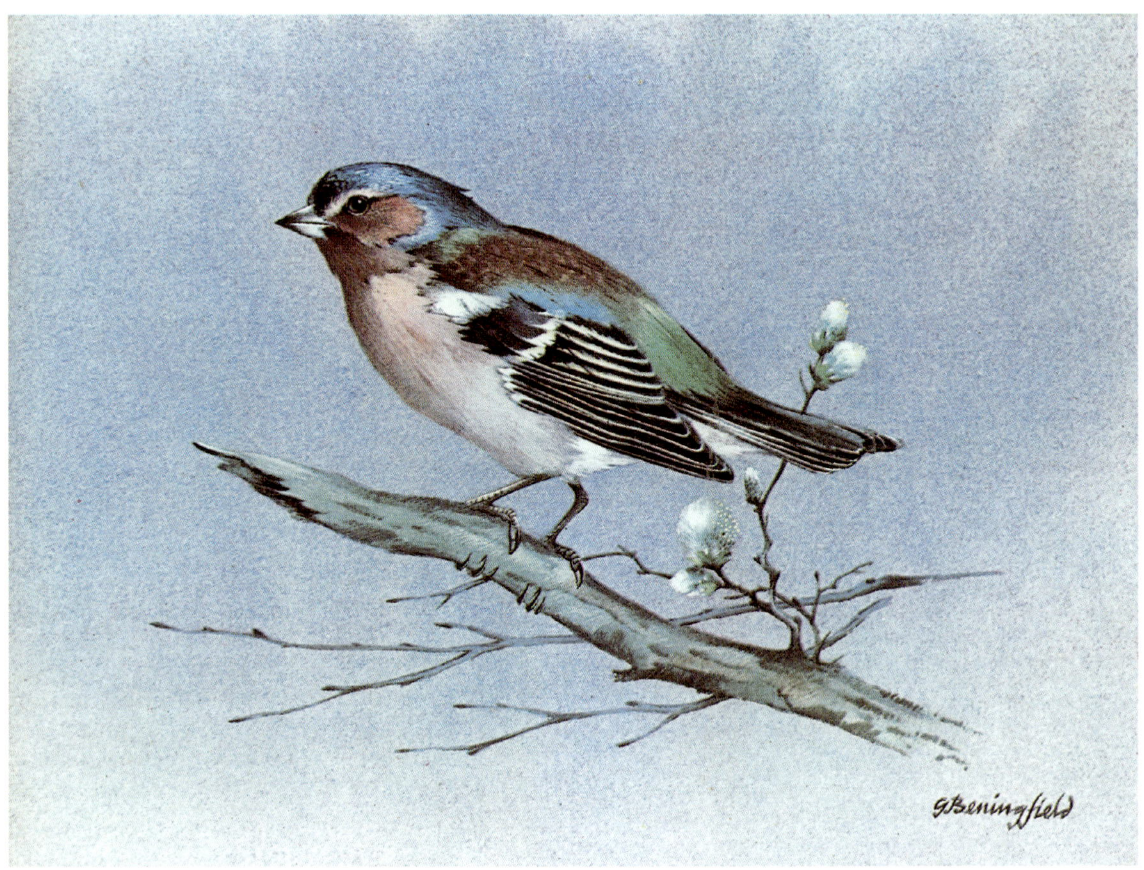

The chaffinch.

work being almost entirely composed of slender twigs, and is very flat, not unlike a miniature Wood Pigeon's nest. The sticks are very artfully woven and matted together; and in the middle of this platform of sticks the cup of the nest is formed of fine rootlets projecting above the frame-work, making the inside as deep as usual. In some nests a little wool or a feather or two are found.

The eggs are from four to six in number, greenish blue in ground-colour, spotted and some-times streaked with dark purplish brown and with larger and paler blotches of pinkish brown. In some eggs the spots are evenly distributed over the entire surface, but in the majority of specimens they form an irregular zone round the large end. The eggs of the Bullfinch are much bluer than those of any of the allied Finches, except those of the Lesser Redpole.'

Long-tailed tits will also create their amazingly intricate nests in an orchard if there is enough cover and if there is holly, bramble, or hawthorn growing among the fruit trees then long-tailed tits will almost certainly nest. Rough areas around the orchard will also attract birds such as the yellowhammer.

Another interesting bird that has started nesting more regularly in Britain is the woodcock and although it often likes denser woods, they are often seen in orchards particularly in winter. It remains to be seen whether they will start breeding in the rough corners of orchards.

We have for many years had quite a large rookery near our little orchard, but we have never had any rooks nests.

BELOW: *The woodcock.*

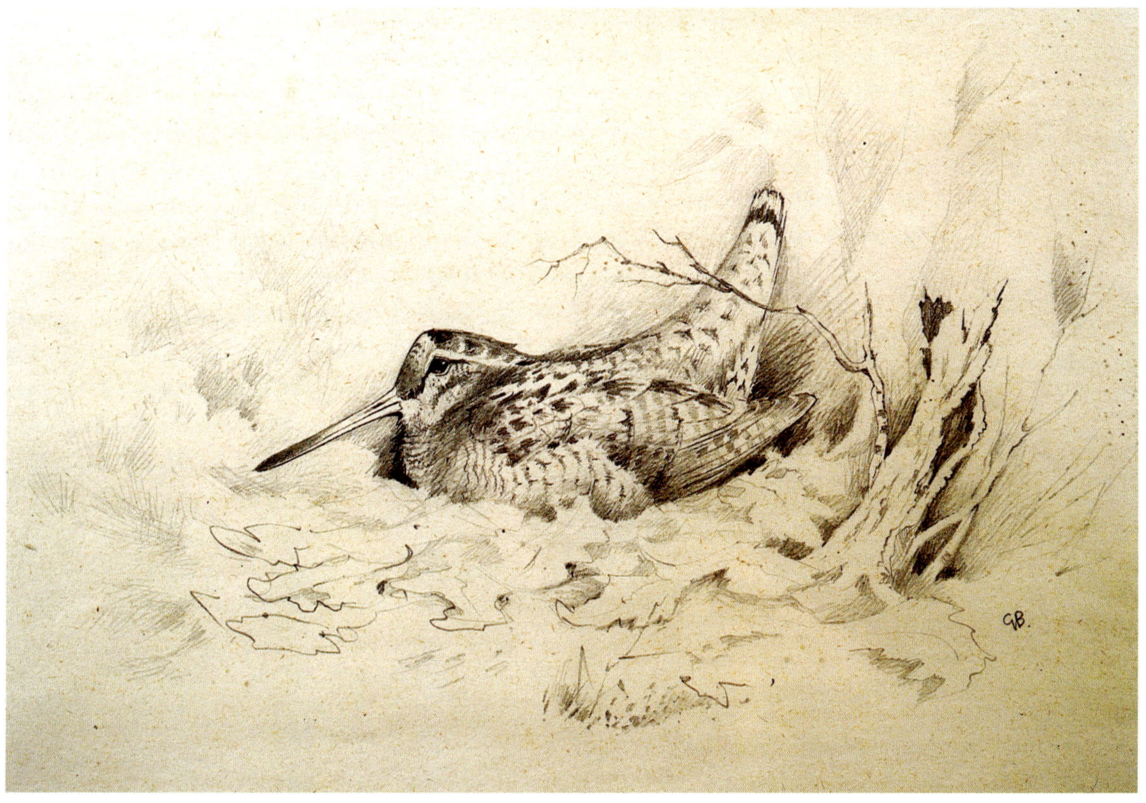

However rooks do often like visiting orchards for the grassland surrounding the trees it is the home of various bugs they can pull out of the soil with their great beaks. If animals graze orchard grass, then of course rooks really love delving into old cow pats for the insects or eggs that might be hidden inside.

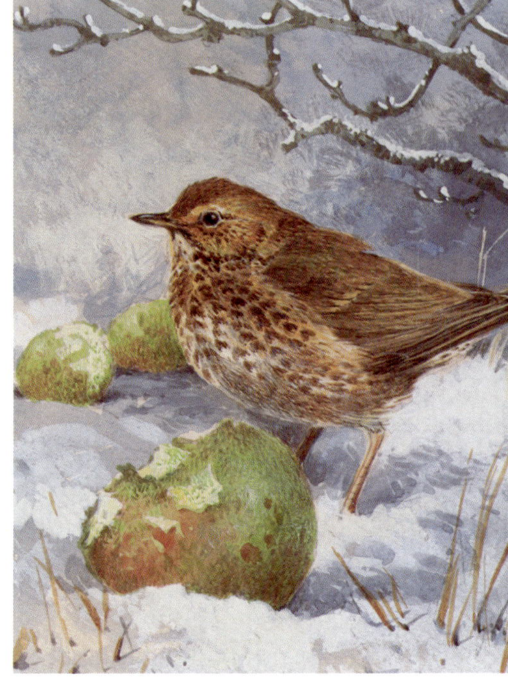

Blackbirds and thrushes – the song thrush and the mistle thrush – also are very fond of orchards for both the worms in the soil, and the fallen fruit in autumn and winter. The first picture that Gordon painted for his fruit collection was of the song thrush looking very cold in the snow; but at least it had had a really good meal on what looks to be a Bramley cooking apple. Blackbirds and thrushes can stay in the orchard the whole year and both sing beautifully to welcome the spring. The song of the thrush is mimicked in verse by Alfred Lord Tennyson, in *The Throstle*:

'Summer is coming, summer is coming.
I know it, I know it, I know it.
Light again, leaf again, life again, love again,'
Yes, my wild little poet.

Sing the new year in under the blue.
Last year you sang it as gladly.
'New, new, new, new!' Is it then so new
That you should carol so madly?

'Love again, song again, nest again, young again,'
Never a prophet so crazy!
And hardly a daisy as yet, little friend,
See, there is hardly a daisy.

'Here again, here, here, here, happy year!'
O warble unchidden, unbidden!
Summer is coming, is coming, my dear,
And all the winters are hidden.

As you read the poem it is almost possible to hear the beautiful song of the thrush; similarly he also wrote a poem in praise of *The Blackbird*.

O blackbird! Sing me something well:
While all the neighbours shoot thee round,
I keep smooth plats of fruitful ground,
Where thou mayst warble, eat and dwell.

The espaliers and the standards all
Are thine; the range of lawn and park:
The unnetted black-hearts ripen dark,
All thine, against the garden wall.

Yet, though I spared thee all the spring,
Thy sole delight is, sitting still,
With that gold dagger of thy bill
*To fret the summer jenneting**

A golden bill! the silver tongue,
Cold February loved, is dry:
Plenty corrupts the melody
That made thee famous once, when young:

And in the sultry garden-squares,
Now thy flute-notes are changed to coarse,
I hear thee not at all, or hoarse
As when a hawker hawks his wares.

Take warning! he that will not sing
While yon sun prospers in the blue
Shall sing for want, ere leaves are new,
Caught in the frozen palms of spring.

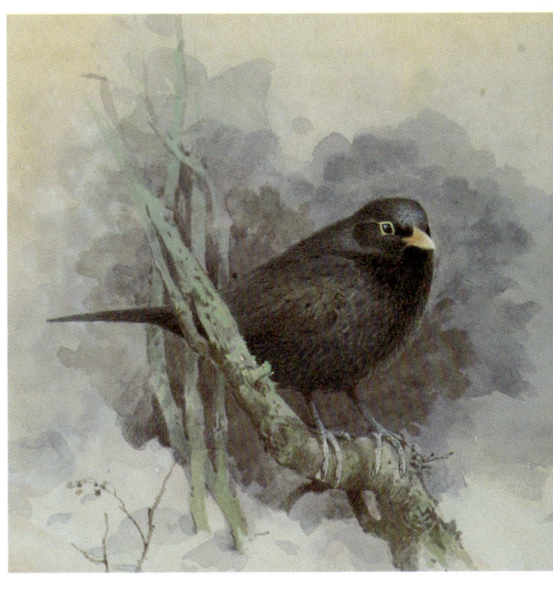

This poem is made even more interesting because it mentions the blackbird using its bill in the 'summer jenneting'. The 'jenneting' of the poem is more commonly known as Joaneting which is a very old variety of eating apple which was grown in gardens and for sale for many centuries up to about the 1920s. It is a very early season apple and ready to be eaten in July; the season only lasts for a few days. It was mentioned by Frances Bacon (1561–1626) in an essay *On Gardens*; he referred to it as 'Ginnitings'; it was also noted by Rae in 1665 and it was described as being 'small, crisp, brisk and eaten straight from the tree'.

As most orchards do have patches of long grass that hold the damp, they are also very good places for slugs and snails and so song thrushes use orchards extensively as a source of snails. They will then either find an anvil stone in the orchard or have one nearby where they can go and smash the shell to eat the snail. Certainly many experts believe that the decline of the song thrush has been caused by a decline in the snail population; farm chemicals as well as the chemicals used in countless gardens simply wipe out the snail population. Consequently a good old traditional orchard is often the last snail reservoir for the embattled song-thrush. Other members of the thrush family also fly into orchards during the autumn and the winter and fieldfares and redwings are very attractive birds. Consequently fallen apples should not be swept up or tidied but they should simply be left where they fall so that our winter visitors can feed well. Often when the birds arrive from Scandinavia they will move along the hedgerows eating hips and haws and then, as the berries run out they will turn to the orchards before finally moving into grass fields for much smaller seeds. One way of attracting fieldfares and redwings into the garden is to throw out any rotting apples, but they should be thrown quite a long way away from the house as, particularly fieldfares, can be quite nervous. If half bramleys are put on bird tables, then many birds will be attracted and the blackbird is particularly fond of a good cooking apple.

In the traditional country garden and on an old-style farm there are often free-range hens; they are also extremely fond of orchards.

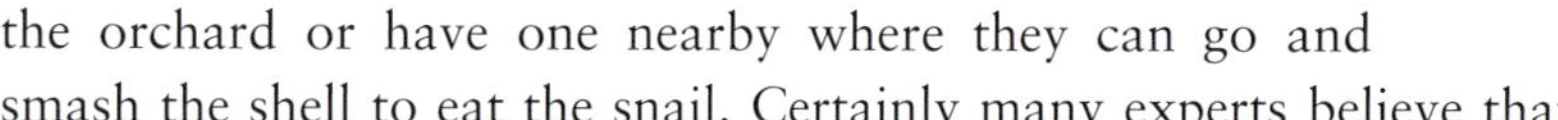

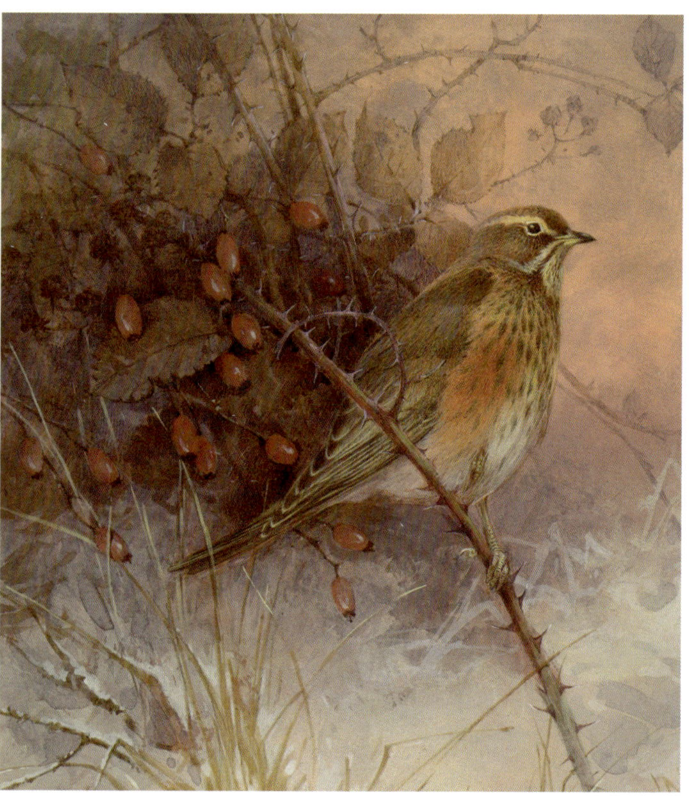

Redwing, a winter visitor appreciative of fallen apples.

It can be a great problem if they then try and roost out because there are many stories of foxes using their cunning to walk round and round an apple tree to make a hen fall out of the branches through the dizziness caused by watching the fox. Whether true or false is not known but we have certainly had roosting hens disappear from trees in the past. The hens not only eat the fallen apples but they love scrapping around in any old 'muck-heaps' around the roots of the trees. If there are patches of long vegetation then a hen will sneak off and lay her eggs there well hidden away – she will then become broody and 'disappear'. The usual response is: 'Oh no, the hen has gone, a fox must have got her' – but then one day she will arrive outside the house with a brood of newly hatched chicks.

Orchards often attract free-range hens.

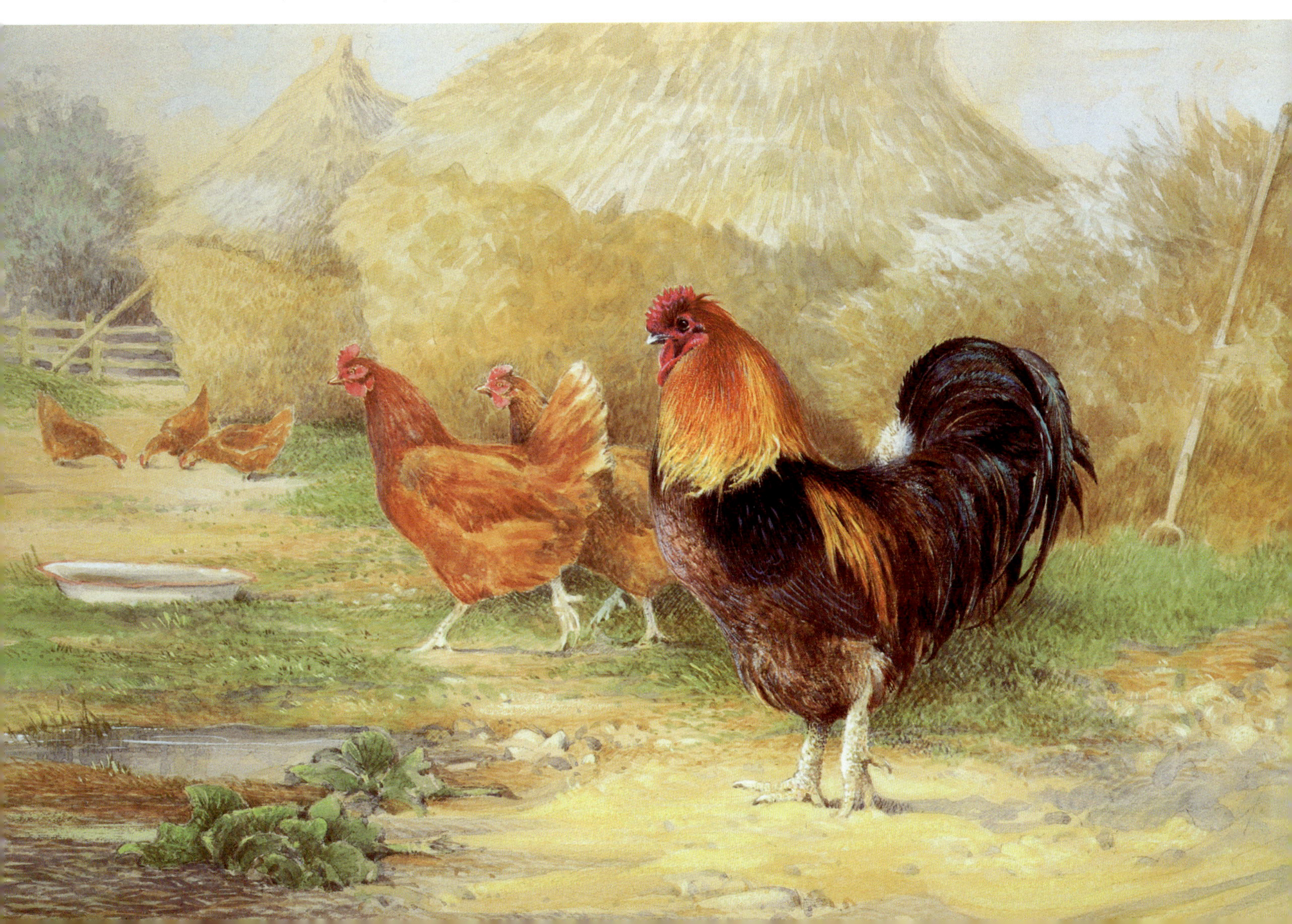

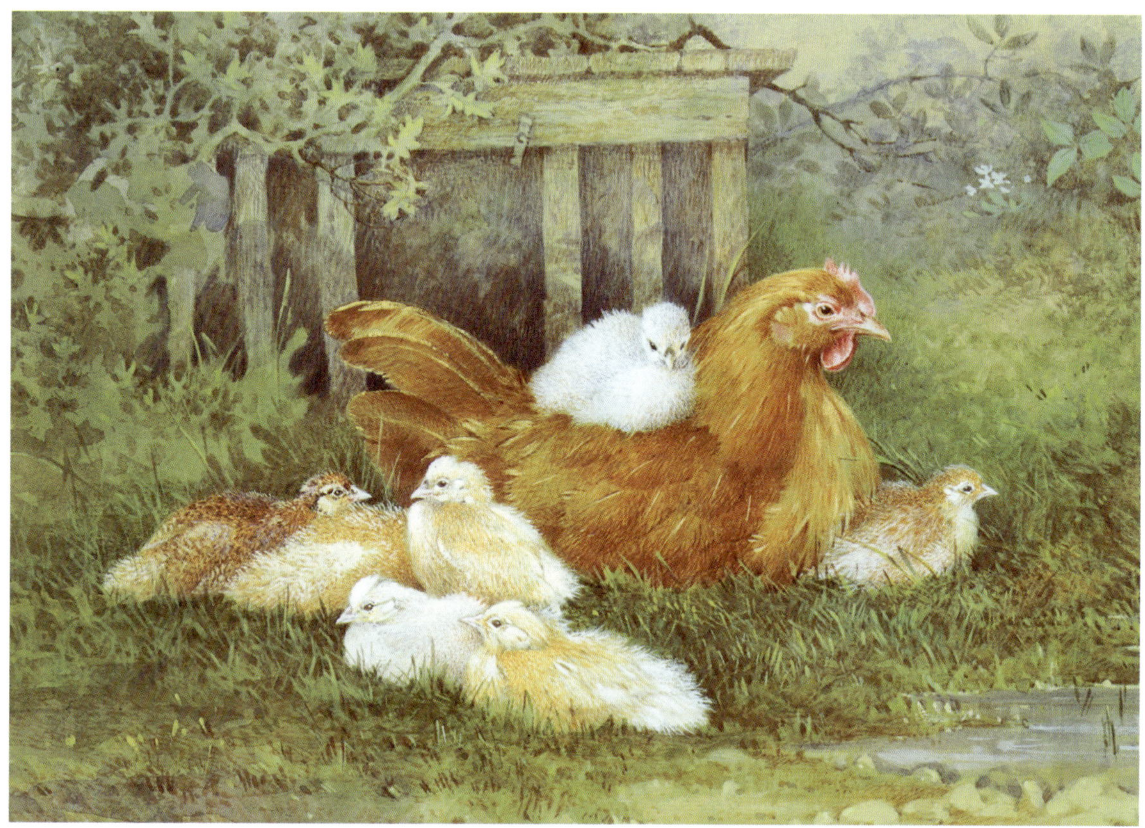

John Clare (1793–1864), the old peasant poet from Northamptonshire, described the old hen's nest in the orchard perfectly:

Among the orchard weeds, from every search,
Snugly and sure, the old hen's nest is made,
Who cackles every morning from her perch
To tell the servant girl new eggs are laid;
Who lays her washing by, and far and near
Goes seeking all about from day to day,
And stung with nettles tramples everywhere;
But still the cackling pullet lays away.
The boy on Sundays goes the stack to pull
In hopes to find her there, but naught is seen,

> *And takes his hat and thinks to find it full,*
> *She's laid so long so many might have been.*
> *But naught is found and all is given o-er*
> *Till the young brood come chirping to the door.*

According to one old rhyme black hens are less successful at hiding their eggs than brown hens:

> *Higgledy, piggledy, my black hen*
> *She lays eggs for gentlemen;*
> *Gentlemen come every day*
> *To see what my black hen doth lay.*

I suppose to be politically correct, and not sexist, as I have mentioned a little verse about a hen, I'd now better give an old traditional verse about a cock:

> *The cock crows in the morn*
> *To tell us to rise,*
> *And he that lies late*
> *Will never be wise:*
> *For early to bed,*
> *And early to rise,*
> *Makes a man healthy*
> *And wealthy and wise.*

If only that was true.

In addition to bumble bees, other insects and butterflies come into the orchard to feed from the nectar in the blossom and to feed from the fruit, both on the tree and fallen and rotting on the ground. The bumble bee is the best known feeder on nectar and pollen and without the bee there would be far fewer apples, pears and plums on the tree. Gordon was extremely pleased to be asked to paint a bumble bee as a stamp (overleaf); he had already drawn a set of butterflies which had been extremely popular and so he was honoured when he was asked to do yet another set. I think that the bumble bee for the stamp is

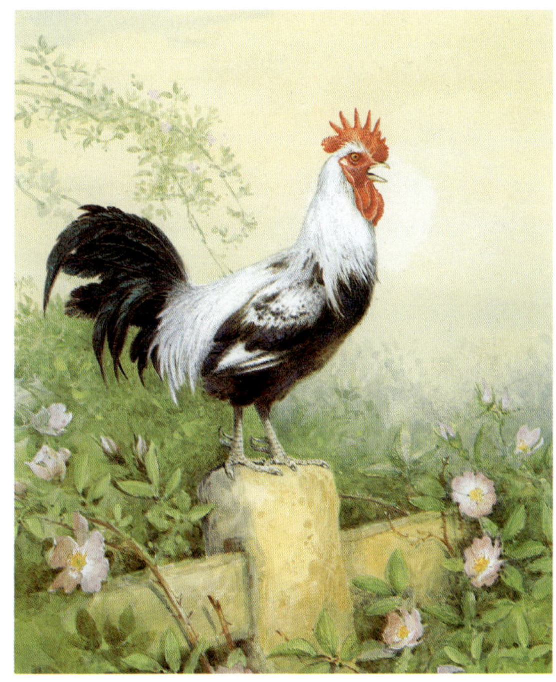

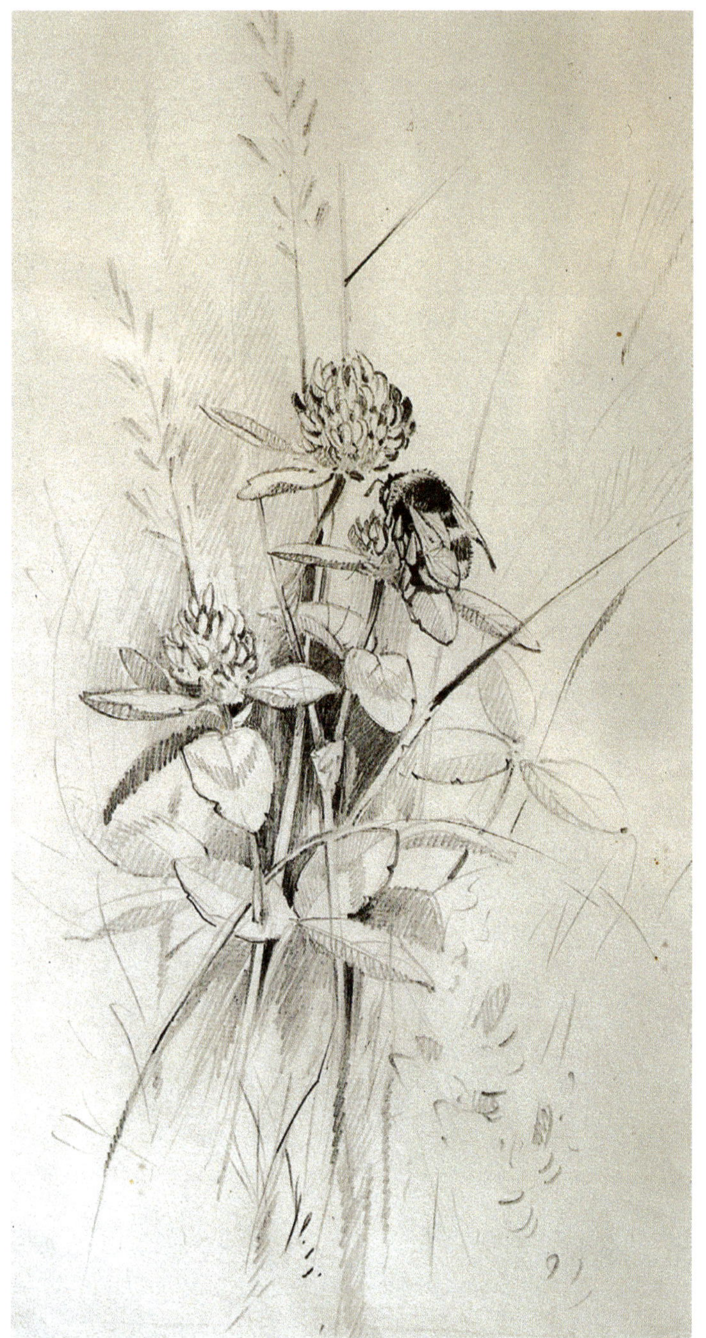

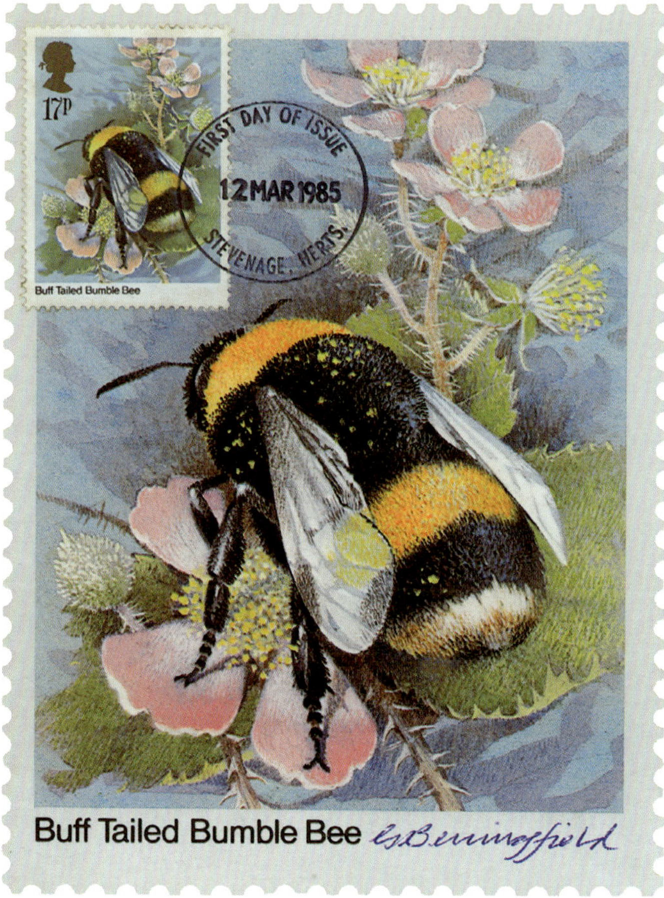
17p
FIRST DAY OF ISSUE
12 MAR 1985
STEVENAGE, HERTS.
Buff Tailed Bumble Bee
Buff Tailed Bumble Bee

one of his best paintings. The others in the set are also important and can be found in a good traditional orchard. Ladybirds are nature's own form of pest control. Fruit trees, like many vegetables in the garden, can be absolutely plagued with aphids – greenfly and blackfly. Yet although they look extremely attractive, ladybirds are very efficient predators and aphids make up one of their main food sources – starter, main course and sweet are all aphids. They like them and eat them in large quantities. Consequently an orchard, a garden, or a field of wheat, barley, or beans that has a good population of ladybirds will not have a very great aphid problem.

It is strange that thinking about orchards and ladybirds brings back memories, it is one of the features of picking fruit that ladybirds can be found on the leaves and on the fruit. While picking a basket of fruit you see so many of these charming little creatures. The dragonfly is another sight of fruit-picking time, patrolling up and down the rows, in and out of the trees. They are astonishingly beautiful as they drone here and there – hovering – accelerating and resting with their brilliant wings open; their bodies seem to light up in sunlight. They are also very efficient predators and they will take damsel flies or even butterflies on the wing and they are really quite ruthless hunters. Their life story is amazing as they spend their winter at the bottom of ponds and ditches and then emerge and change into such remarkable creatures, patrolling and hovering. They are one of the sights of late summer and the emperor dragonfly is the largest and the most beautiful.

It is very fitting that the last one of the set should be the grasshopper. As with so many species, as gardens and fields have been tidied up and sprayed with chemicals so grasshoppers have disappeared. Yet in many old orchards they have hung on. Now it is almost exciting to hear the shrill chaffing sound of the grasshopper again, it should be the sound of high summer, and it still is in a few places. I know that Gordon was so pleased when the Countryside Restoration

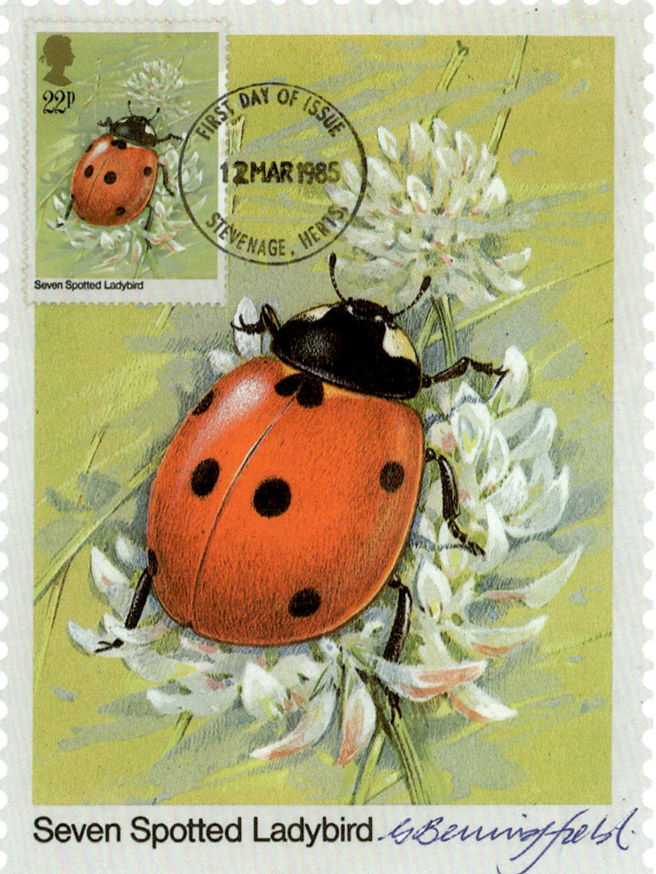

Seven Spotted Ladybird

Trust acquired old flood plains in Cambridgeshire that had been ploughed for intensive wheat production. The CRT planted it with Miriam Rothschild's wonderful traditional hay meadow mixture and it pleased him so much to see old grasses and wildflowers come back so quickly. An added pleasure was that grasshoppers quickly returned too, so it was possible to hear that wonderful grating noise on a hot day and also see them jumping ahead as you walked through the long grass. Grasshoppers are important for birds, particularly the young of skylarks, yellowhammers, partridges and pheasants, as they are high in protein and if there is a flourishing insect and grasshopper population then there will be far more young birds and nestlings survive to become adults. It was a good idea to use this group of four stamps to try and remind people of the importance of our simple but beautiful creatures.

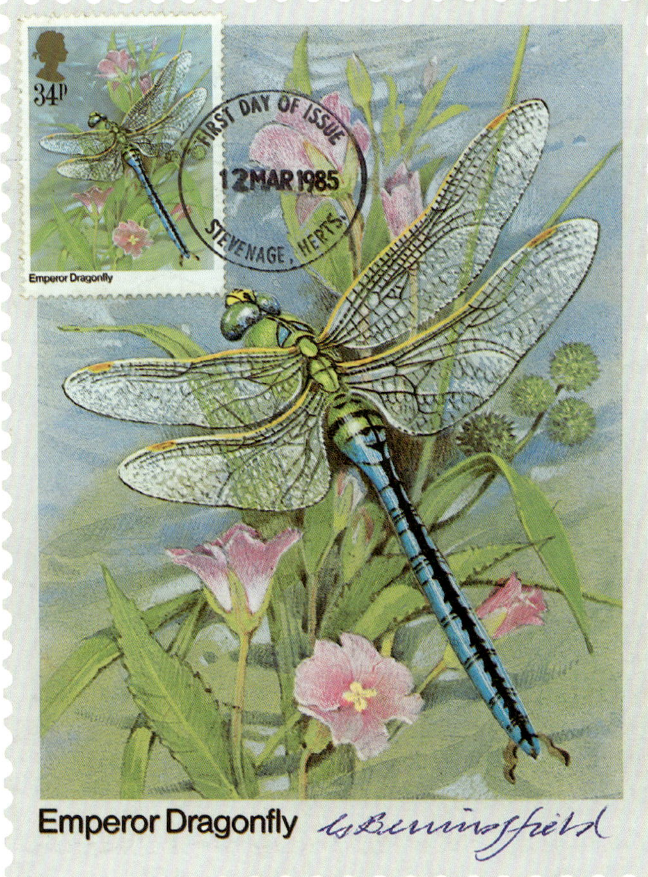

Emperor Dragonfly

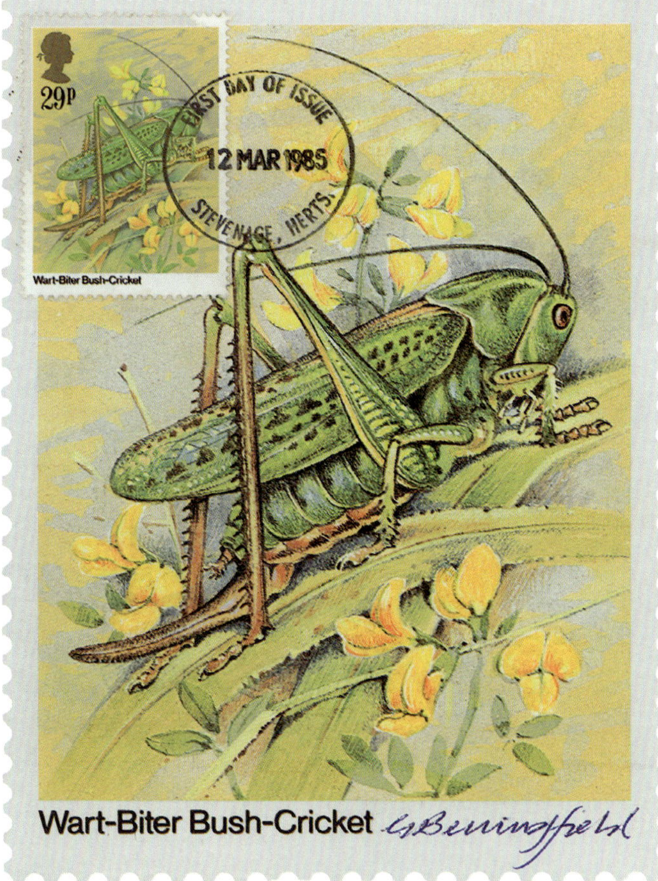

Wart-Biter Bush-Cricket

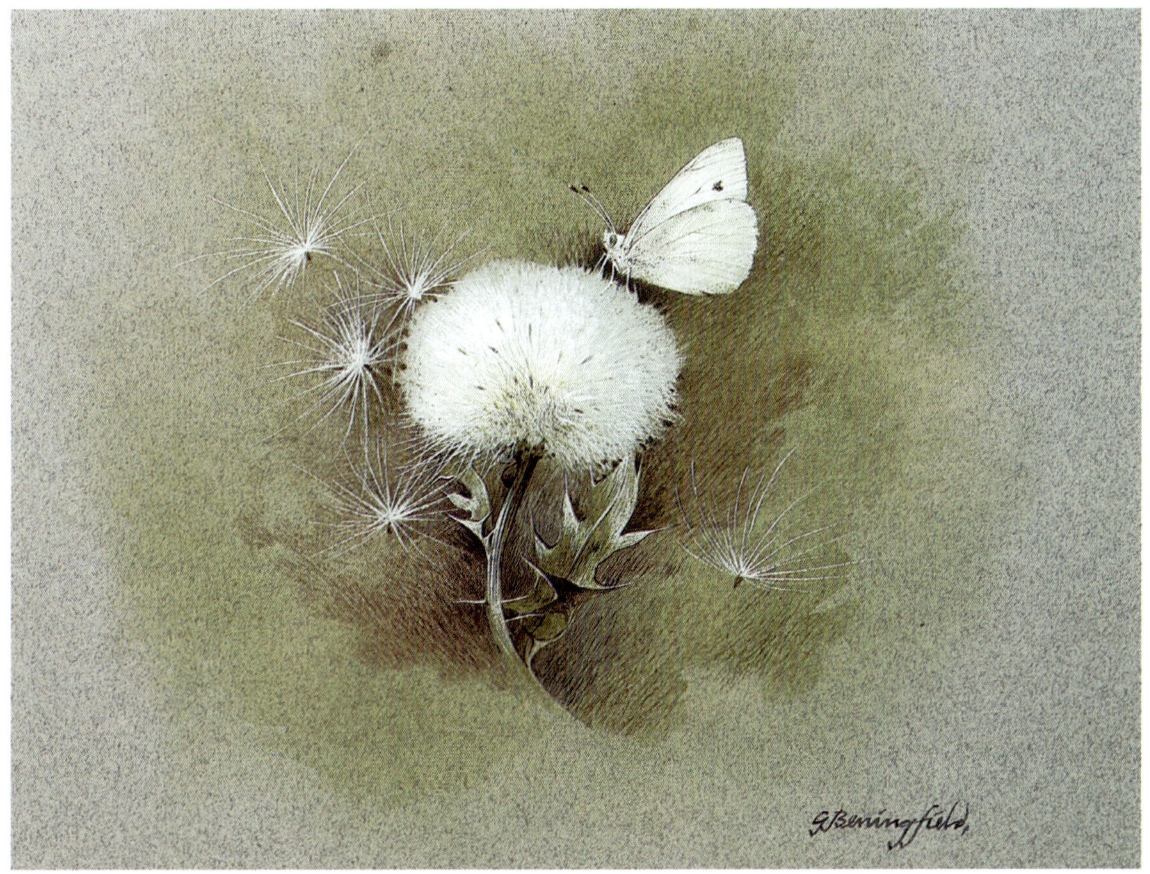

Small white on thistle seed-head.

There is another creature that inhabits orchards in large numbers in late summer and that is the wasp. Although wasps are much maligned, and I have to say unfairly maligned, if they are left alone they will not sting and of course they serve a very useful purpose in eating up old and rotting fruit as well as all sorts of other old and rotting pieces of vegetation. The only trouble starts when they begin eating apples and plums that we want to pick, then they are not helping us, but competing with us and it is not funny to pick a Victoria plum with a wasp feeding on it. The wasp might get very angry, but the person stung will get even angrier and the whole wasps' nest will have to watch out.

Butterflies too like Victoria plums, and any other plum, and the most famous of all the fruit-eating butterflies is the beautiful red admiral. It is a fantastic butterfly and Gordon painted it

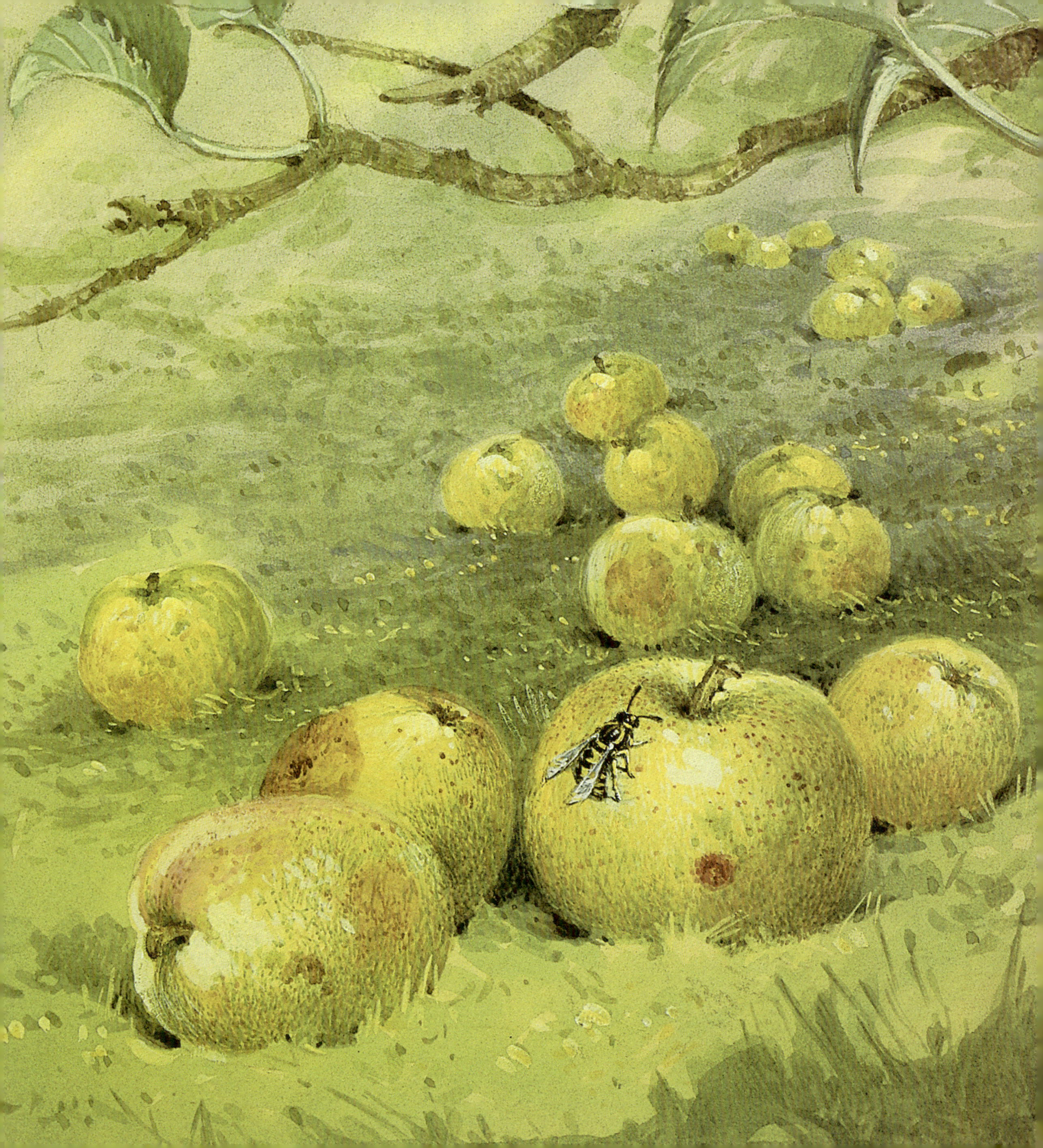

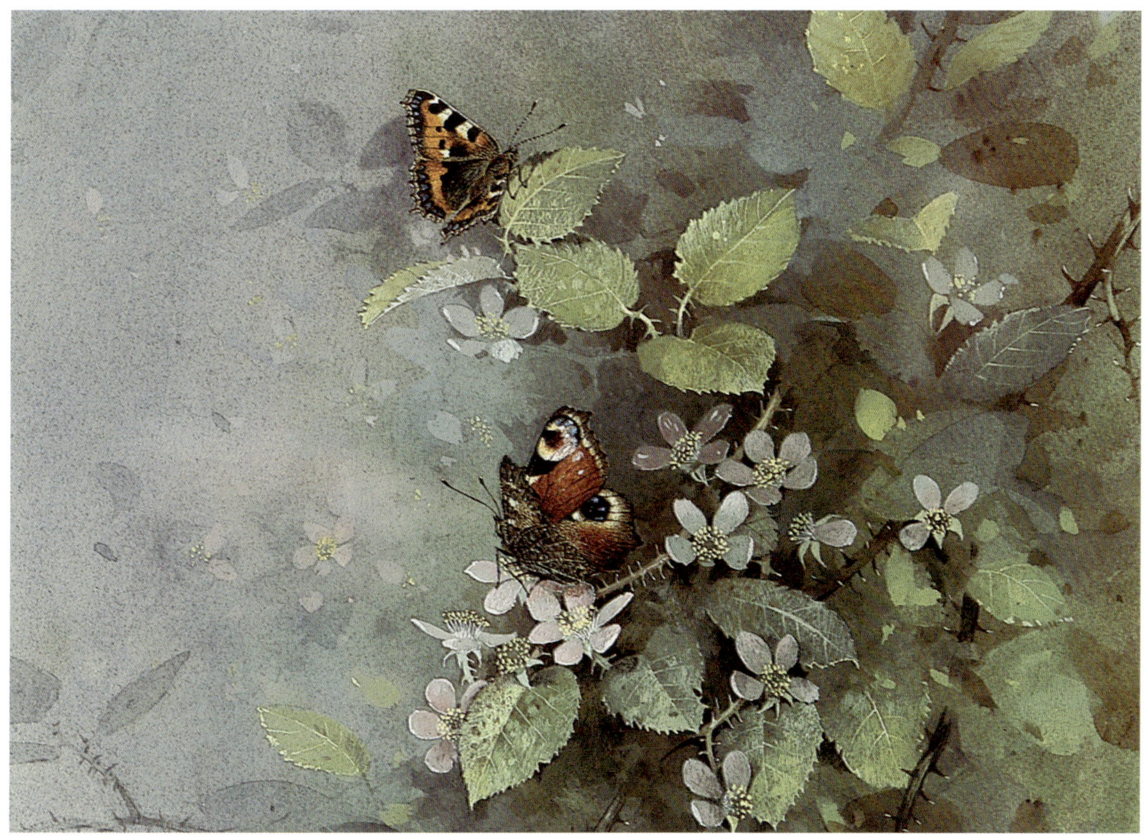

LEFT: *Wasp attracted by windfalls.*
ABOVE: *Small tortoiseshell and peacock.*

many times on apples, on plums, on flowers, and on brambles because it is such a spectacular creature. All butterflies are amazing; the red admiral can smell and taste through its feet and it can often be seen treading on stinging nettles which is where it lays its eggs and where the caterpillars hatch and so it has to make sure that it is on the right food plant for its young. Each year red admirals migrate to Britain from Southern Europe in large numbers. Many experts are beginning to think that with our climate getting warmer some are managing to survive over winter. As a result there are many sightings these days of very early red admirals flying alongside our other early flyers, small tortoiseshells, peacocks and brimstones. But in the wildness, among the flowers and 'weeds' other butterflies too regularly frequent orchards. The large white, the small white, the green veined white, the holly blue, the orange tip and many more. Another of Gordon's quite

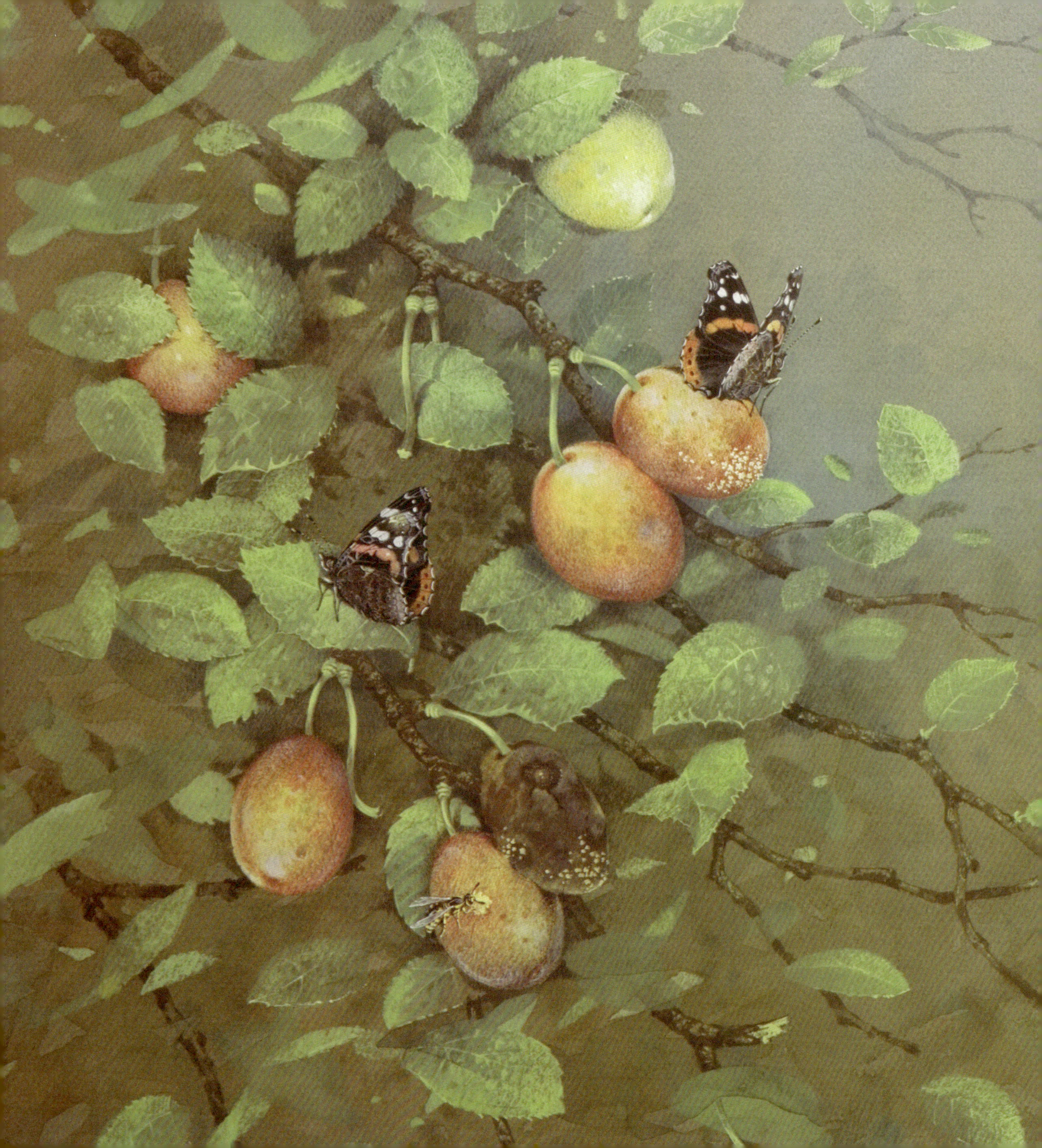

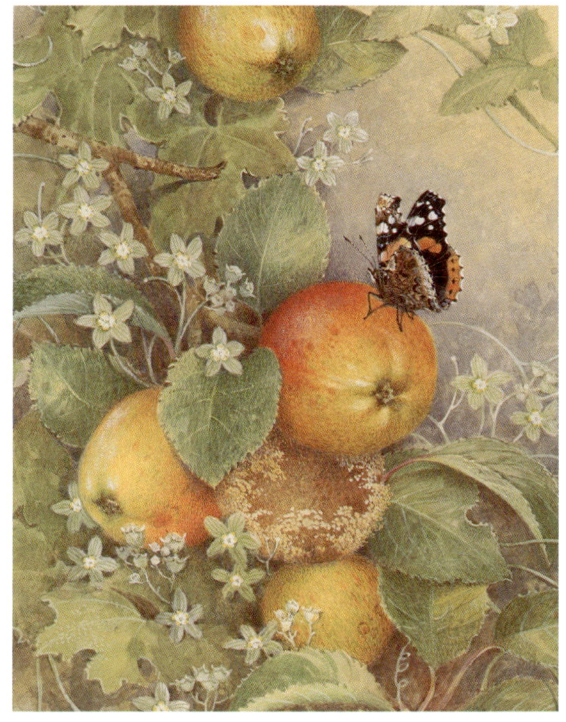

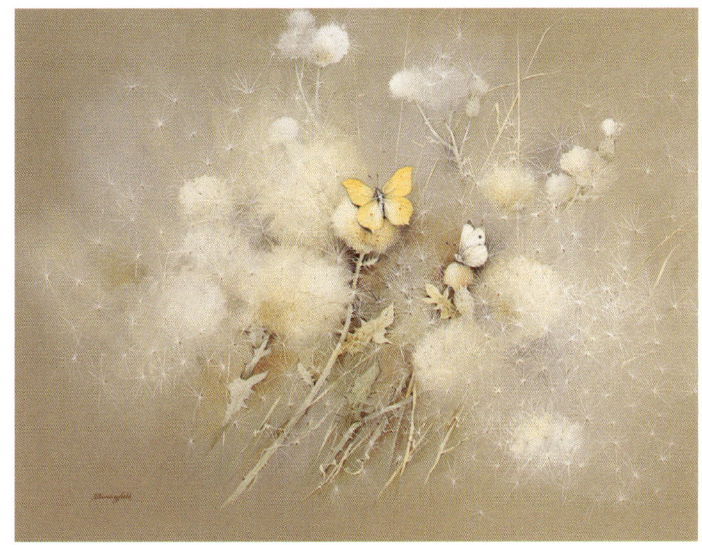

OPPOSITE AND LEFT: *Red admirals on Victoria plums and apple.*
ABOVE: *The brimstone on thistledown.*

remarkable paintings is of a brimstone on thistledown. Thistledown in the wind coincides with apple-picking time and it would have been at that time that Gordon painted the picture. Consequently it is wrong just to think of orchards as places for fruit. Orchards can be areas of vibrant light and beautiful colour. So, thinking of orchards can bring back memories and again the link between butterflies and memories reminds me of a WH Davies poem, *The Ways of Time*:

As butterflies are but winged flowers,
Half sorry for their change, who fain,
So still and long they lie on leaves,
Would be thought flowers again –

E'en so my thoughts, that should expand,
And grow to higher themes above,
Return like butterflies to lie
On the old things I love

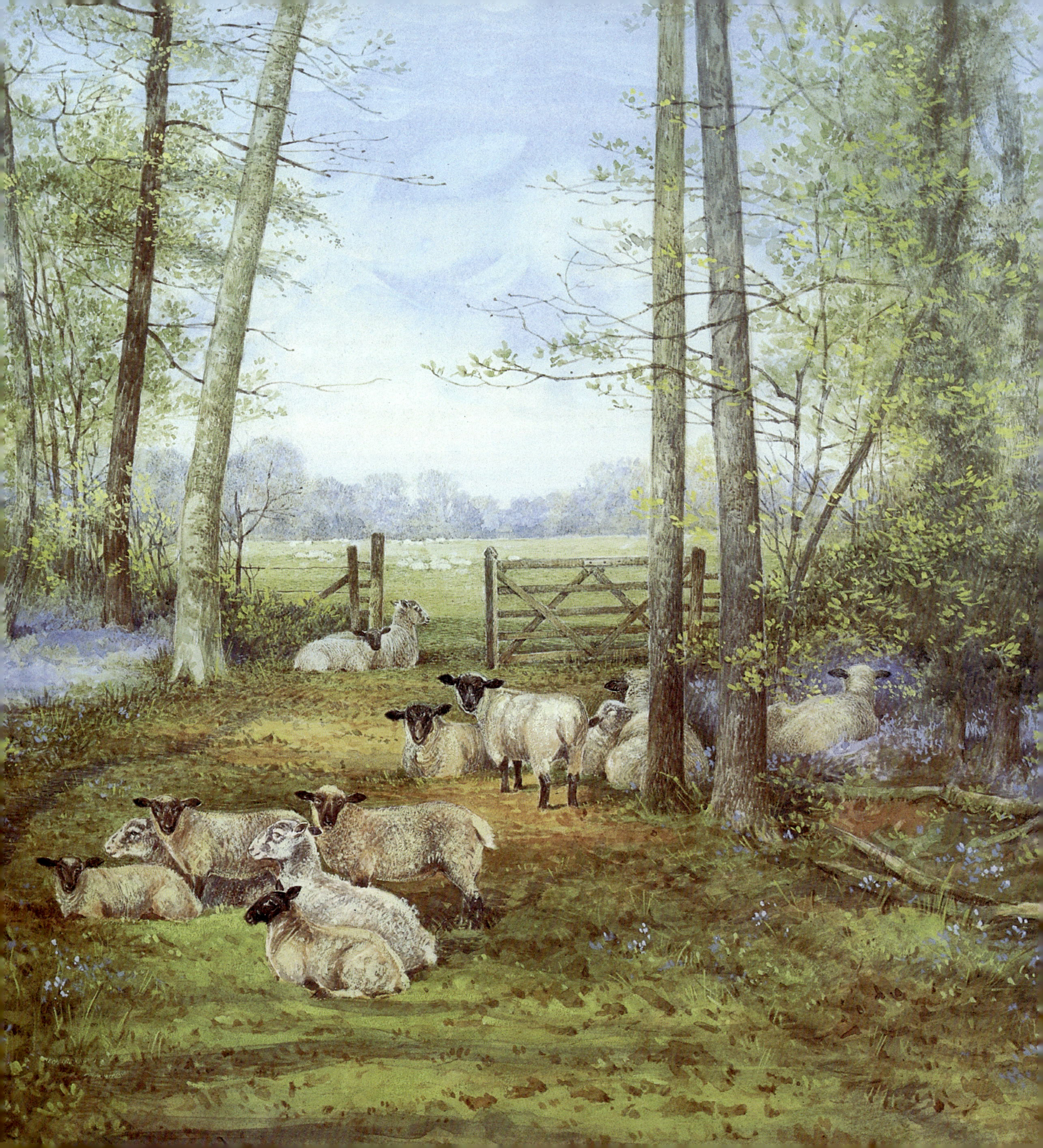

CHAPTER FIVE

Animals of the Orchard

Animals of all shapes and sizes, with two legs and four, love orchards as well as the birds, bees and butterflies that use them. Domestic and wild, welcome and unwelcome, they all love apples, plums and pears when they are ripe. Many traditional farmers let their livestock into their orchards to graze and to eat the late summer windfalls which they do with relish. Donkeys, horses and ponies will all allow themselves to be caught, if the would-be catcher has an apple in a pocket. We have caught Sarah and Sally's ponies many times when they were younger by luring the awkward beasts to us with the promise of an apple. They eat the apples noisily and obviously with great enjoyment.

Pigs make even more of a meal of fallen fruit than horses. They dribble and eat enthusiastically open mouthed, smacking their lips together with obvious complete enjoyment. Indeed the way they chomp their jaws is even more disgusting than the way in which football managers chew gum. Gordon always loved seeing pigs, painting pigs and drawing pigs and the Gloucester Old Spot was one of his favourites. In these pictures he has caught their characteristics perfectly. They are a wonderful old variety of pig and one of those that the Rare Breeds Survival Trust has worked so hard to maintain. It has to be said too that they make delicious meat and it reminds me of this verse of Ogden Nash:

> *The pig, if I am not mistaken,*
> *Supplies us sausage, ham and bacon.*
> *Let others say his heart is big –*
> *I call it stupid of the pig.*

LEFT: *Leave a gate open and sheep will go through it – to the orchard, wheat field or even the garden.*

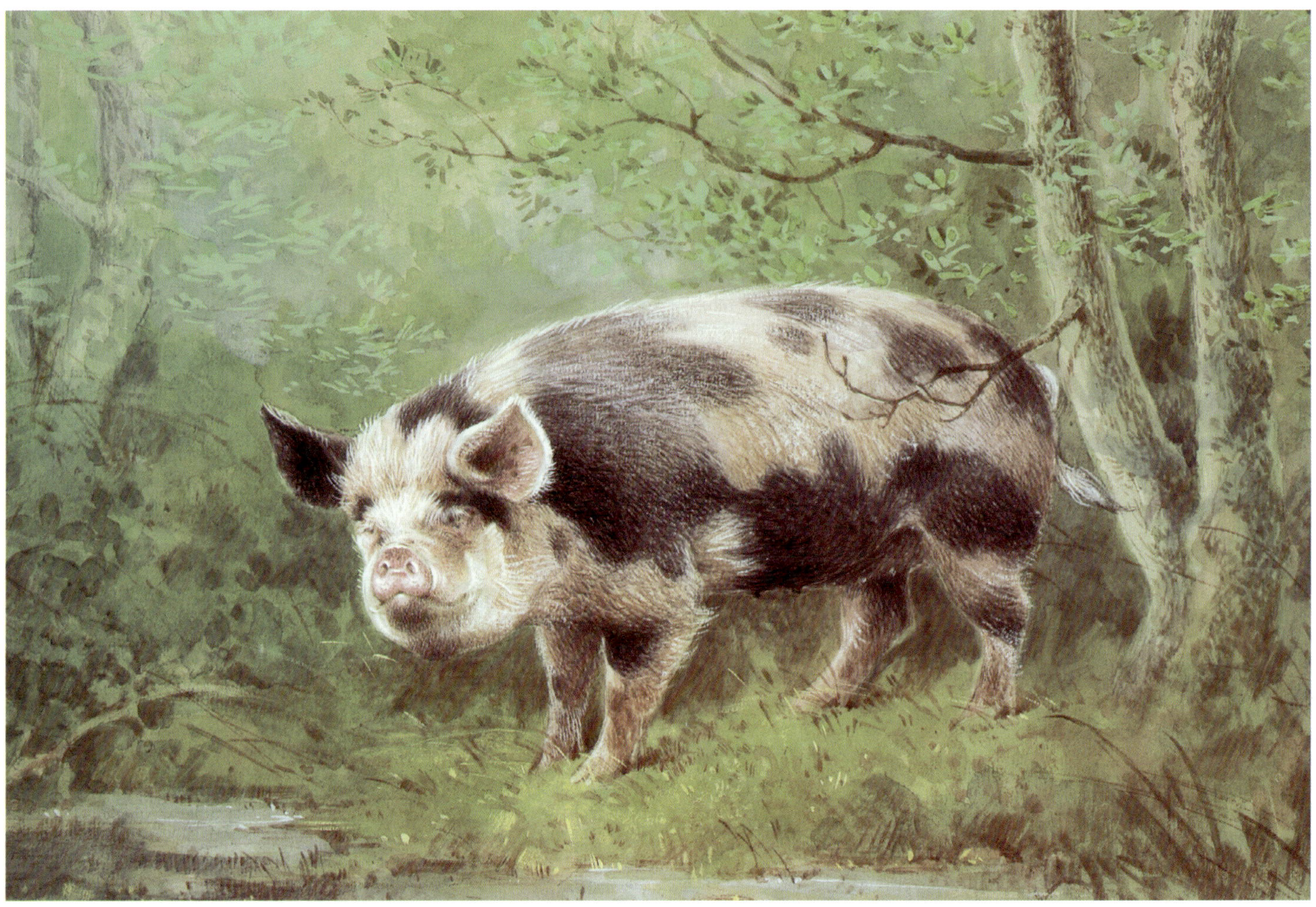

ABOVE AND RIGHT: *The wonderful Gloucester Old Spot.*

The meat of traditional pork has more fat in it than some of the modern breeds of pig giving it more flavour, but looking at the health and welfare of animals objectively pigs once needed to put on fat to help them get through the winter and one of the traditional ways of getting the pigs fat was to let them into the orchards and into the forests. 'Commoners' often had rights to let their pigs go into the woods where they would eat acorns and beech mast, lucky pigs would also find windfall crab apples and wild pears to eat too. The meat of the Gloucester Old Spot is really delicious and it makes that rarity – magnificent crackling. With apple sauce and sage and onion

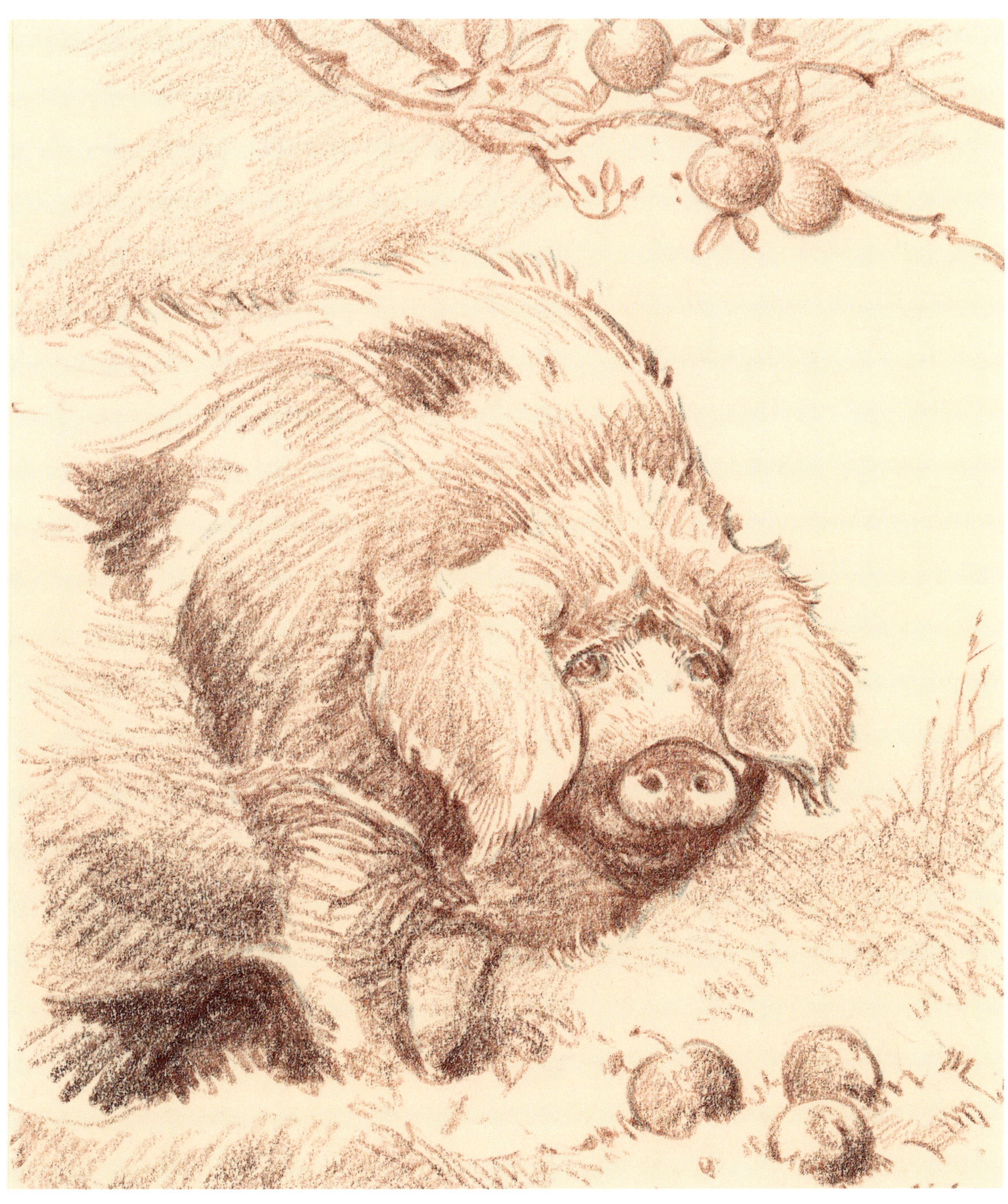

stuffing it is a delicious meal. The bacon too is first rate. It is ironic that in the picture we have the pig and the apple – the pork and the apple sauce.

One of the dangers of picking plums and apples in an orchard where pigs are allowed to live is that pigs are very bright animals and they watch the activities of the pickers. Consequently to put an overflowing basket on the ground such as the one Gordon painted, and leave it unguarded, is a very dangerous thing to do as the pigs will quickly make for it and regard the contents as a great prize. These pigs are lucky pigs; Edmund Blunden wrote of *The Poor Man's Pig* – a not so lucky pig:

Already fallen plum-bloom stars the green
And apple-boughs as knarred as old toads' backs
Wear their small roses ere a rose is seen;
The building thrush watches old Job who stacks
The fresh-peeled osiers on the sunny fence;
The pent sow grunts to hear him stumping by,
And tries to push the bolt and scamper thence,
But her ringed snout still keeps her to the sty.

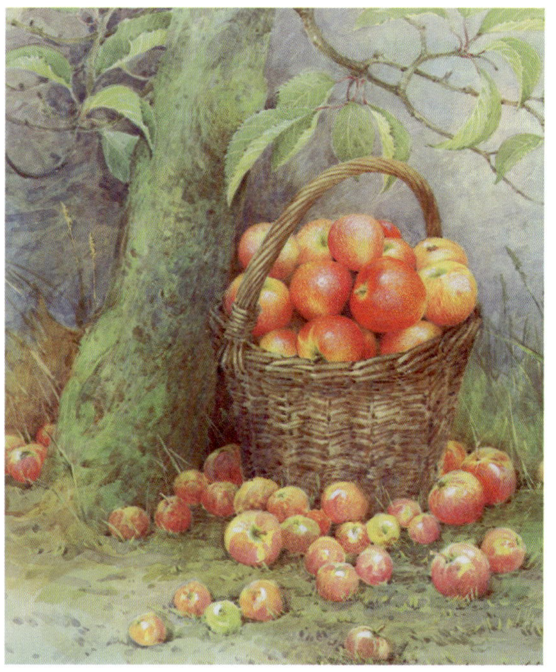

Then out he lets her run; away she snorts
In bundling gallop for the cottage door,
With hungry hubbub begging crusts and orts,
Then like the whirlwind bumping round once more;
Nuzzling the dog, making the pullets run,
And sulky as a child when her play's done.

Some farmers let their cattle into their orchards to graze the grass and eat the windfalls – they will also eat the leaves too if they get the chance to browse the lower branches. The Countryside Restoration Trust's David Powell certainly lets his traditional Herefords into his cider apple and perry pear orchard in Much Marcle, and Robin also lets his heifers into his small orchard in Cambridgeshire. They get the benefit of the lush grass and they act as the mower to stop the orchards getting as overgrown as mine. In this area we are lucky to have some most attractive Belted Galloway cattle which are owned by the Boxmoor Trust of which

Gordon's good friend – naturalist and writer Dennis Furnell is Chairman. They are wonderful hardy cattle and Gordon's sketch of them makes a lovely picture. One of the paintings that we found was actually owned by a one-time neighbour who now lives in Scotland and we have also included the picture of a Friesien. At one time of course most farms in Britain had its own little herd of dairy cows but dairy farming has suffered hugely over recent years and dairy herds have vanished even faster than orchards. Again Ogden Nash had a little rhyme about cows which I think is apt:

The cow is of the bovine ilk
One end is moo, the other, milk.

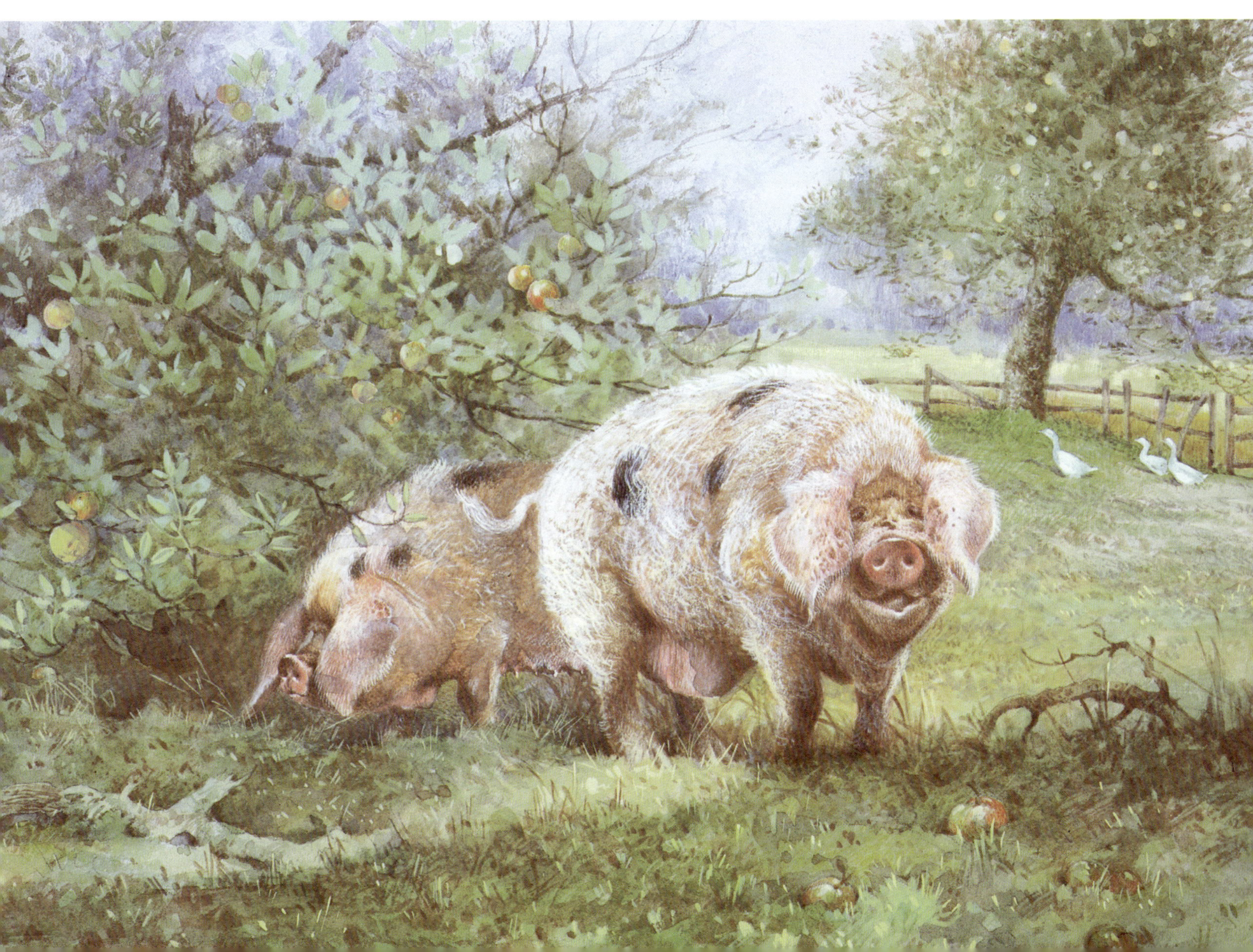

Robert Louis Stevenson also wrote poetry as well as books and his work included a very good little poem about *The Cow* which includes the prospect of apple tart and cream:

The friendly cow, all red and white,
I love with all my heart:
She gives me cream with all her might,
To eat with apple-tart.

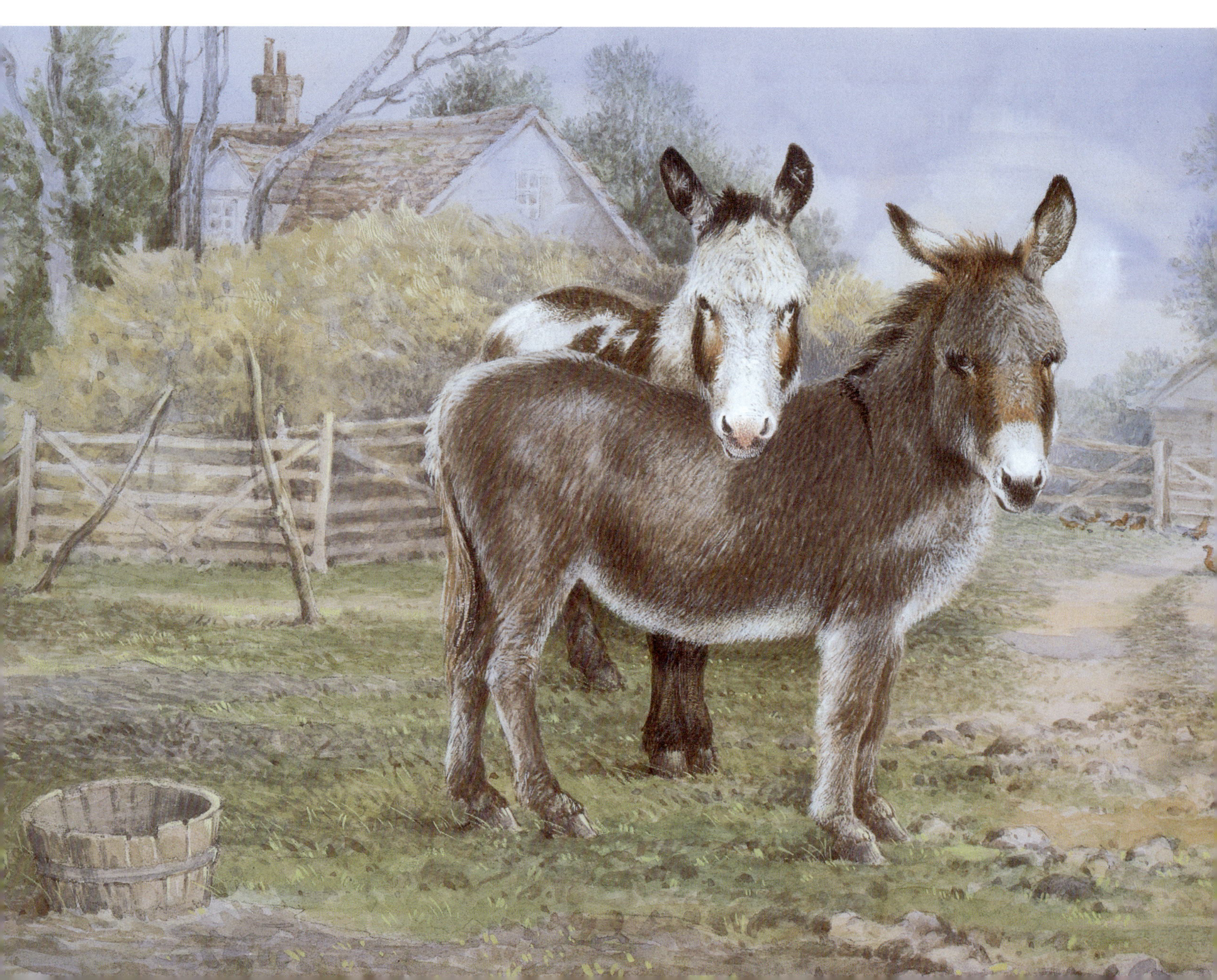

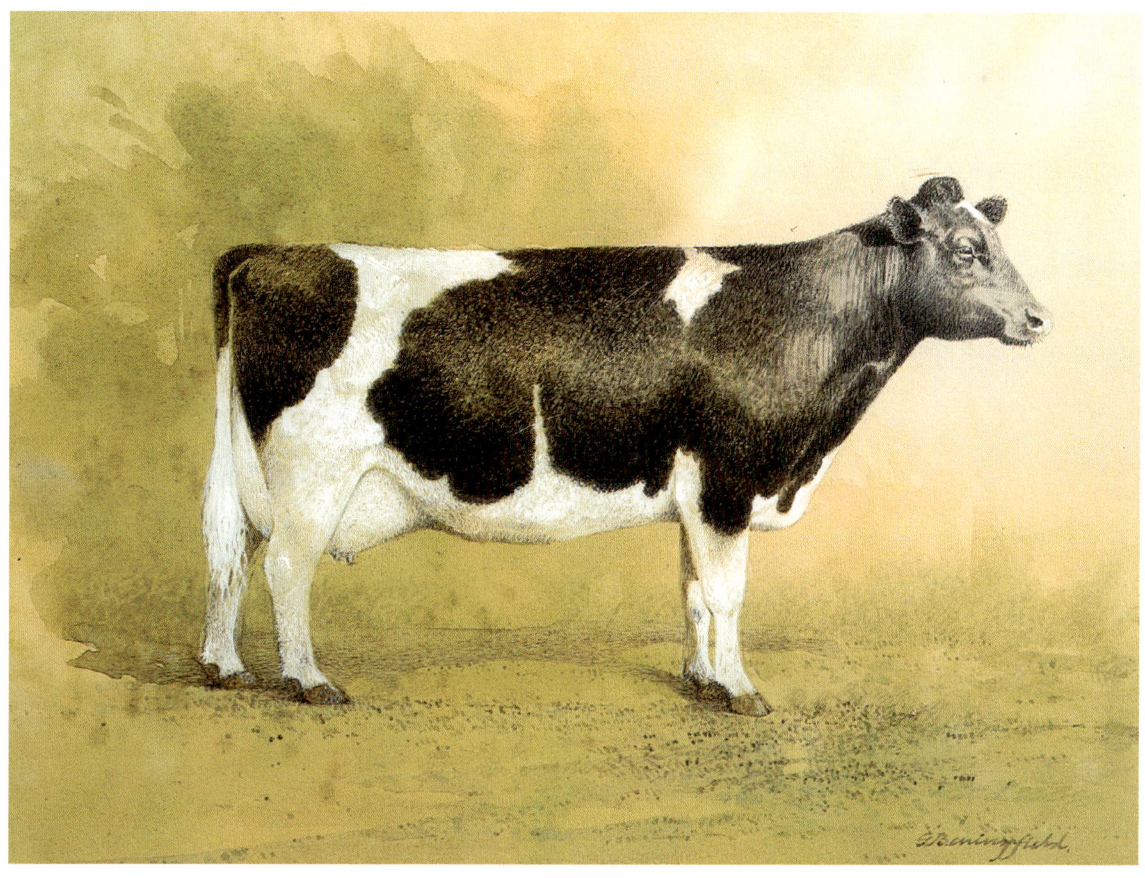

LEFT: *Donkeys in a traditional farmyard.*
ABOVE: *The British Friesien – a once familiar dairy cow throughout the country.*

She wanders lowing here and there,
And yet she cannot stray,
All in the pleasant open air,
The pleasant light of day;

And blown by all the winds that pass
And wet with all the showers,
She walks among the meadow grass
And eats the meadow flowers.

My favourite poem mentioning cows is of course WH Davies's *Leisure*. If only we would all take more notice of these brilliant verses; perhaps our politicians ought to take the time to stand and stare in order to understand farming and the countryside:

What is this life if full of care,
We have no time to stand and stare.

No time to stand beneath the boughs,
And stare as long as sheep or cows.

No time to see, when woods we pass,
Where squirrels hide their nuts in grass.

No time to see, in broad daylight,
Streams full of stars, like skies at night.

No time to turn at Beauty's glance,
And watch her feet, how they can dance.

No time to wait till her mouth can
Enrich that smile her eyes began.

A poor life this if, full of care,
We have no time to stand and stare.

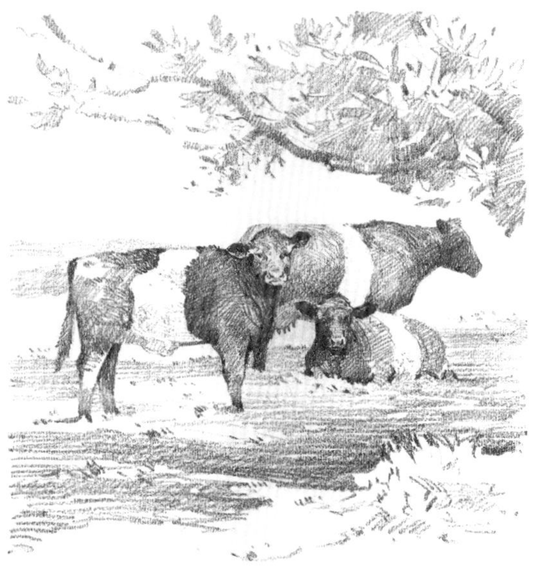

ABOVE: *Belted Galloways.*

Sheep are other lovers of the orchard and again I know that at lambing time Robin lets his pregnant ewes into his orchard so that he can keep watch over his flock by night as well as the day. I love the two paintings of the sheep by the open gates. Sheep quickly know when gates are open, whether by accident or design, and these particular sheep have a knowing look about them. A gate left open and the sheep will find it: it takes a good dog, or a loud shout, to let them know whether they have been good sheep or errant sheep. Sheep also like windfalls. Because of the structure of their mouths and teeth they do not find it all that easy to eat them, but once the size has been reduced, like all the other examples of farm livestock they do love apples. They love plums even more, because the smaller size means they can chew them far better – stones and all.

RIGHT: *Oh dear: the gate's open and the sheep are out again.*

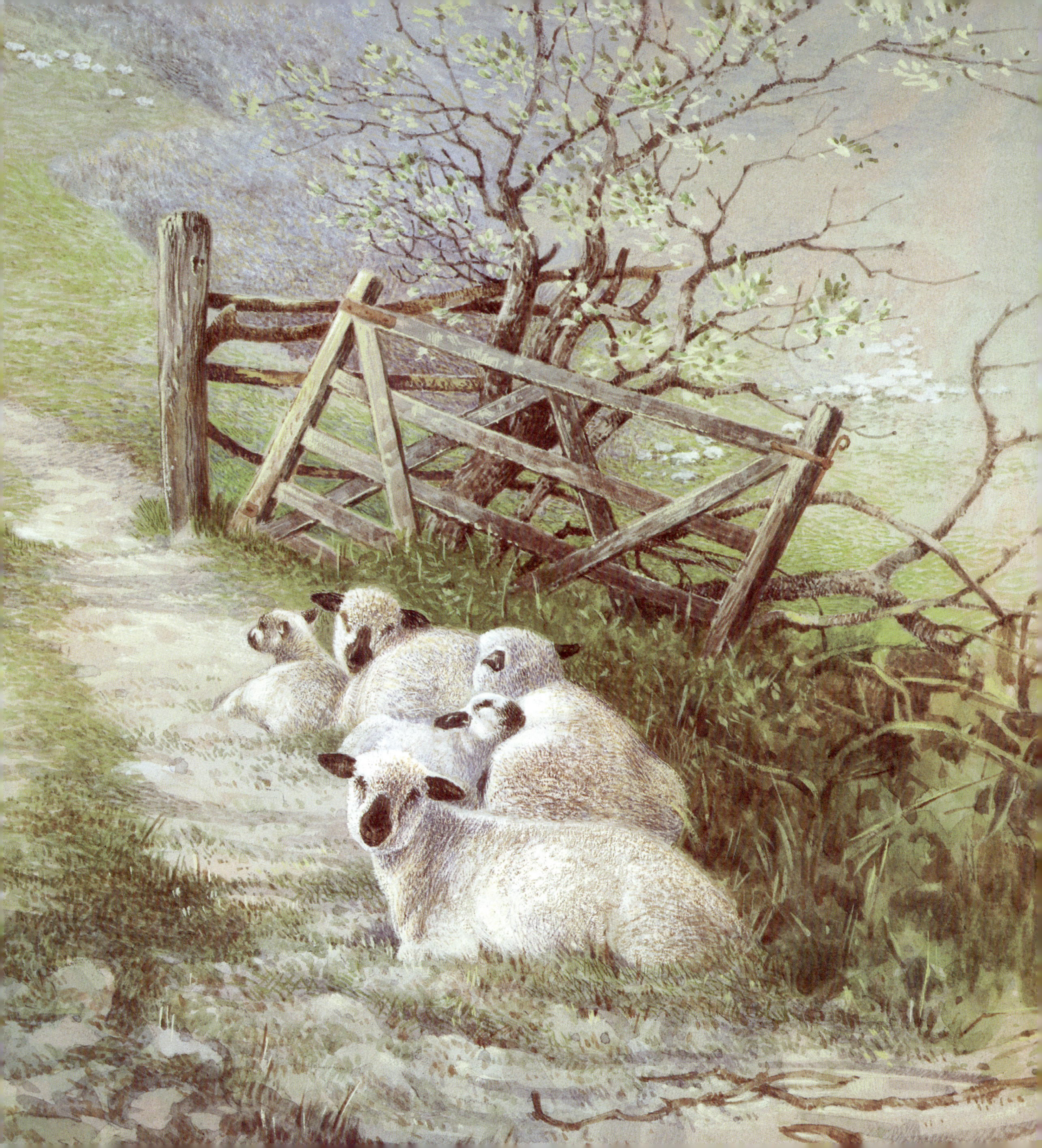

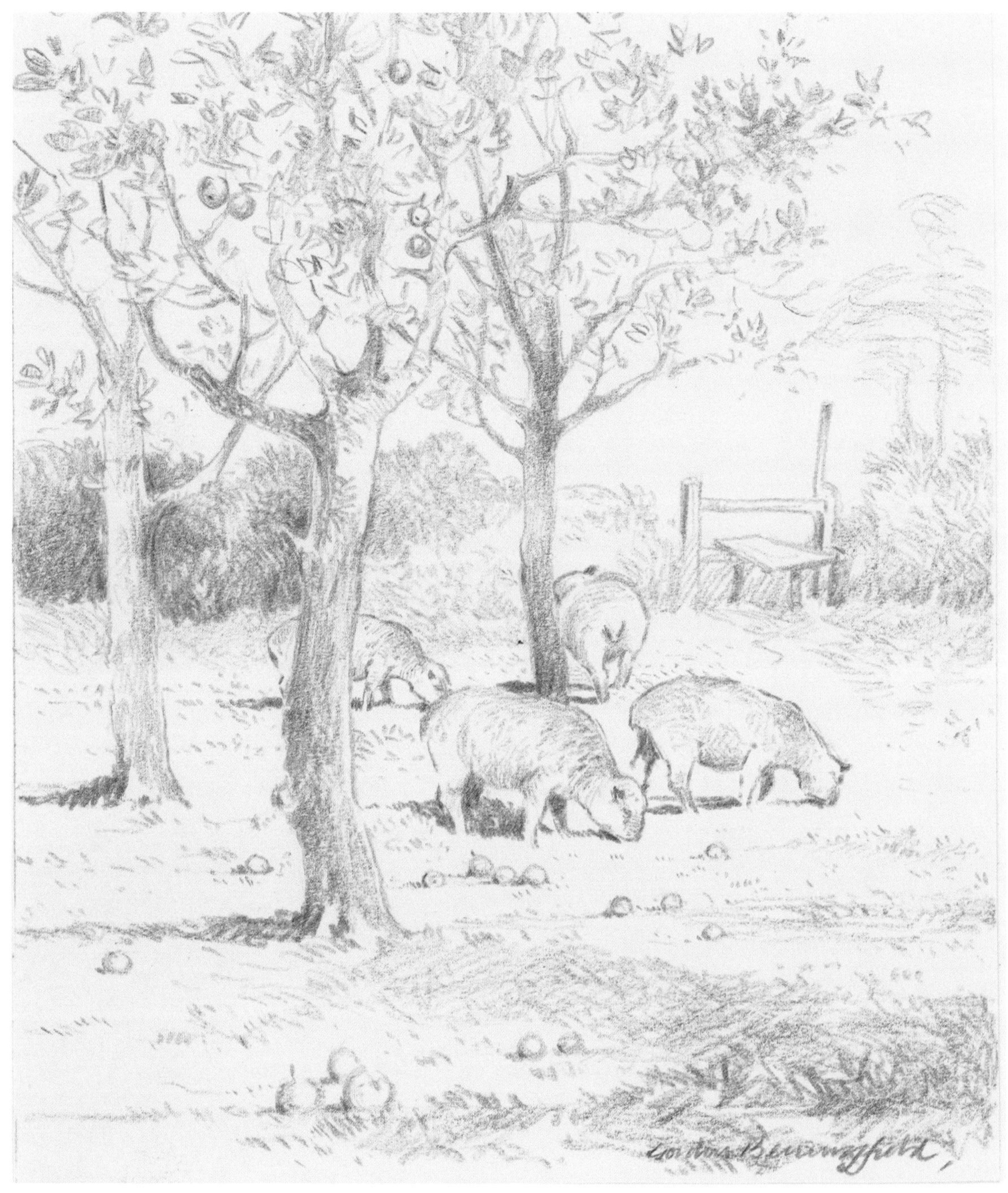

Plum stones and indeed apple pips are the great give-away to show that foxes frequent orchards. At plum time the droppings of foxes will be full of stones showing how the foxes must really enjoy damsons, greengages and the wild bullace. The bigger stones of the Victoria plum will be found later in the season as will apple pips. I do not make a habit of dissecting fox droppings but the pips and stones are so noticeable at the fruiting time of the year.

Badgers are lovers of windfalls and clear tracks will develop in late summer from the badger sett to the orchard and there they will snout and rootle about finding fallen apples, plums and pears. Quite often fallen apples will collect worms or insects underneath them and so the badger will have a double feast, the worm and woodlouse – and then the apple – main course followed by pudding. The badgers

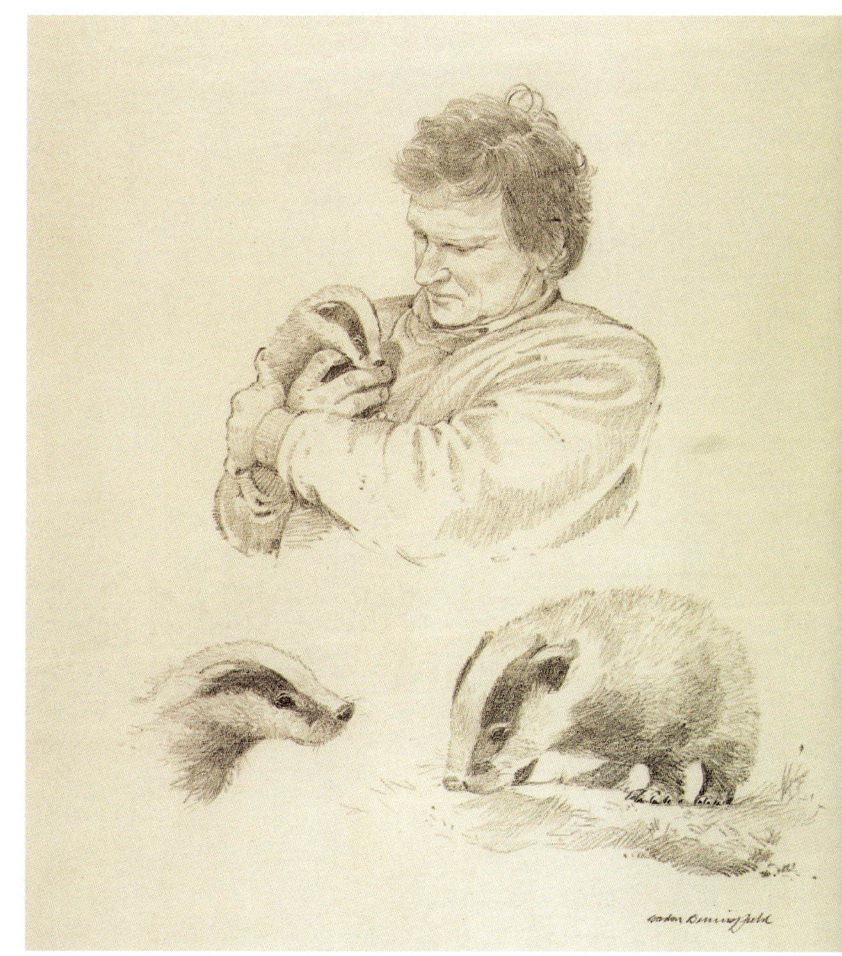

ABOVE: *Gordon's friend 'Badger' Walker with a badger cub.*

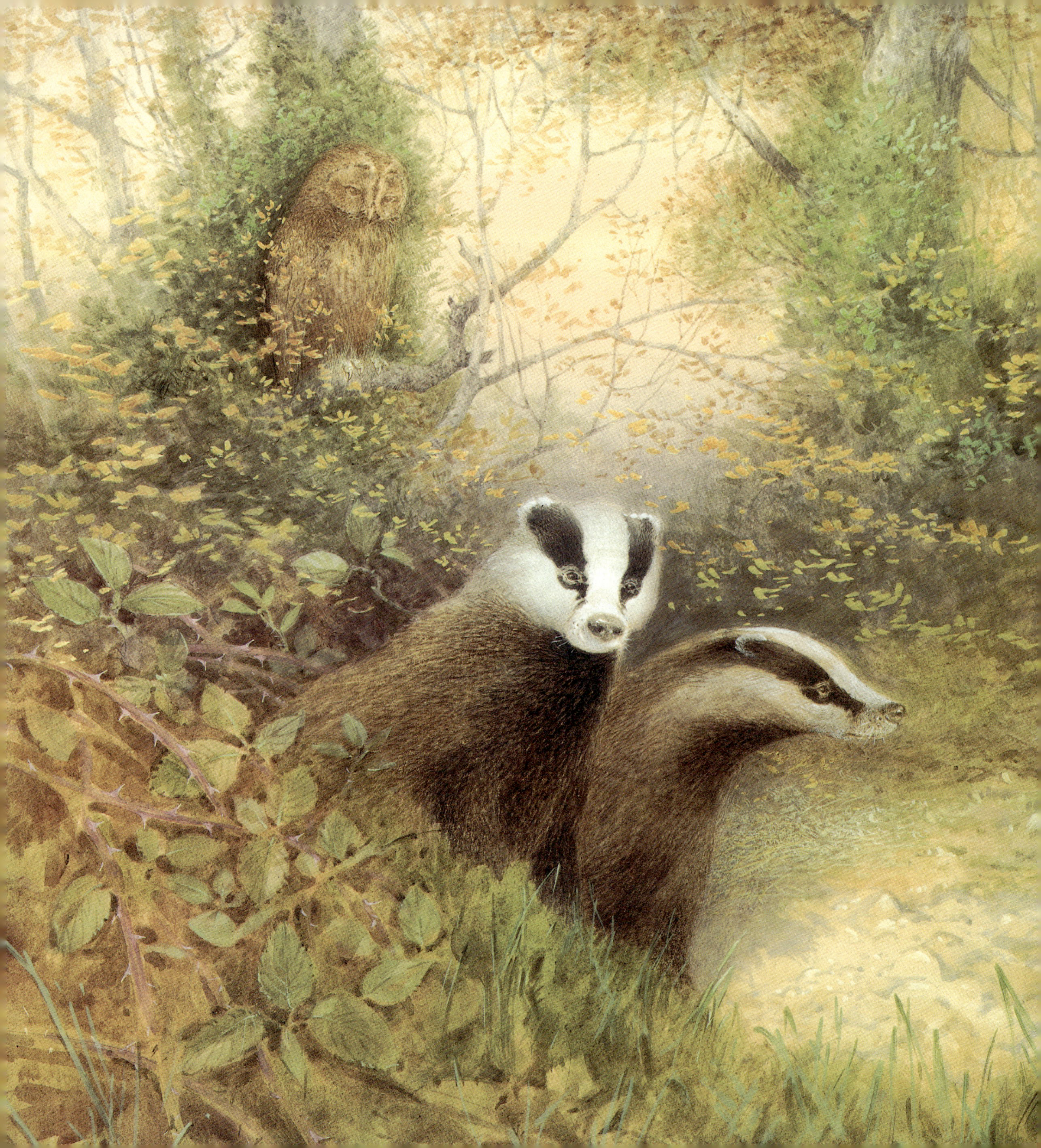

are very attractive animals and it is good to see them trundling about in orchards. Again, I love the painting that Gordon did of the two badgers outside the sett, with the tawny owl above them. He spent many hours watching badgers and they were one of his favourite animals.

We found another new animal picture just over the fields from here owned by Gordon's very old friend, Derek Christopher. Derek was the village Bobby at one time and he is a great lover of horses, hunting and racing, and his expertise on breeding and horse management is sought after by all kinds of people from the mounted police, to serious racers and point to pointers. He is very

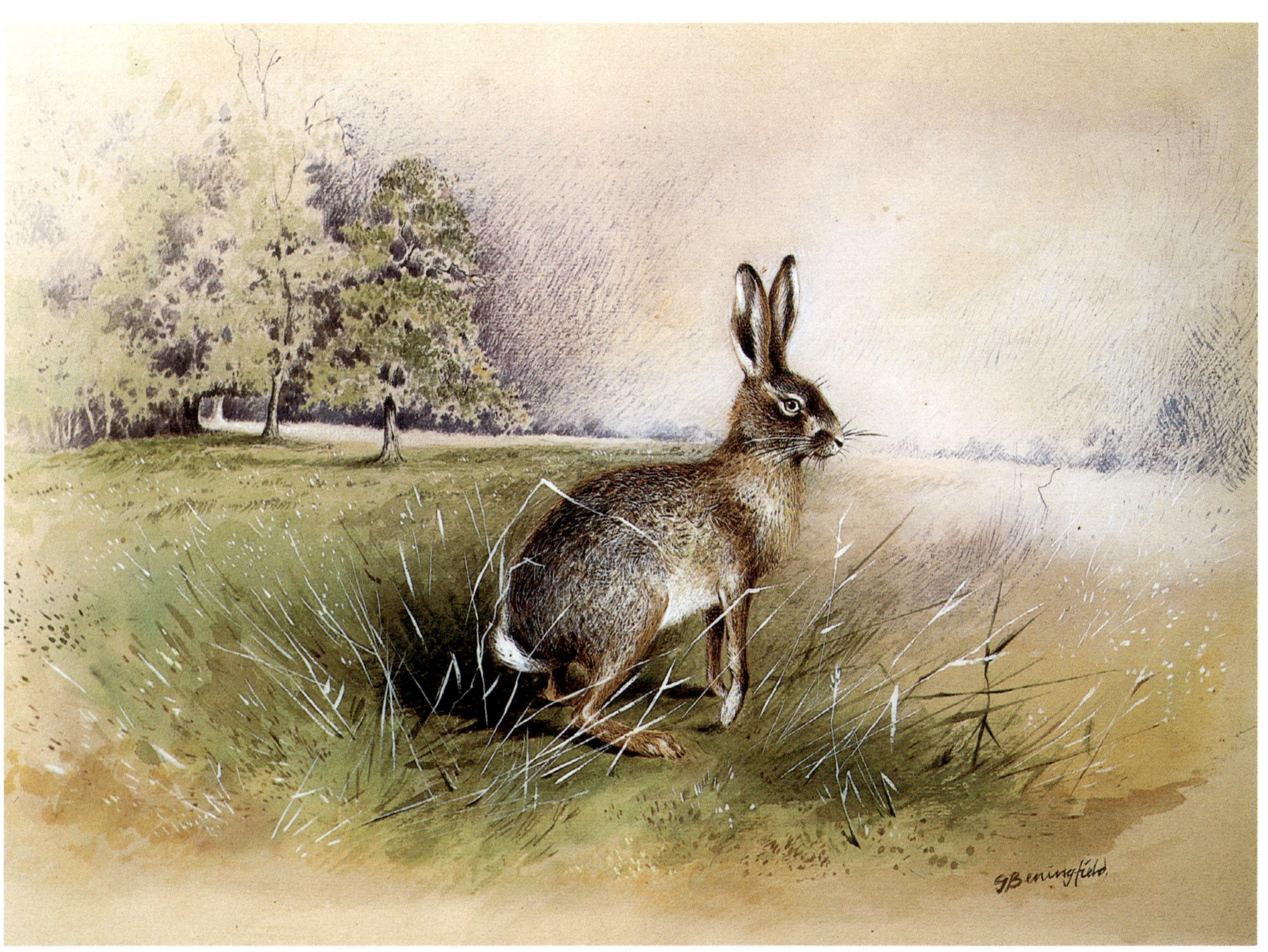

fond of his hare picture which is one of Gordon's earliest. Again it is very true that hares like orchards. It gives them concealment; the long grass means that the young leverets get shelter and of course they also enjoy the fallen fruit. Hares like a wide variety of food and although they are normally associated with open fields they also take to woodland and to orchards extremely well. The Mad March Hare can also be a playful hare, and its other side was caught by John Clare:

The birds are gone to bed the cows are still
And sheep lie panting on each old mole hill
And underneath the willows grey green bough
Like toil a resting – lies the fallow plough
The timid hares throw daylights fears away
On the lanes road to dust and dance and play
Then dabble in the grain by nought deterred
To lick the dewfall from the barleys beard
Then out they sturt again and round the hill
Like happy thoughts dance squat and loiter still
Till milking maidens in the early morn
Gingle their yokes and start them in the corn
Through well known beaten paths each nimbling hare
Sturts quick as fear- and seeks its hidden lair.

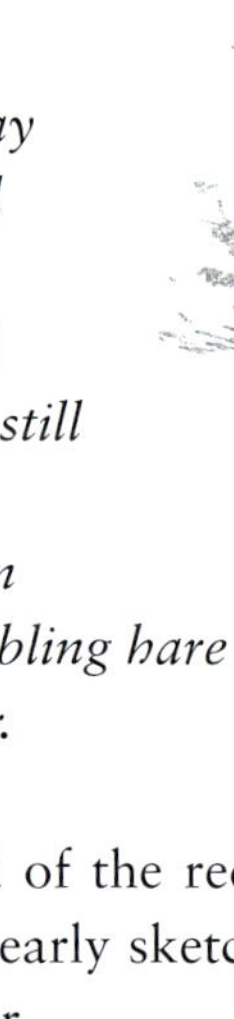

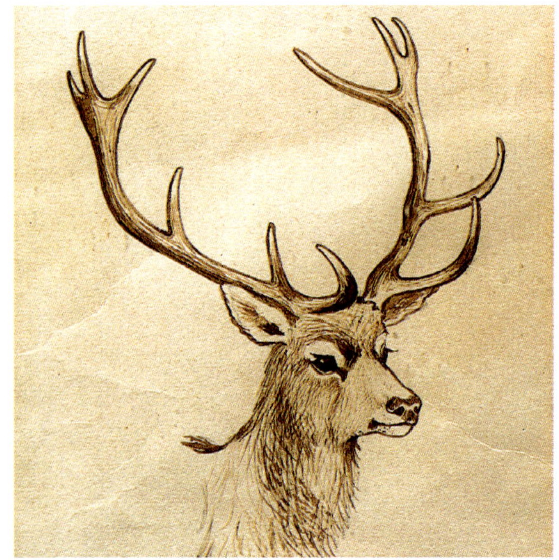

I have included the head of the red deer here as deer love apples and this is a very early sketch of Gordon's which he did for Derek Christopher.

Smaller animals make use of orchards for food and for breeding; the long grass and wild places are ideal areas for harvest mice. With their prehensile tail, and ability and agility, they can weave their nests in long grass and brambles and they can also take to the trees to sample the fruit up in the branches. Many people do not realise just how mice and voles can climb. Wood mice can climb into trees after fruit whether they are searching for ripe blackberries or for apples and plums. Once the fruit has fallen then it is not a problem, but they have no trouble climbing and

RIGHT: *Harvest mouse.*

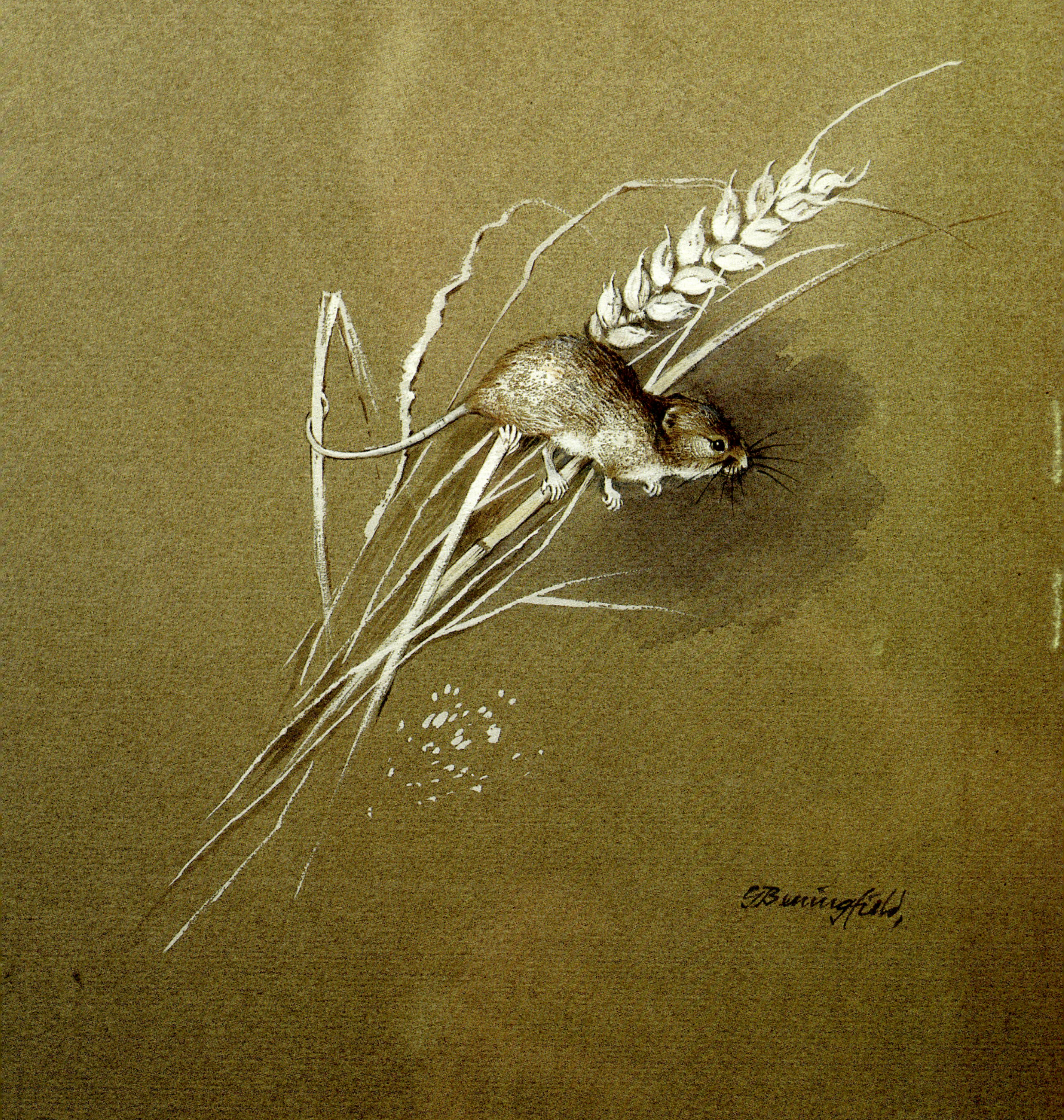
Buningfeld

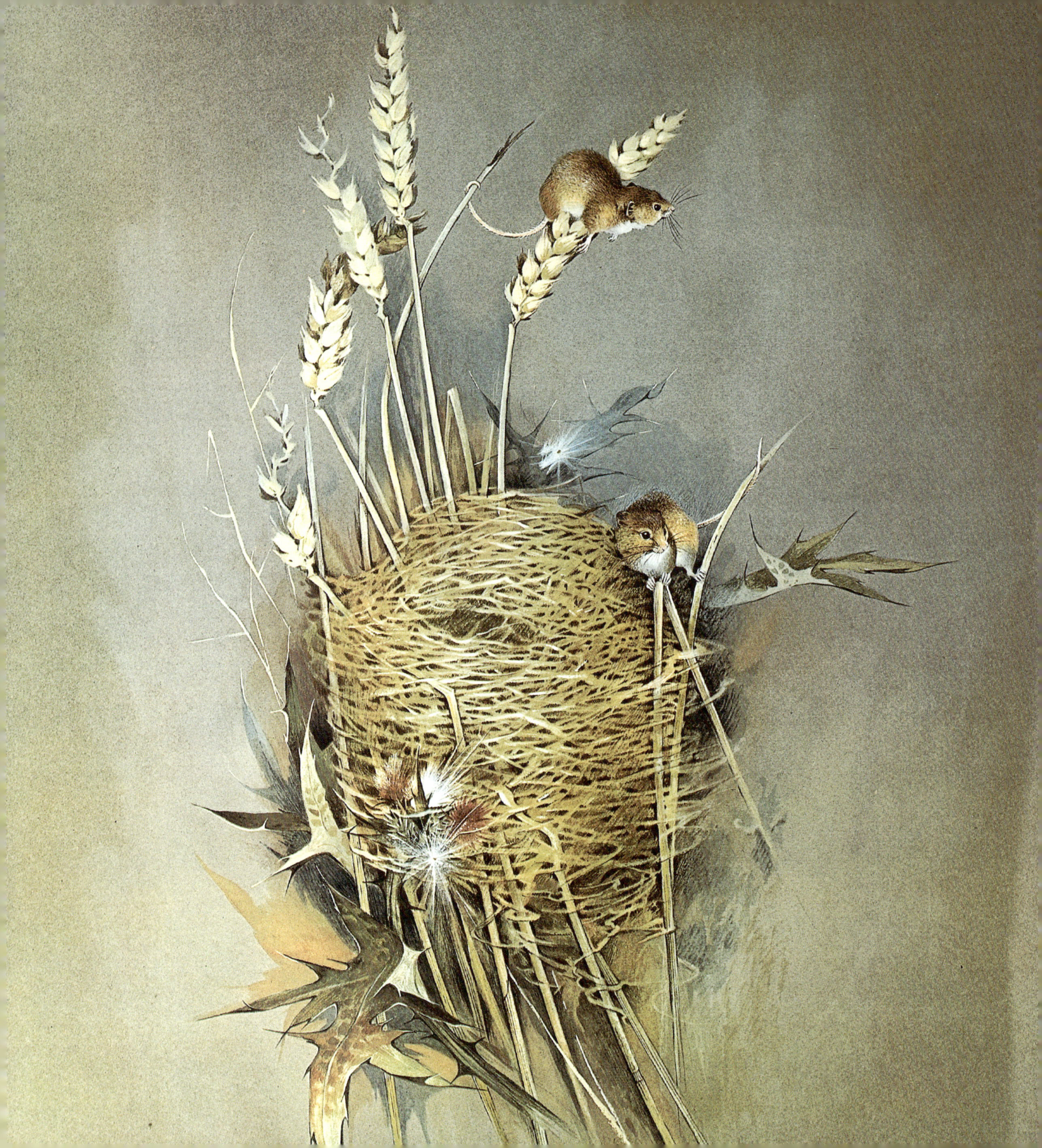

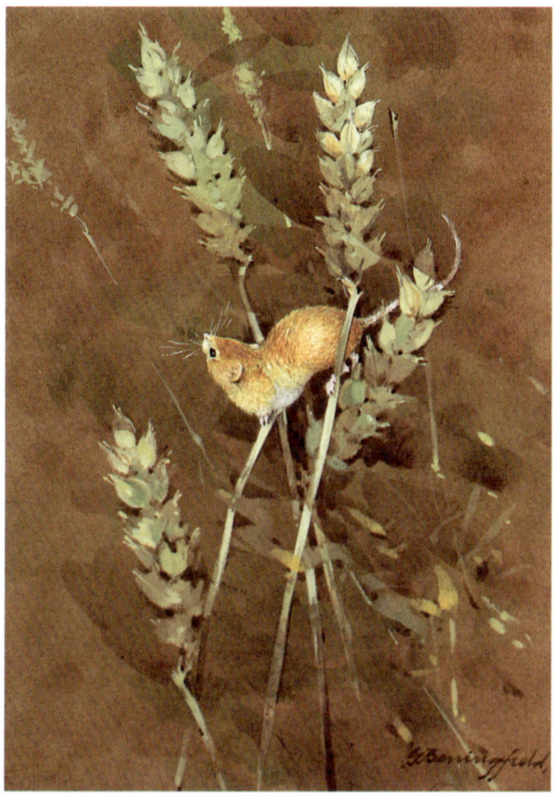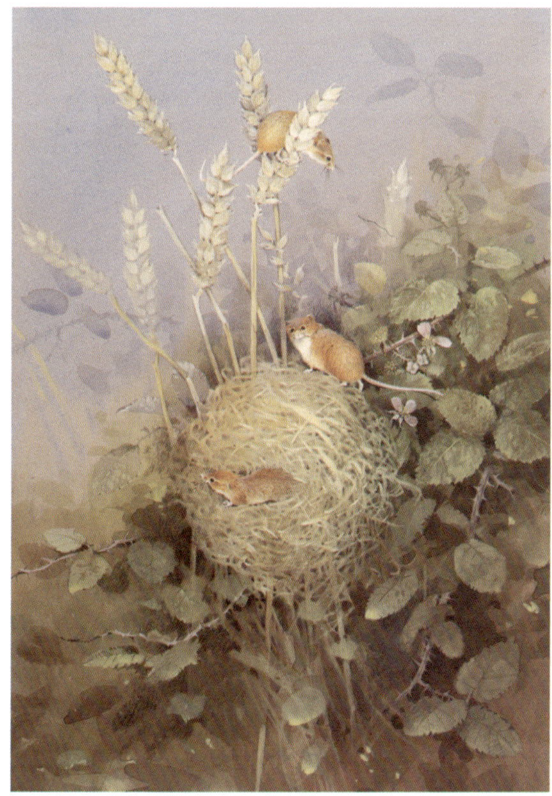

Harvest mice and their intricate nests.

climb well. As I was writing this chapter Robin told me of watching a vole climb about eight feet from a clump of cow parsley up into one of his garden trees next to his bird-feeding area.

Dormice need no second invitation to climb and they live much of their lives up in the trees and scrub. Their diet goes beyond the actual fruit because they also like the blossom and will eagerly feed on the leaves of apple and plum blossom. After a winter of hibernation, blossom leaves make a very welcome and nutritious food for the spring.

This inevitably brings us to one more animal of the orchard, because if there are mice and voles living, breeding and feeding in an orchard then domestic cats will surely follow. Cats take a huge toll of our wildlife and so the mice have to be forever on their guard. Consequently if the mice regard the orchard as their pantry, then the cat also regards the orchard as its *restaurant*, but not for the apples – for the animals and birds that feed on the fruit – hence the *City Mouse and Garden Mouse*, by Christina Rossetti:

The city mouse lives in a house,
The garden mouse lives in a bower;
He's friendly with the frogs and toads,
And sees the pretty plants in flower.

The city mouse eats bread and cheese,
The garden mouse eats what he can;
We will not grudge him seed and stocks,
Poor little timid, furry man.

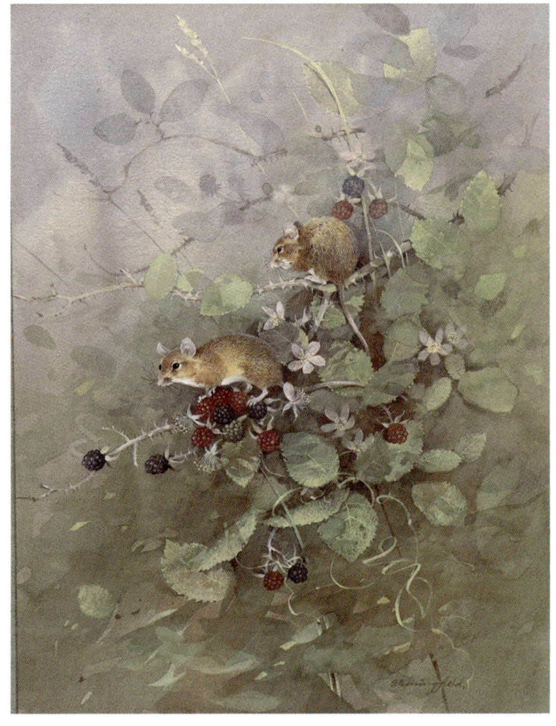

ABOVE: *Climbing wood mice after blackberries.*
RIGHT: *Dormice – eager for both fruit and bloom.*

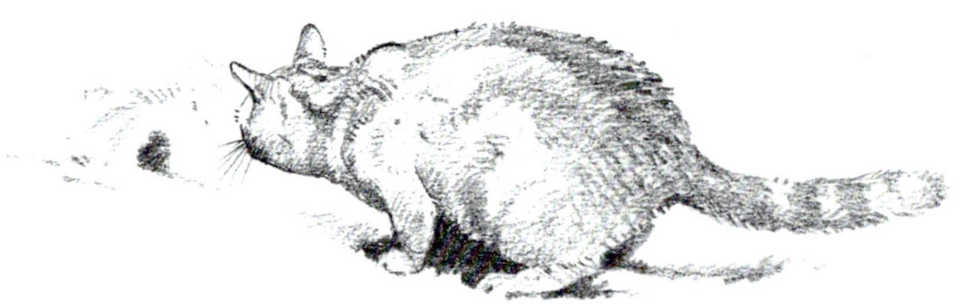

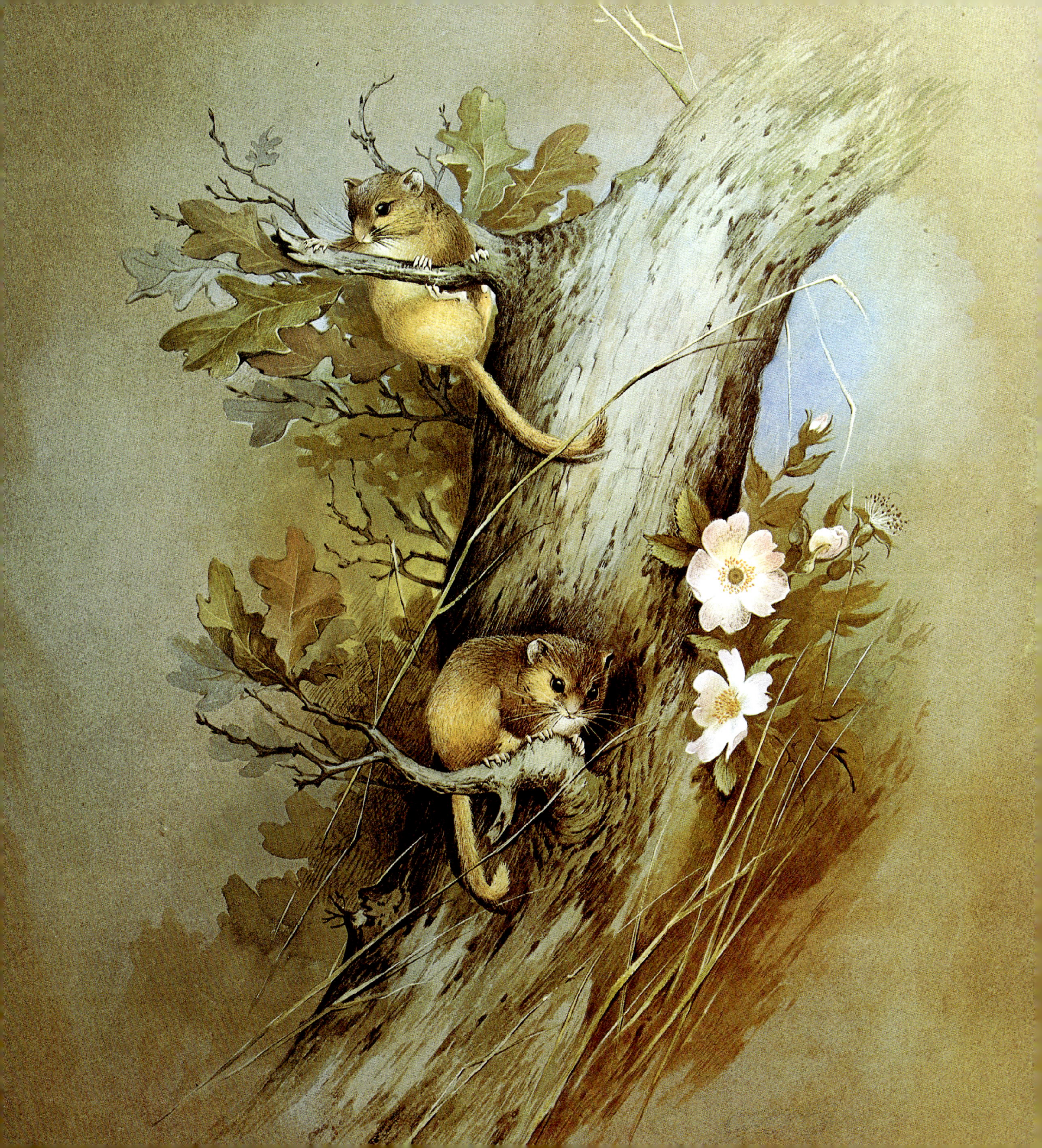

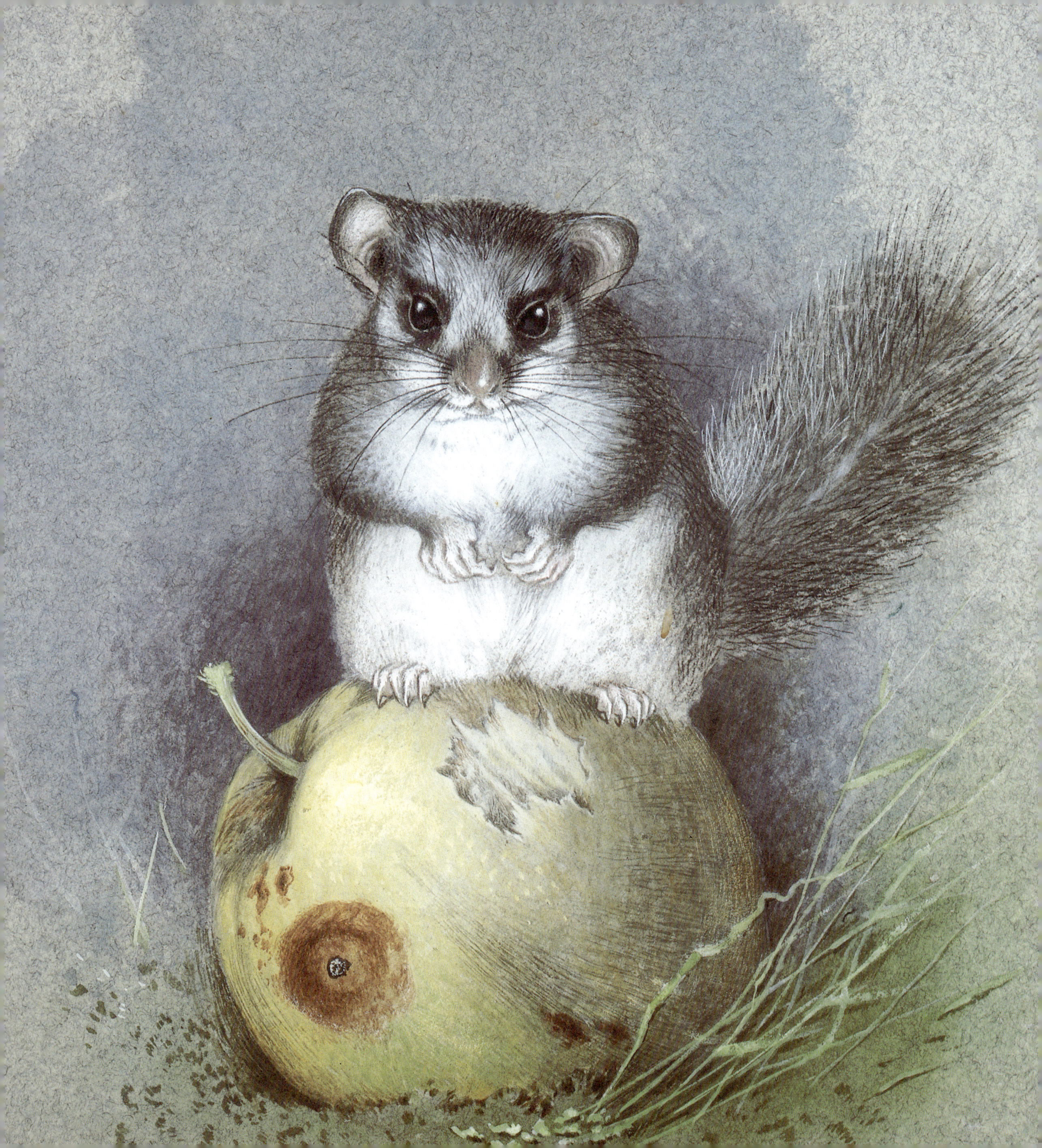

CHAPTER SIX

Perry, Puddings and Pies

I have started this chapter with a picture that Gordon really liked painting because in the garden we have visits from the edible dormouse. The edible dormouse is twice as large as the ordinary wild dormouse and is an animal of mainland Europe; it looks like an extra friendly grey squirrel. However, it was introduced into an area north of London in 1902 and it has successfully colonised small areas in Hertfordshire and Berkshire, and that area includes our garden. Obviously because it is called the edible dormouse some people like eating it. However, although we get them in our orchard I am relieved to say that we only eat the apples. Although they were introduced into this country we have always welcomed seeing them, and of the two objects in the picture we would only eat the apple.

One of the great sadnesses about the decline of orchards, big and small, over recent years is the fact that as a result, many ordinary people seem to have become even further separated from the land and further separated from where their food actually comes from. As watchers of the torrent of television cookery programmes, they imagine that their taste buds and their cooking abilities are becoming more cosmopolitan and sophisticated, in fact by ignoring the simple pleasure and delights of local fruit and easy cooking they are denying themselves feast after feast.

Obviously the purpose of having an orchard is to gather the fruit, and that fruit whether it be apple, pear, plum, cherry, quince, or whatever, can provide food fit for a king, and food that can be simply prepared, but remains very, very tasty. I suppose the simplicity of the apple as food is summed up in Gordon's picture of the worker's lunch or the worker's 'docky'. At one time whether it was in the harvest field or sitting in a barn in mid-winter many farm workers would find in their 'docky bag' an apple, a chunk of bread, probably with a bit of butter or margarine, and some cheese. I should explain that in the old days farm workers would start their day very

LEFT: *An edible apple with an edible dormouse – baked apple and baked dormouse – in France that is.*

early with breakfast but then they would have 'docky' halfway through the morning, and cheese, an apple and a chunk of bread made a wonderful 'docky'. Many people when they go out for a meal today often mention a 'doggy-bag', this is corruption of 'docky bag', which was the bag for carrying food. It is called 'docky' simply because this was an unofficial break for rest and food that developed into a regular break. Because of this the farmers would 'dock' their workers the time they took for the break, and so it became 'docky'. Even so it was ten minutes or quarter of an hour that broke up a long morning and was very welcome.

But an apple and cheese can also be a wonderful way of finishing off an orthodox meal and at Christmas, apple and mince pie or apple and Stilton can be delicious. Yes, an apple and cheese can be perfect partners and

an apple without cheese, is like a kiss without a squeeze.

At Christmas a kiss with a squeeze can be stolen with the help of a sprig of mistletoe.

I do things slightly differently. I start my day with an apple – grated on porridge. It is so refreshing and on top of all that I then put yoghurt. What a good, low fat way of starting the day, although I do have to admit on some occasions I give myself a treat by sprinkling it all with a little bit of brown sugar. The grated apple can be any sort from a beautiful Russet or Cox to a straight-foward Bramley. I mustn't forget the under-used Newton too – it is a fine apple – although it is meant mainly for cooking – the longer it is kept, the sweeter it seems to get.

I had better say too that the purpose of this chapter is not to turn *Beningfield's Orchards* into a cookery book, but it is just to give a few very simple and easy recipes, that many people may already be familiar with, but which emphasise the value and versatility of British fruit. Those who do not know them ought to try them, because British apples, plums and pears are so good and apples in particular can be used as savoury or sweet and, for good measure, they can even be made into a delicious cake for afternoon tea, if anybody has time for afternoon tea these days.

I suppose the most famous of all apple foods is quite simply apple sauce. A good apple sauce makes a meal containing pork, duck or goose that much better; even sausages can be eaten with apple sauce. The taste and texture of the meat is brought out perfectly with added apple. It is so easy; all you have to do is peel and cook a good cooking apple with sugar until it is soft and pulpy. Even Robin could make apple sauce if he concentrated for a few minutes and it is well worth those few minutes.

With traditional pork from a Tamworth or a Gloucester Old Spot then it does make a

RIGHT: *'Docky time'. An apple, a chunk of cheese and a piece of fresh bread, all laid out on a spotted handkerchief – perfect.*

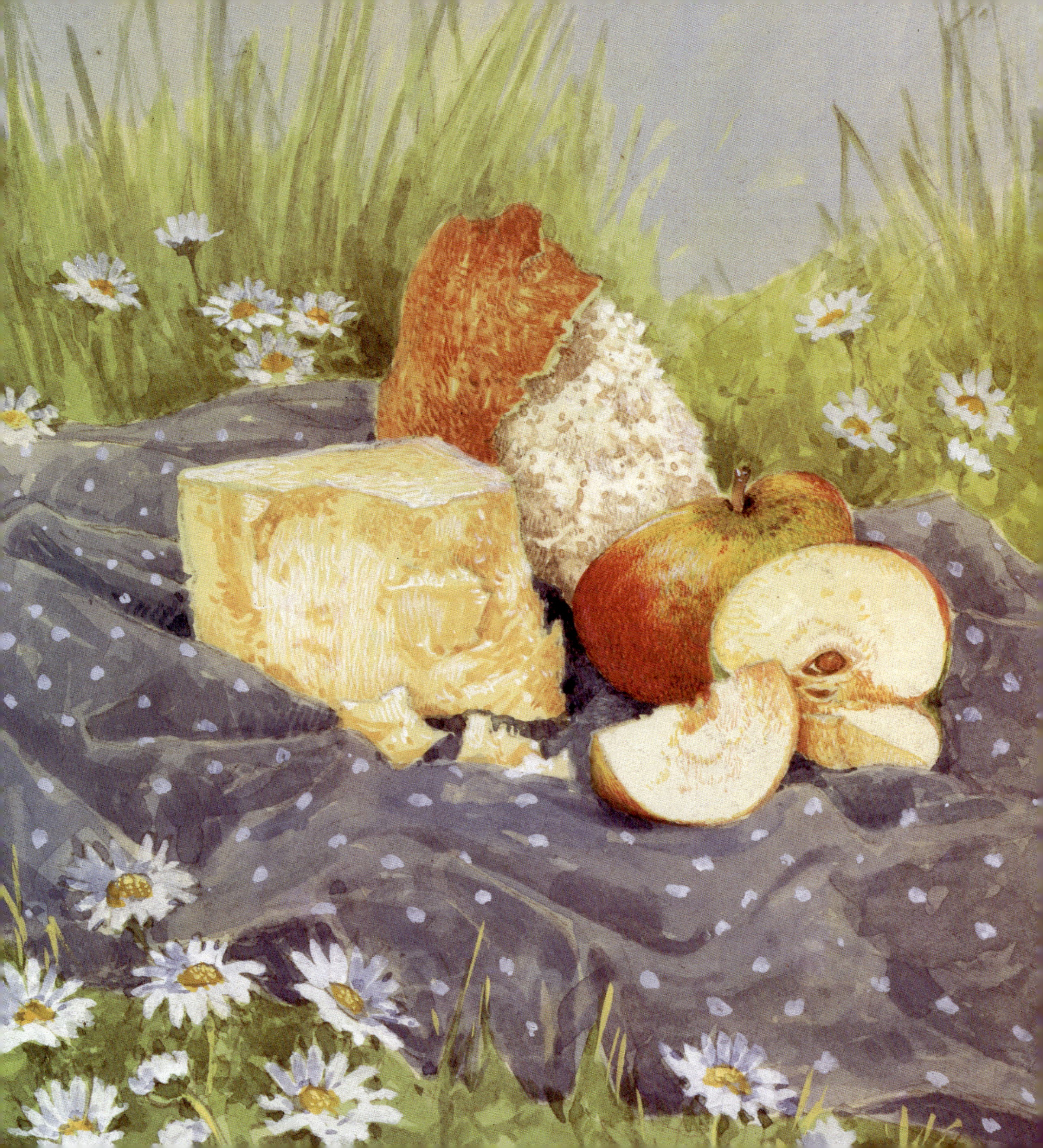

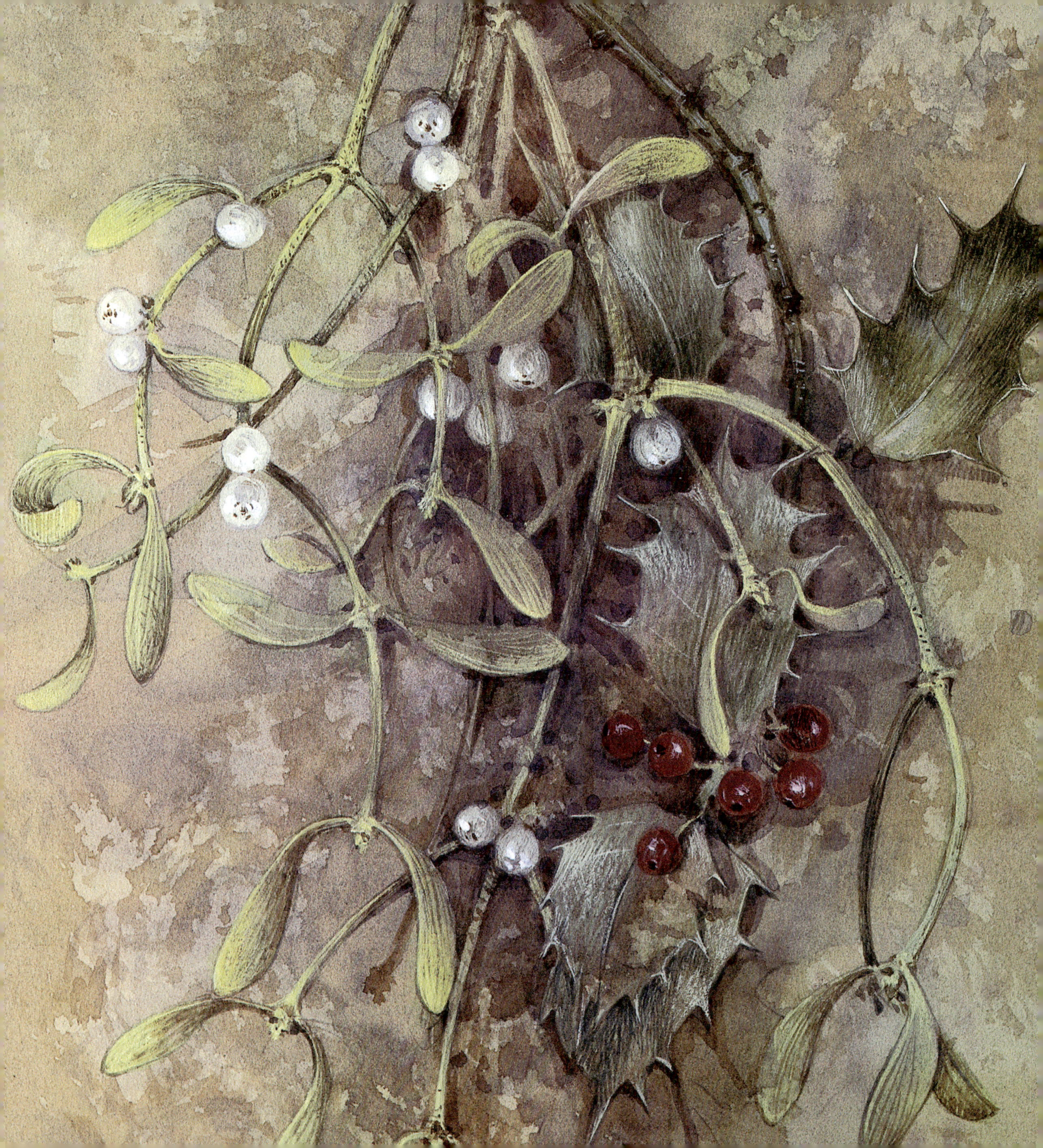

wonderful meal. Similarly at Christmas time the flavour of goose or duck is enhanced with apple sauce and sage and onion stuffing. The other savoury addition that helps to make a perfect meal is apple chutney. Apple chutney with salads and cheese really adds flavour. It should be remembered as well that chutney can be made from pears; by switching the apple ingredient with pears, then a beautiful pear chutney can be made and used in exactly the same way as apple. In addition chutney also adds flavour to any meal involving cold meat. Chutney is very easy to make and experiments can be carried out to perfect the chutney to taste. The simplest is:

> 2 lbs apples
> 2 lbs green tomatoes
> 1 lb onions
> 1 lb sugar
> 2 pints vinegar
> 1 oz chilli (optional)
> 1 lb raisins
> 2 tablespoonfuls of salt

It is very easy to prepare and cook:

Peel and core the apples before cutting them up, cut up the tomatoes into chunks, and then peel and chop the onions. Place into a large pan and remember that it is best not to cook apples in aluminium containers because the acid in the apple can react with the aluminium. Bring to the boil, stirring until the sugar has dissolved. Then simmer until nicely brown, thick and smooth for about $1\frac{1}{2}$ hours. Pour into jars and cover and you have a delicious chutney.

Another really scrumptious cold addition to meat is apple and red cabbage. We always used to have this on bonfire night with chicken legs, sausages and jacket potatoes and it is really superb. One of the joys of making apple and red cabbage is that it is all done by guesswork, and so with this one, practise makes perfect as the ingredients are at their most basic.

> 1 red cabbage shredded
> 1 onion chopped
> 2 large cooking apples, peeled and chopped
> 6 tablespoonfuls of vinegar

LEFT: *Mistletoe and hollyberries – different Christmas fruit.*

3 tablespoonfuls of dark brown sugar
Salt and pepper
6 or 8 cloves *some people are not too fond of cloves, but I think they do add a
very subtle taste to the whole mixture.*

Mix all the ingredients together and put into a casserole dish, cover with foil *(foil is not
a very traditional way of cooking but makes it simple)* and cook for 1½ hours at 160°C.
Just check after ¾ hour to see that the mixture is not dry, add more water if required.

Now comes a great family favourite and it is wonderful winter fodder; I got this recipe from my
sister-in-law, and anybody who has not tried sausage and apple casserole has missed a real treat.

1 lb best sausages from your local butcher – *please note that some sausages in
supermarkets are really awful and it is important that quality sausages are bought.
It really is a crime that the quality sausage has been devalued by some retailers,
selling second-rate apologies.*
2 large onions
1 leek
1 tablespoon of plain flour
2 eating or cooking apples, peeled and chopped
salt and pepper
1 pint of cider or apple juice

Using traditional cider puts a bit of zip into the whole mixture.
Fry the sausages for about 5 minutes, just enough to brown. Put into a casserole
dish then fry onions and leek for 5 minutes. Add flour, salt, pepper and cider, cook for
2 minutes, then add apples. Cook for another 2 minutes then pour over the sausages.
Cover with foil and cook for 1 hour at 180°C. Serve with mashed potatoes and green
vegetables – life may be never be the same again.

Another cooking casualty in modern Britain has been the steamed pudding, and steamed apple
and blackberry pudding is almost a meal in itself. It is delicious and Gordon loved it. It is very
simple to do. The base is:

8 oz self raising flour
4 oz sunflower margarine

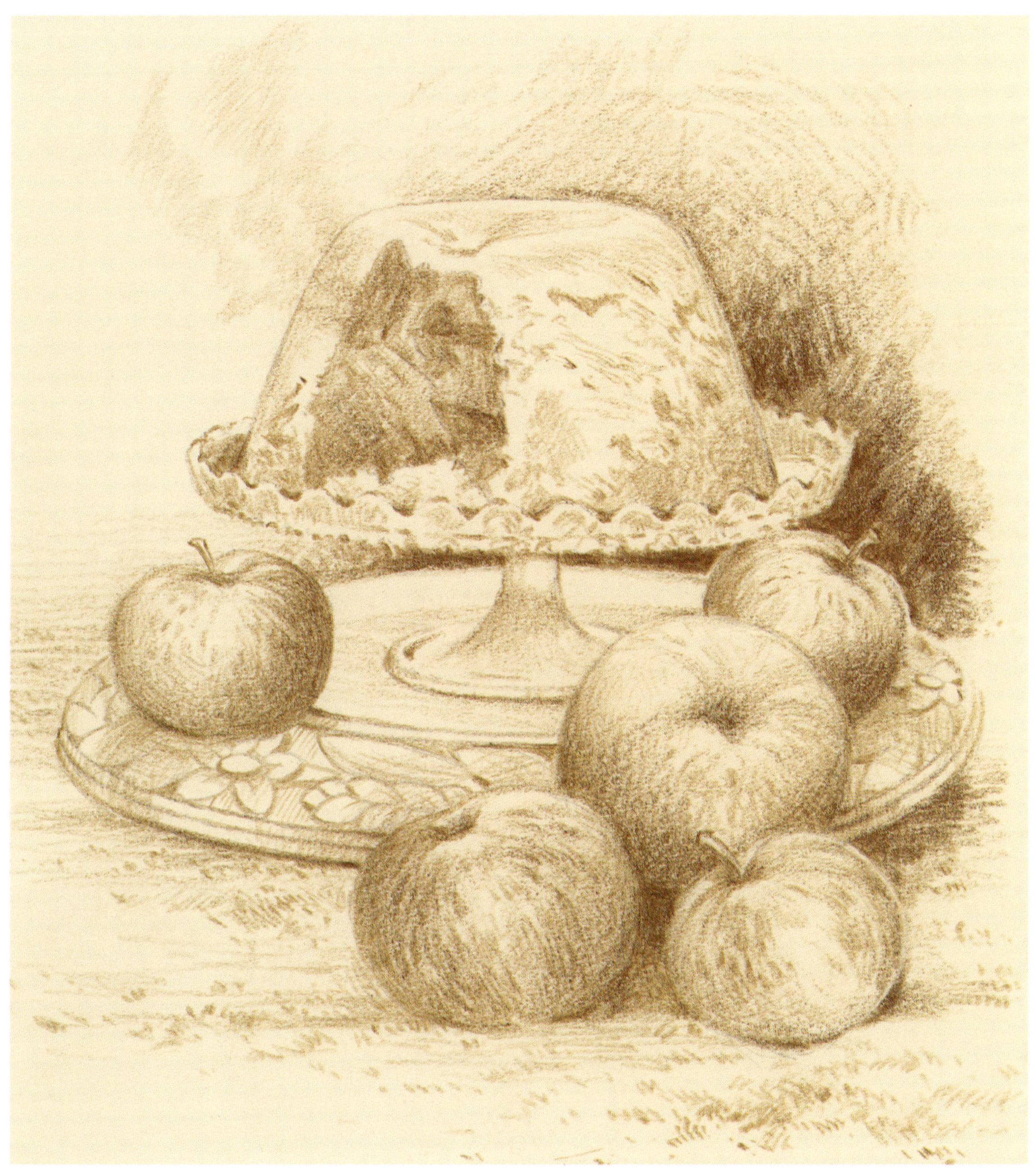

A delicious apple and blackberry pudding.

pinch salt
cold water to mix
Filling:
1 lb cooking apples, peeled and sliced
½ lb blackberries
4 oz sugar

Grease a pudding basin, mix flour, fat, pinch of salt and add enough cold water to make a soft but not too sticky dough. Roll out three-quarters of the dough to fit the basin, leaving a quarter to cover the top. Fill basin with fruit and sugar, add 2 tablespoons of water. Then cover with remaining pastry. Cover pudding with greaseproof paper and foil. Steam for 1½ hours.

Then eat it with custard and fall asleep in front of a log fire.

Although this pudding is wonderful in season, of course one of the good things about freezers is that this season can be extended because blackberries can be added to apples for the whole winter.

Traditional apple pie can be just as good and can be served hot, warm or cold, and eaten with cream, ice cream or custard. Some people even eat it with cheese. The recipe is simple:

8 oz short crust pastry
2 lbs cooking apples
6 oz sugar
juice of half a lemon adds a bit of oomph
4 cloves
milk to glaze
icing sugar to serve.

Make the pastry and leave to chill for 30 minutes. Heat the oven to 220°C or 425°F. Core, peel and slice the apples and drop them into a bowl of water which includes some lemon juice. Roll out ⅔ of pastry and line a shallow pie dish – about 7 inches. Place apple on pastry. Sprinkle with sugar and lemon juice, put in cloves and then carefully put the remaining pastry on top of apples, making it slightly domed. A little china blackbird in the middle of course makes the dome the exact elevation, and so it can take on an even more appealing shape than the dreadful London Dome. The edges should be sealed with water, press firmly all the way round and brush the top with milk and sugar. Bake for 20 minutes and then reduce the heat to 180°C or 350°F and

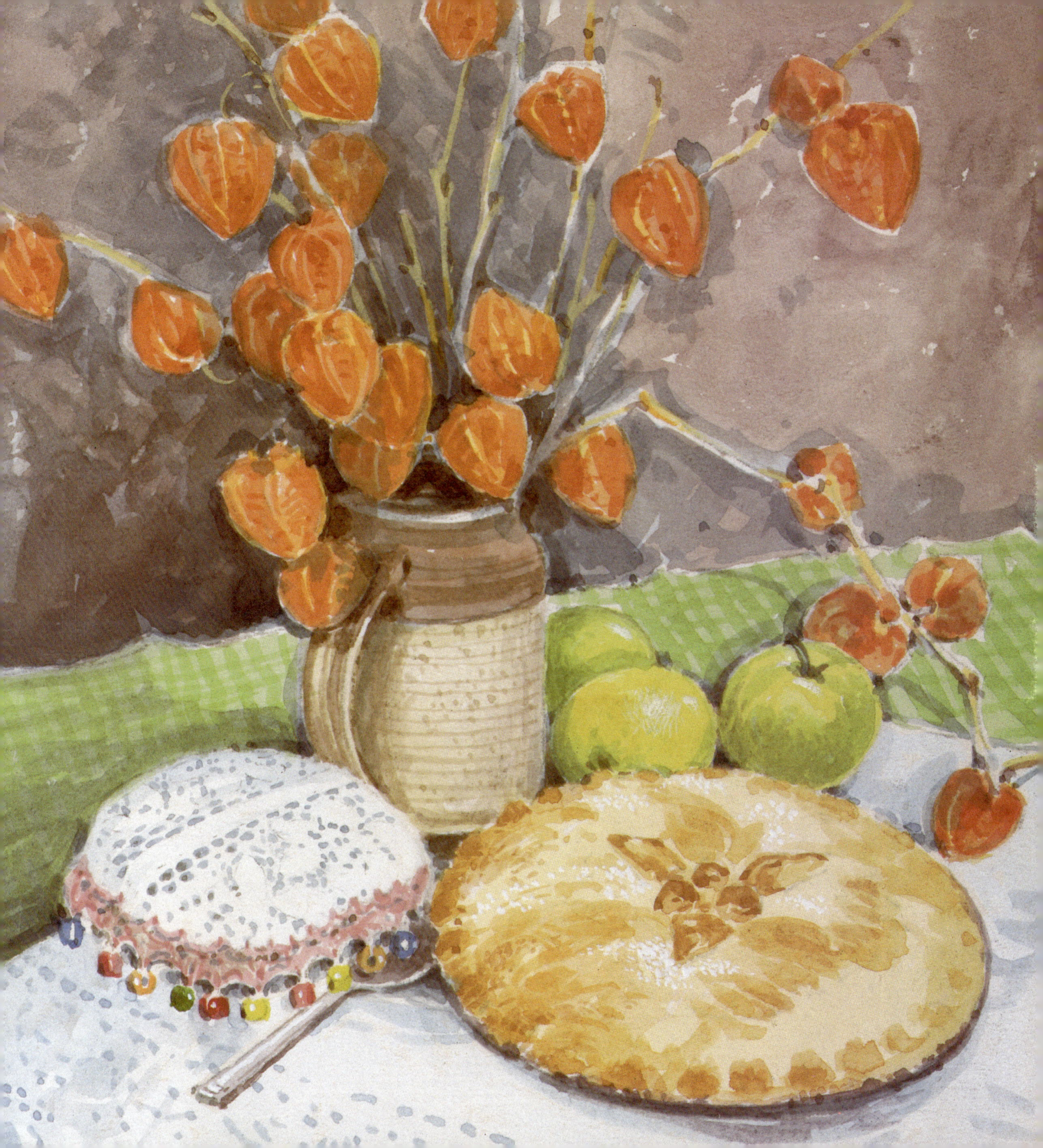

continue to cook for another 15–20 minutes until the top is brown. It can be sprinkled with icing sugar for the tubbies, or it can be left as basic for the thinnies.

The traditional English apple pie can be turned into the traditional English *blackberry and apple pie* by simply adding blackberries. For those who really like apple pie however, there is a warning:

> *There was young lad from St Just*
> *Who ate apple pie till he bust;*
> *It wasn't the fru-it that caused him to do it,*
> *What finished him off was the crust.*

Simpler fare can be straightforward stewed apples but they too can make a delicious dish and even men can stew apples if they try hard enough.

First make a syrup by heating sugar and water. The amount of sugar will depend entirely on taste and the variety of apple, whether it is sweet or sour. The best starting point is about 4 oz of sugar to 1 lb of fruit and $\frac{1}{2}$ pint of water. Peel, core and slice the apples; when the sugar has dissolved in the warm water add the apples until they are covered and cook gently for 10–15 minutes until they are tender. It is important not to boil the mixture or the fruit will turn into pulp. Drain the apples very carefully and put in a warm serving dish; boil the syrup very fast until it thickens and pour over the fruit, stir and it can be eaten on its own or with custard, then the wonderful taste can be fully appreciated.

Slightly more up-market but something we used to love, and something I still love, is pears in red wine.

> 4 pears peeled and left whole
> 4 oz sugar
> $\frac{1}{2}$ pint water
> $\frac{1}{2}$ pint of red wine
> 1 teaspoonful of arrowroot
> Stick of cinnamon
> Rind from one lemon

Dissolve the sugar in the water and wine and add cinnamon and lemon rind. Bring to the boil then add pears and poach slowly for about 25 minutes. Remove the pears and

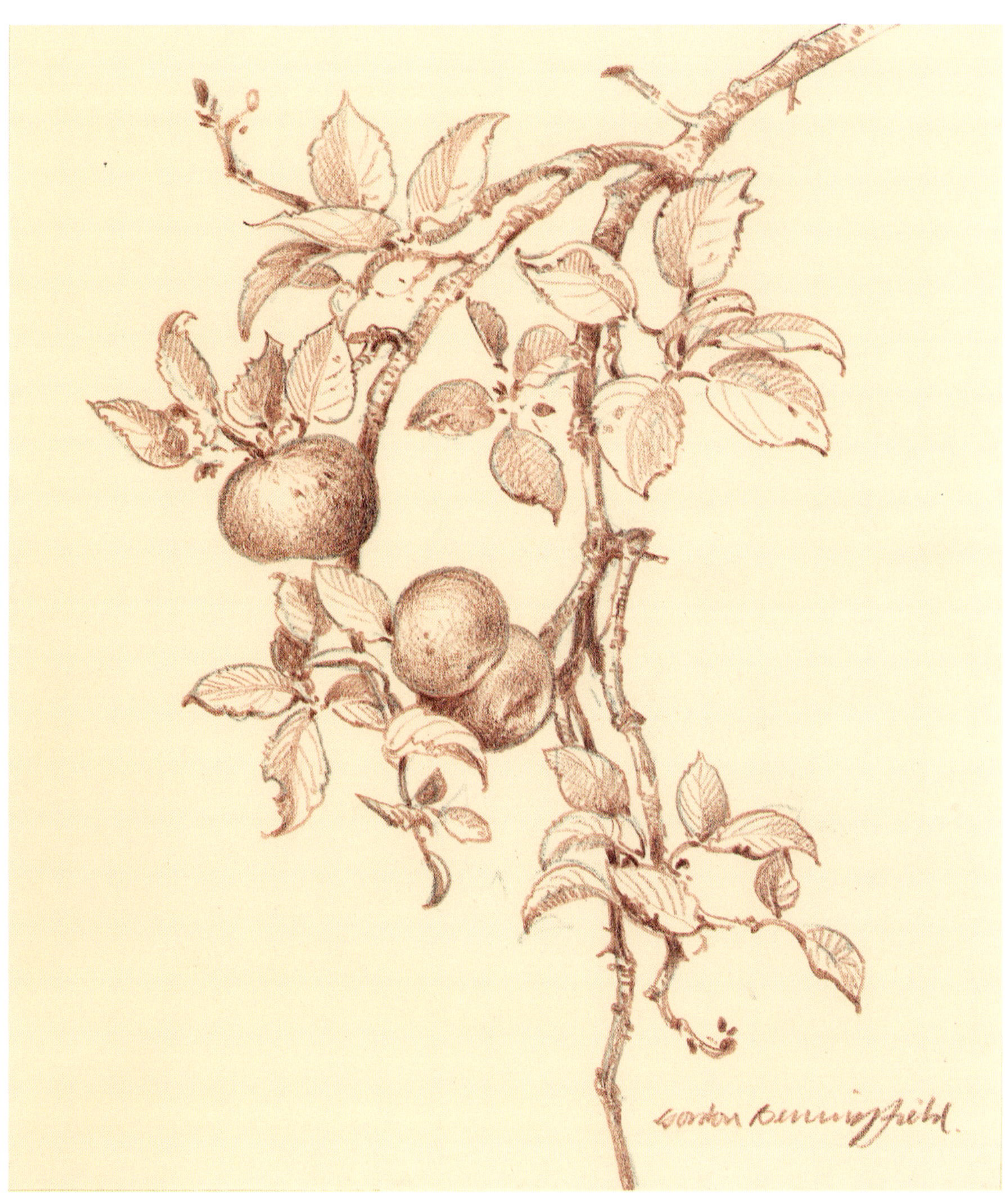

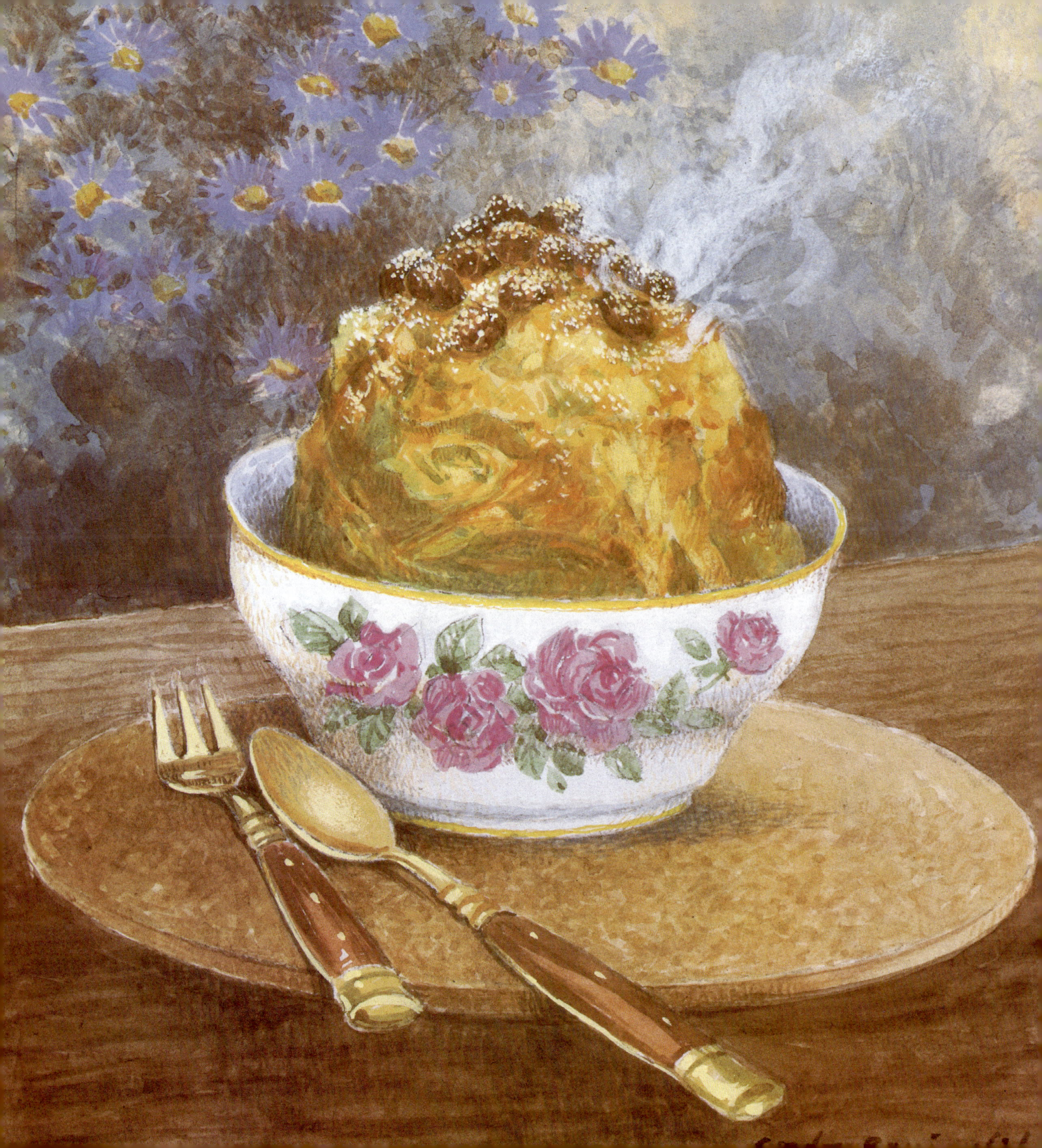

strain the syrup which should come to about $\frac{1}{2}$ pint. Mix 1 teaspoonful of arrowroot, add to the syrup and stir until boiling. Cook slowly until the liquid is clear, arrange the pears in a serving dish and pour over the wine sauce. Serve with cream or ice cream – it is fantastic.

Another simple apple dish is baked apple. It is very easy to prepare and again can be delicious.

All you have to do is wash and core the apple, with a nice big Bramley per person. Score a line around the middle of each apple with a sharp knife and then stand the apple in a buttered dish. The secret of baked apple is what to put in the centre once the core has been removed. Brown sugar or sultanas, raisins and brown sugar make wonderful fillings but it is entirely up to the eater and a great variety of fruits and nuts can be tried. The apple is then baked in a not too hot oven for about 45 minutes until the outer skin is brown and the apple is soft. It is as simple as that and can make a wonderful pudding or supper.

Apple dumplings are another traditional and popular dish and easy to make:

> 8 oz plain flour
> 2 oz margarine
> 2 oz Flora white
> pinch of salt
> water to mix
> 4 cooking apples cored and peeled
> brown sugar to taste

Make pastry, roll out and cut around a plate large enough to cover the apple. Place apple onto pastry round and fill centre of apple with brown sugar. Dampen edges of pastry with water and fold around the apple. Brush with milk, sprinkle with castor sugar. Decorate with pastry leaves if desired, or if you are feeling artistic. Bake until pastry looks golden brown, test to see if apple is cooked. This simple but excellent meal should take about 30 minutes at 180°C.

Apple turnover is another traditional apple dish and is like a large dumpling. The filling is easy:

> 1 lb Bramley apples, peeled and sliced
> 2 oz sugar

A little water
Pastry:
8 oz plain flour
2 oz lard
2 oz margarine

Cook apples, sugar and water slowly until soft. Add a few cloves according to taste.

Mix dry ingredients together until crumbly. Add 3–4 tablespoons of water, add slowly – do not make the pastry wet or sticky. Cut pastry into four pieces and roll out using a 6-inch cutter or a saucer to cut around. Place the stewed apple in the centre of pastry circle and dampen around the edges. Draw pastry up to centre and pinch edges together between thumb and forefinger. Brush turnover with milk and sprinkle with castor sugar. Bake at 180°C for 25–30 minutes until golden.

Apple crumble is another really good traditional sweet and it is just as easy to make a *plum* crumble or a *pear* crumble using the same basic recipe.

The apple crumble base:
1 lb cooking apples, peeled and sliced
4 oz sugar
2–3 tablespoons of water
Cook slowly until soft.
Place in pie dish.
Topping:
8 oz flour
4 oz marg or butter
3 oz sugar

Rub ingredients together until crumbly and place on top of the stewed apples, then sprinkle 1 oz of brown sugar on top. Bake at 180°C for 30–40 minutes until golden. For a change I sometimes put 6 oz flour and 2 oz of muesli, this gives a more crunchy topping.

I should add that with all the pies, puddings and crumbles, plums can all be used and plum pie is delicious. The other advantage of using plums is that there are an enormous number of little rhymes to say with each stone on the edge of the plate –

She loves me, she don't;
she would if she could;
she loves me, she don't;
she would if she could.

'*Rich man, poor man, beggar man, thief*' – it foretells of love and loss of love plus the social status of the intended partner. Consequently sometimes eating plum pie can give great happiness, but on the other hand it can also give tremendous sadness and foreboding.

Robin's mother used to make a wonderful plum treacle and it can be made with Czar's, Early Rivers, or any type of plum.

Line an 8-inch flan dish with short crust pastry
Pour in 2 tablespoons of golden syrup
Fill with halved and stoned plums

Bake in a moderate oven for 40–45 minutes. Serve hot or cold with cream or custard. It can also be made with rhubarb or gooseberries.

Once smitten by plum treacle then late summer will never be the same again.

Apple fritters were another of Gordon's favourites and they too are very easy to make.

4 oz flour
1 egg
$\frac{1}{2}$ pint milk
pinch of salt
apples, cored, peeled and cut into rings.

Sieve the flour, salt and add egg and milk. Beat thoroughly until a smooth batter. Coat apple rings with batter and place into hot fat. Fry until golden, drain on kitchen paper and sprinkle with cinnamon and sugar.

Another fattening and traditional meal is to put slices of apple into Yorkshire pudding and then serve with a spoonful of golden syrup.

So if lunch and dinner are survived, there is always tea and apple cake to follow. It is a very, very pleasant and tasty experience.

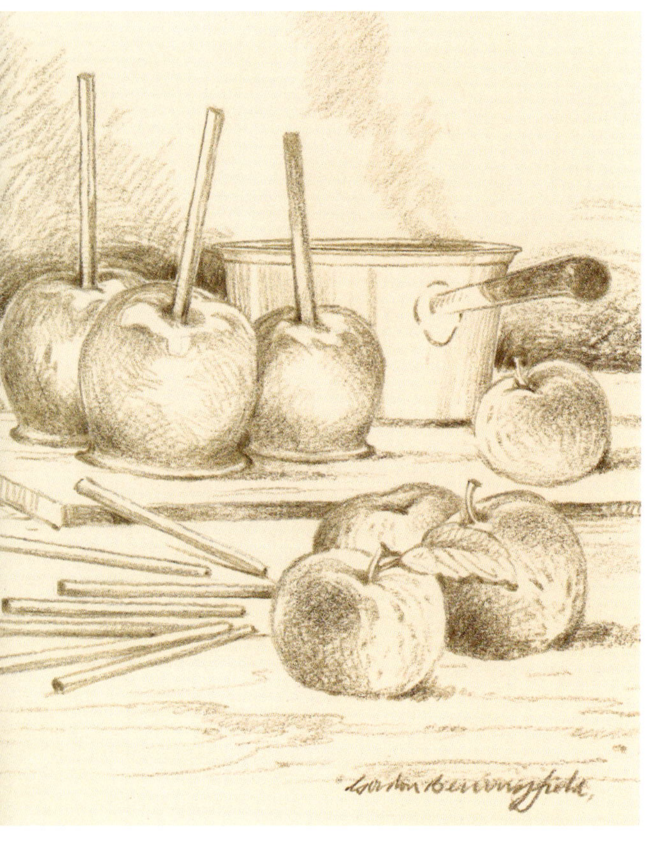

ABOVE: *Toffee apples –*
a traditional treat.

8 oz self raising flour
4 oz butter or margarine
4 oz castor sugar
2 cooking apples, peeled and chopped
1 egg
3 tablespoons of milk

Rub flour, fat and sugar together; add chopped apples, beaten egg and milk. Mix well and place into a well greased tin. Bake at 170°C for between 50–60 minutes until the cake is well and truly done.

For those who want to be even more adventurous there is always Upside Down Caramel Apple Cake.

5 oz self raising flour
2½ oz butter or margarine
2 oz dark brown sugar
2 cooking apples, peeled and sliced
pinch of salt.

Grease a round tin – not loose bottom – with butter, then sprinkle with dark brown sugar. Place the sliced apples in a circular pattern in the sugar. Make the topping by rubbing flour, fat and salt together, add enough water to make a soft dough. Roll out and place on top of the apples. Bake for 30 minutes at 180°C. Turn out onto a plate so that the caramel apples are on top. Delicious served hot with cream.

But even after all this there are still many fruit traditions to be eaten or should I say drunk, because there is perry, that wonderful alcoholic drink made from pears, which sits very comfortably alongside cider. There are also many other great traditional drinks like Damson Gin, Sloe Gin and even Quince Gin.

Cider has for many years been the traditional drink of the West Country and to this can be added Cider Brandy which is very warming and very strong. There are still many large and small companies throughout the West Country, and indeed in some other parts such as Norfolk and

Suffolk where traditional cider and perry are made. The fanatic can even make home-made apple or plum wine which can be extremely potent. But the traditional cider drinker who also likes beer should be careful as:

> Cider on beer makes good cheer
> Beer on cider makes a bad rider.

For the uninitiated try Quince Gin. The quince is one of our oldest and most traditional of fruit and this recipe was given to Robin by Oliver Tynan, a wonderful tree planter and volunteer of the Countryside Restoration Trust. Many tree planters consider it to be even better than Damson or Sloe Gin. The recipe is simple:

> 4 pints of diced quince
> add 4 lbs of sugar and
> 2½ pints of export Gin

The mixture should be put into a gallon jar and shaken every day for 3 months.

By Christmas it should be perfect and it will help get the moderate partaker through the worst months of winter with a wonderful evening glow.

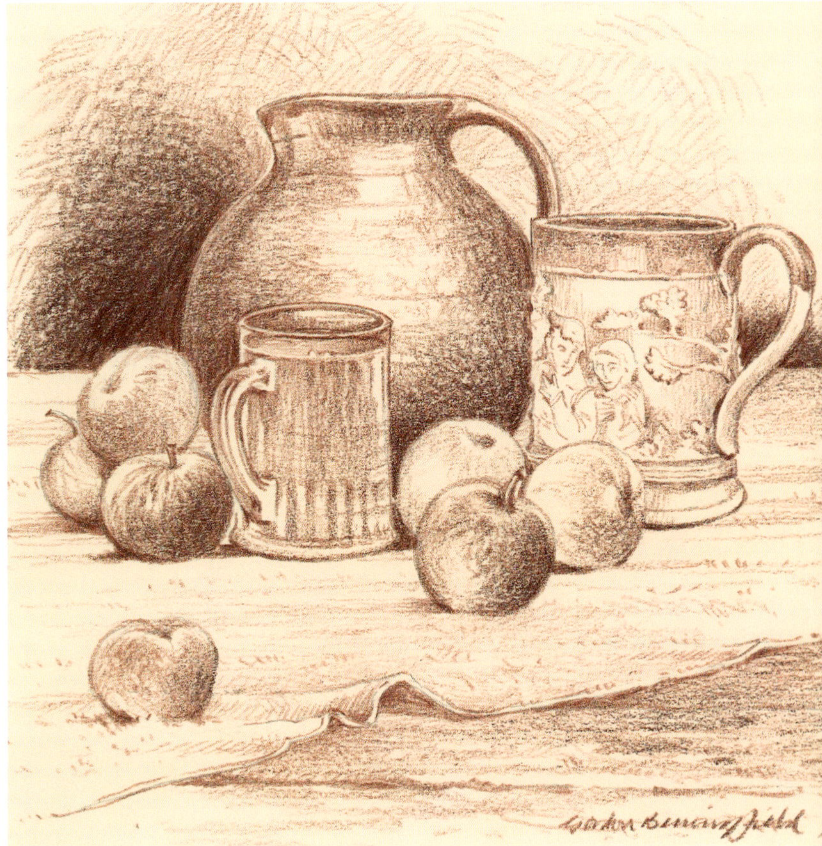

The miracle – apple juice into cider.

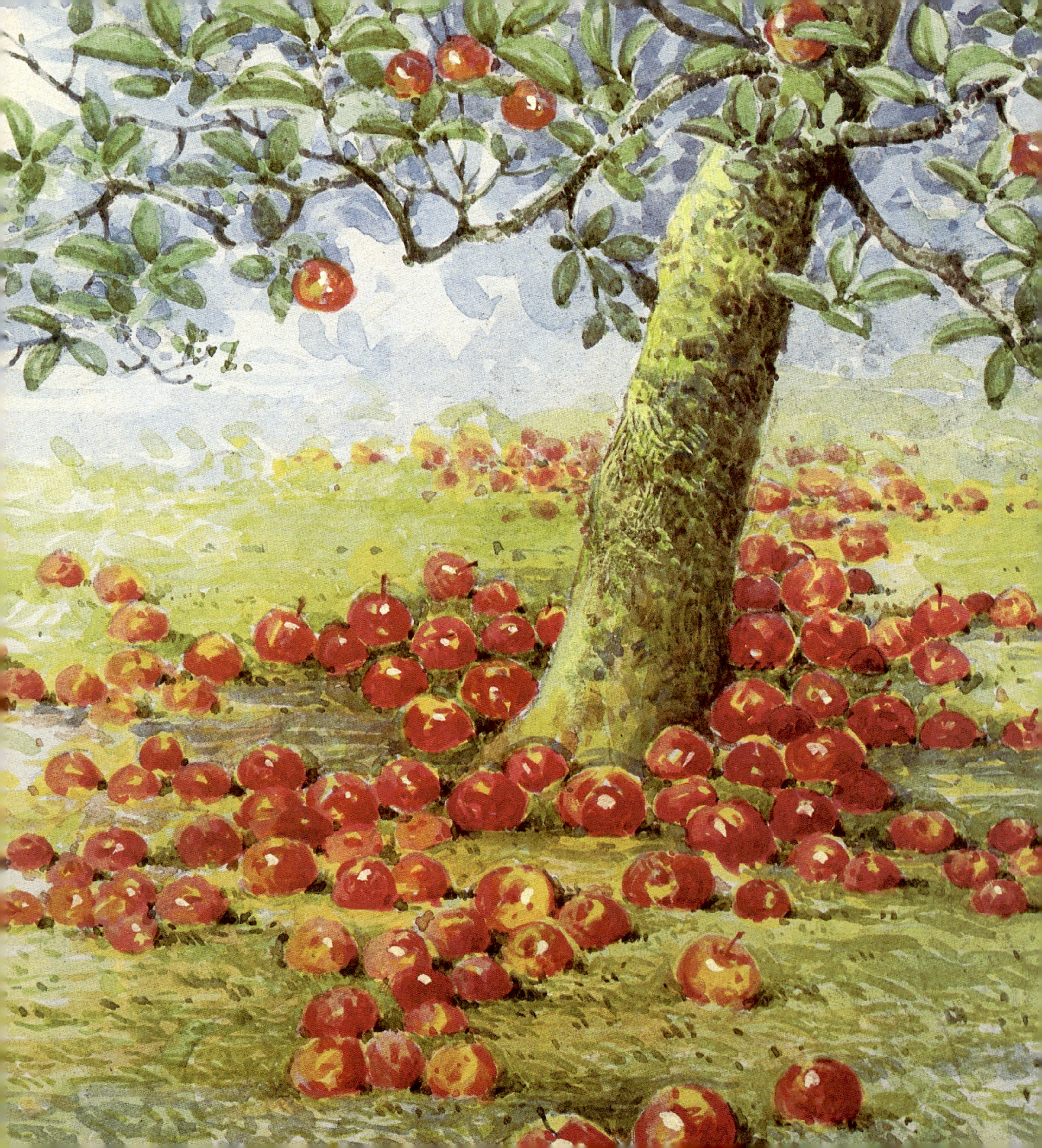

Backword

It has been rewarding to be put back in touch with our traditional orchards through the pictures of *Beningfield's Orchards*. As if to emphasise the point it has been a wonderful year for apple blossom – the best I can remember. The plum, pear and apple trees have been a complete picture. Orchards and individual trees have been awash with blossom and the scent has hung in the air with a perfect sweetness. It has been one of those springs in which Robert Browning's poem *Home Thoughts From Abroad* has never been more appropriate:

> *Oh, to be in England*
> *Now that April's there,*
> *And whoever wakes in England*
> *Sees, some morning, unaware,*
> *That the lowest boughs and the brush-wood sheaf*
> *Round the elm-tree bole are in tiny leaf,*
> *While the chaffinch sings on the orchard bough*
> *In England – now!*
>
> *And after April, when May follows,*
> *And the whitethroat builds, and all the swallows –*
> *Hark! where my blossomed pear-tree in the hedge*
> *Leans to the field and scatters on the clover*
> *Blossoms and dewdrops – at the bent spray's edge –*
> *That's the wise thrush; he sings each song twice over,*
> *Lest you should think he never could recapture*
> *The first fine careless rapture!*

> *And though the fields look rough with hoary dew,*
> *All will be gay when noontide wakes anew*
> *The buttercups, the little children's dower,*
> *– Far brighter than this gaudy melon-flower!*

The blooming orchards have been matched by the flowering hedgerows and it really has been a spring of blossom like no other. With the sloe blossom and the crab apples as prolific in their flowering as the apples of the orchard, it has been a season of bursting buds and scented air. Even non-fruiting trees such as lilac have bloomed in profusion, adding to a cocktail of fragrance which has helped make a remarkable spring.

As I write, the blossom has faded and the fruit set. The delicate petals have fallen like snow and already the forming fruit promises an abundant harvest. But this abundant harvest, this tradition, is under threat like at no other time. British fruit continues to be largely ignored by the large supermarkets and the varieties of local fruit for sale diminishes each year, as does the actual amount sold. In 1990 Britain was 19 per cent self-sufficient in orchard-produced fruit, by 2001 this had fallen to a mere 10 per cent, with the country importing over 2,700,000 tons of fruit. It is a tragedy and a waste. It reduces biodiversity; it reduces choice to customers, and as we have seen from this book it is in effect, an attack on our wildlife and on our traditional countryside.

Incredibly, at this time too, the Government is threatening to hasten the decline of the traditional orchard. In restructuring the dreadful and wasteful Common Agricultural Policy, which has turned and is turning farming into an industrial process over much of Europe, a new system of subsidy payment is threatening to bypass traditional orchards. The only way orchard owners can claim their subsidy is to grub up their trees and turn once beautiful areas of fruit and wildlife production into ordinary fields. It is a nonsense. If the land was covered with grass and old trees without fruit, the subsidy payments would be made, but because these areas are covered with fruit-producing trees then the subsidy does not cover them. Fortunately it seems that this absurd situation can be reversed, but the real question is: 'How on earth was it contemplated in the first place?' It shows a complete lack of rural awareness; our leaders and bureaucrats, with their tidy urban minds do not understand all the various links and relationships between traditional farming, the environment, people and wildlife.

So what can be done to save our orchards? Every reader of this book can help in a practical way. During harvest it is so important for people to ask for British fruit. In whichever supermarket they go they should take the trouble to ask for British plums or apples and request choice. The

RIGHT: *The orchard harvest goes far beyond fruit and totally beyond the understanding of politicians. Butterflies and wildflowers are part of the additional orchard harvest.*

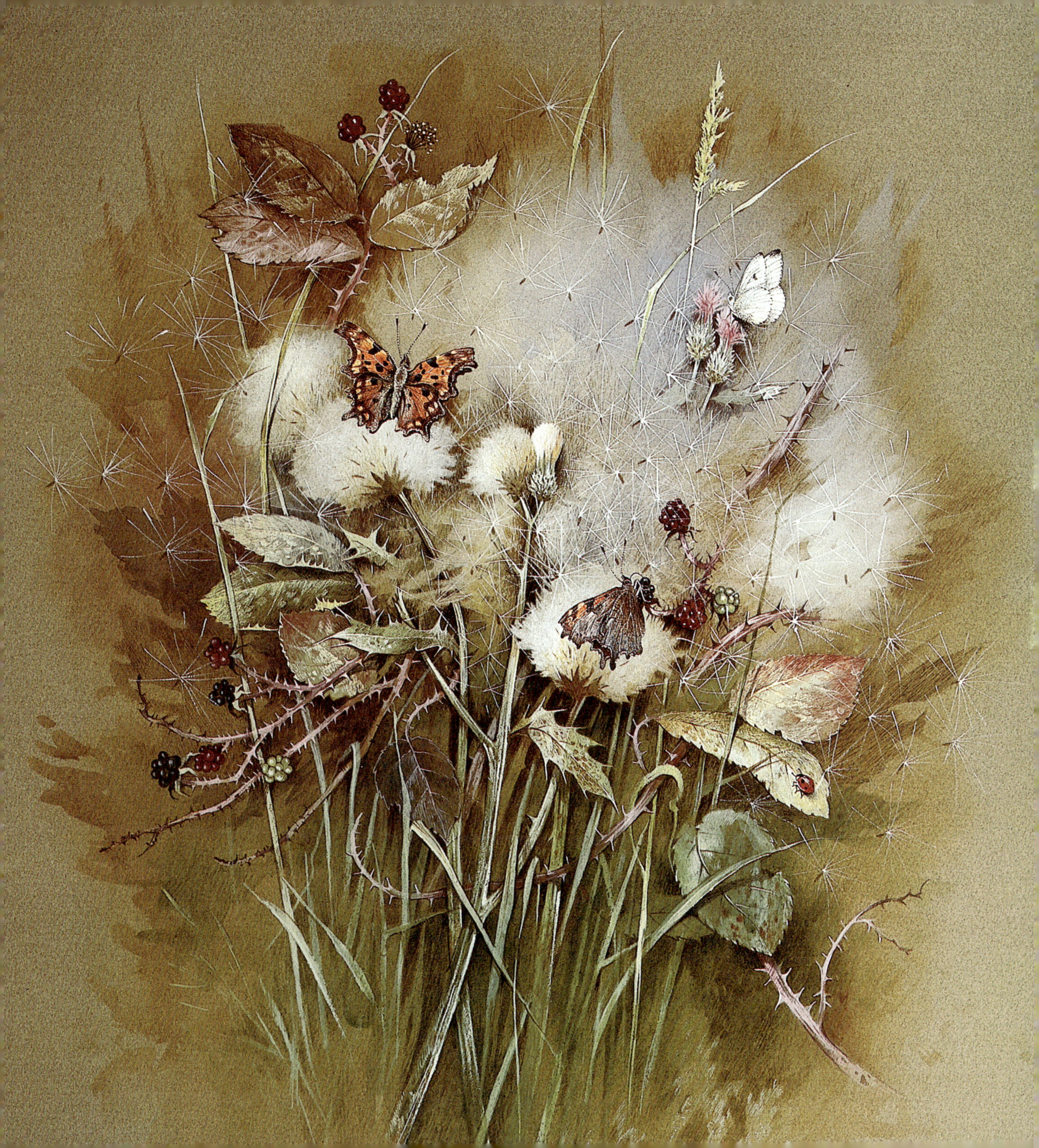

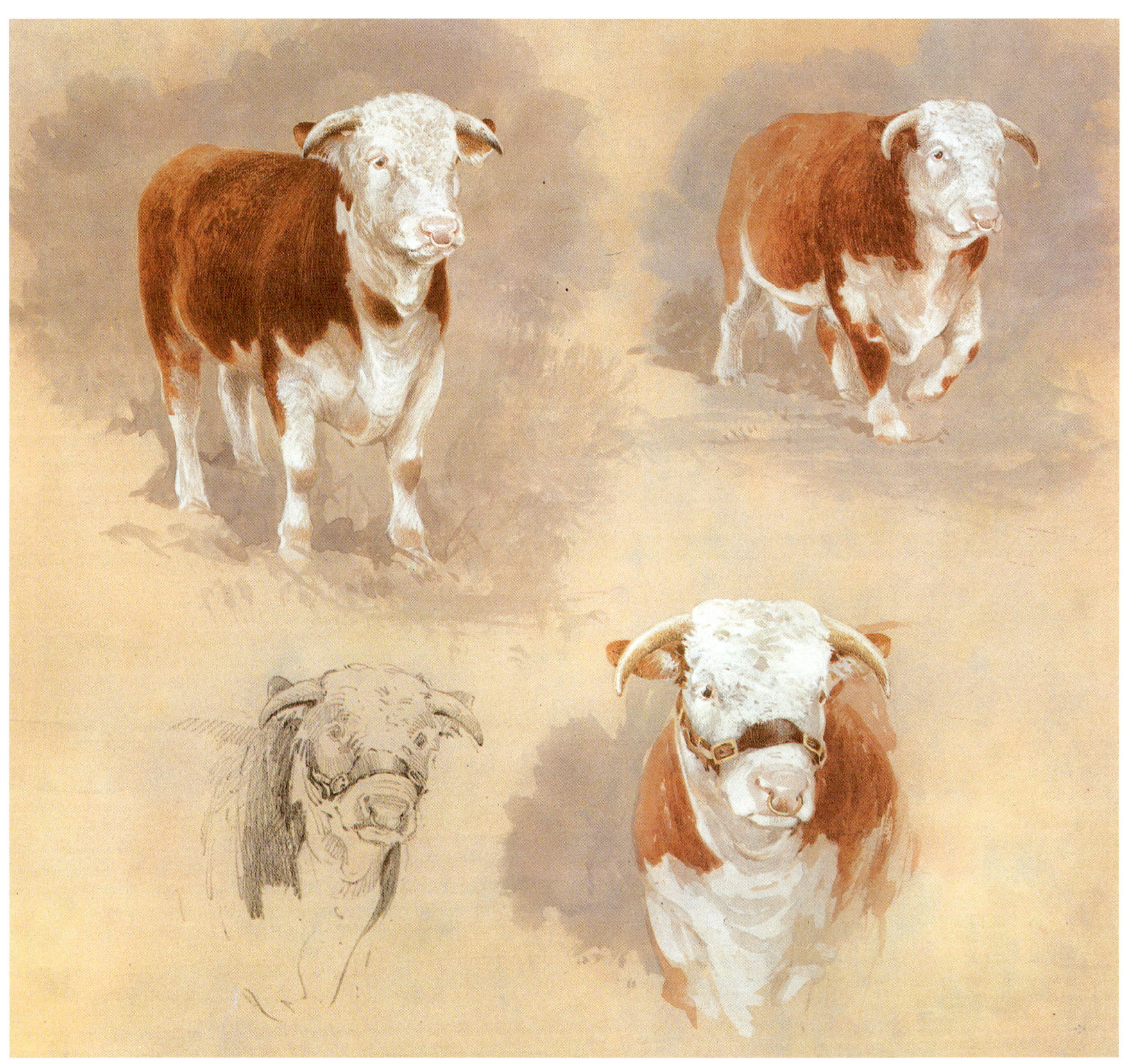

supermarkets boast of 'choice', *but that choice should be customer choice, not supermarket choice* which is based on cheap fruit from abroad. At the moment supermarket fruit represents globalisation at its most absurd, bringing in apples, plums and pears from thousands of miles away when better quality fruit grows on our own doorstep. Food miles are miles that increase greenhouse gases, they increase global warming, and they increase food ignorance with supermarket customers losing an appreciation of season, quality, and home-produced food. Better still don't shop at supermarkets; shop at the corner shop, the village shop, the market or the Farmers' Market – all selling home-produced fruit.

For the benefit of those who doubt the impact of the supermarkets I am including two simple tales. I am doing so reluctantly as I don't want *Orchards* to become a rant or an illustrated political pamphlet – I want to write nothing that detracts from Gordon's wonderful pictures. But quite by coincidence during the course of helping to prepare this book I came across two East Anglian fruit growers – both of whom have had their orchards devastated by the power and the ignorance of the supermarkets.

Just as worrying is the fact that both growers wish to remain anonymous and neither wishes me to mention the supermarket concerned out of fear of legal action. Readers should remember that the British legal system is no longer concerned with justice or the rule of law, it is about proving *points of law* at vast expense. In effect this means that the law can only be used by those with money; i.e. supermarkets, the government, newspapers etc., or those with no money at all; i.e. those on legal aid. In other words, to most members of the public – fruit growers included – the law, and protection under the law is totally beyond them. The best example of the misuse of law – aided and abetted by various politicians and members of the Establishment was the Labour politician, newspaper owner and businessman Robert Maxwell. He was also a criminal and a fraudster, whose dishonesty was protected by the use of our expensive legal system with threats of writs for libel and slander; indeed I am only able to describe him here as a crook of the worst kind because he is dead – some legal system which relies on death for the emergence of truth!

My first orchard owner in the Fens has reduced the area of his trees to just 45 acres. Astonishingly he still grows thirty varieties of plum – but the supermarkets will only take two British types – Victoria and Marjorie. The other eating varieties they regard as too small and they will only take plums with a diameter of 38 millimetres or more – which immediately rules out Early Rivers and Czars, our best desert plums.

Victoria plums will usually yield between 10–12 tons to the acre – but to get them to grow to 38mm the growing crop has to be pruned – so that there are fewer plums; the remaining plums then grow larger – yielding only 7 tons an acre. He sells no cooking plums to the supermarkets – as it is supermarket policy to sell plums only for raw eating. Consequently there is no longer a

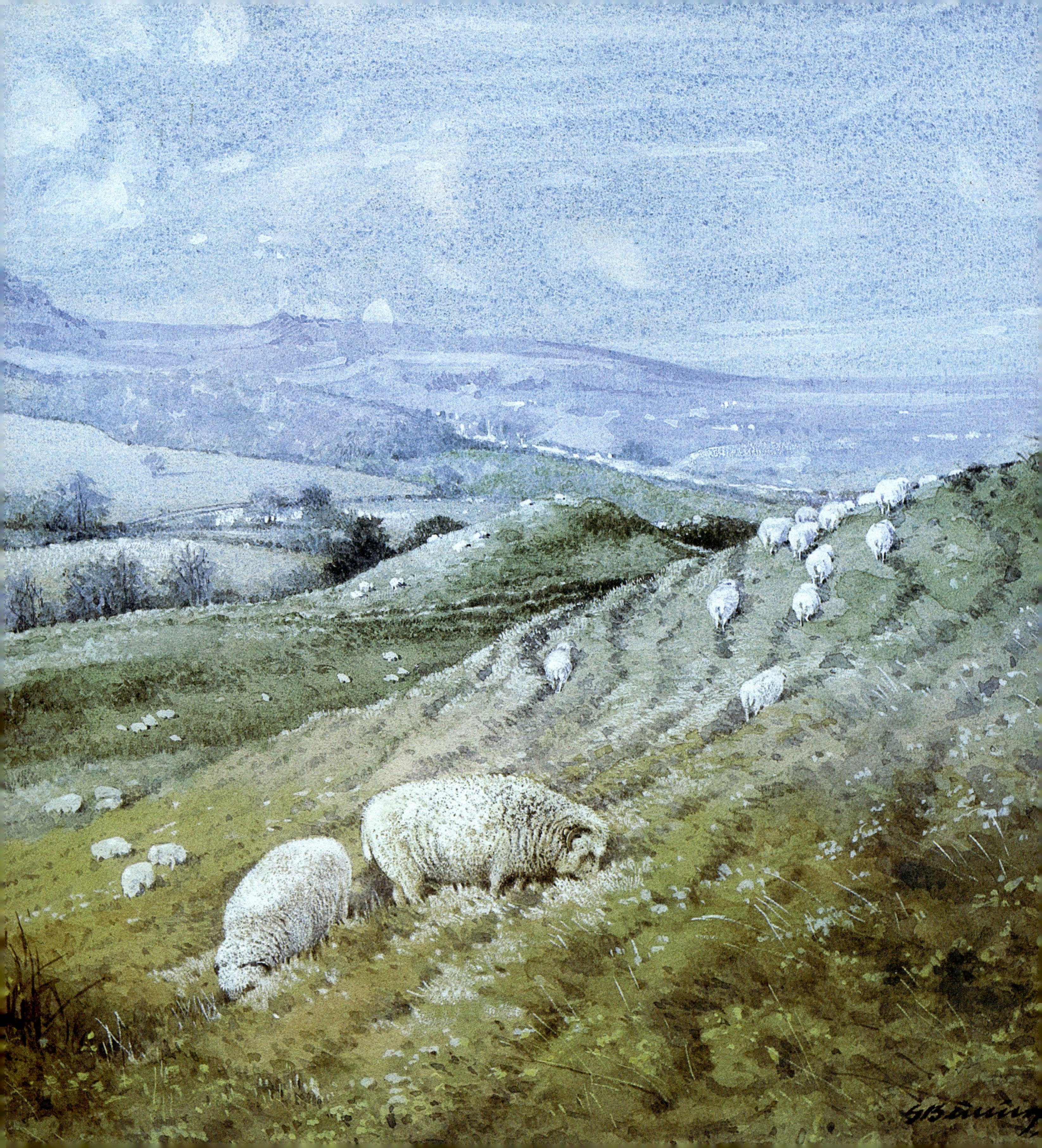

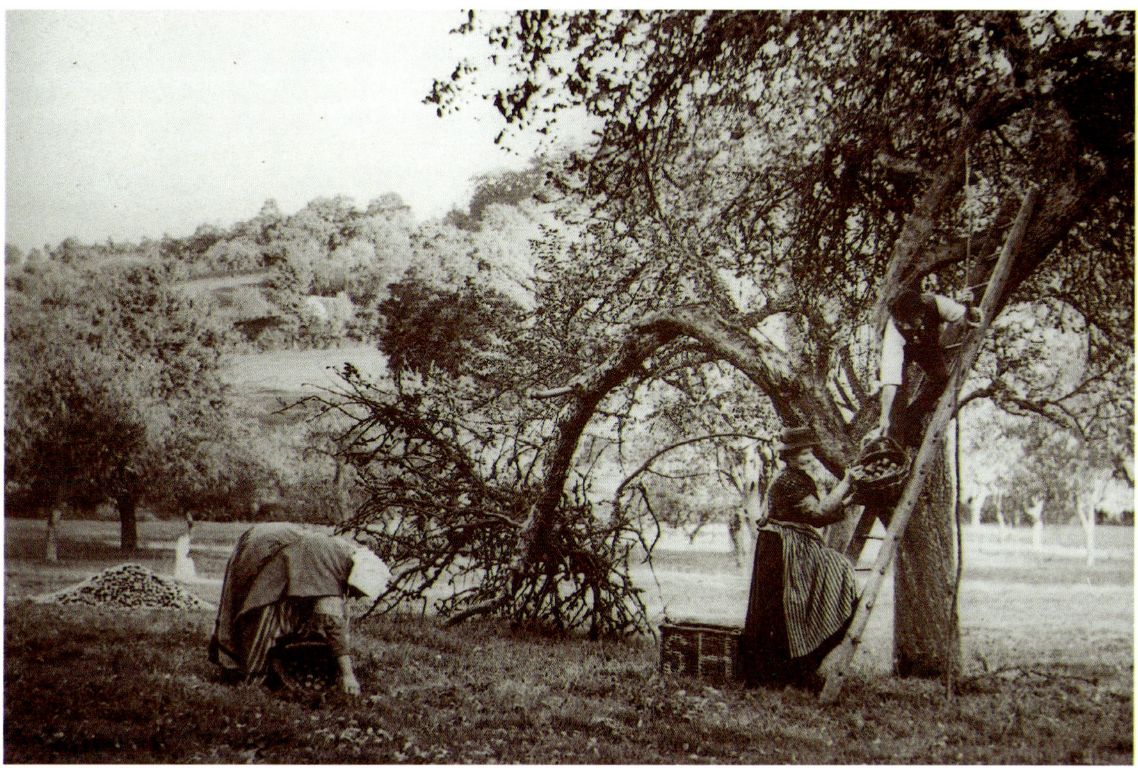

ABOVE: *Traditional picking and gathering of the cider apples – from Weston's photographic archives.*
LEFT: *Gordon's view of Dorset – very similar to the landscape of Turnastone Court Farm.*

market for a beautiful cooking plum, such as the Monarch, and most people under 50 these days fail to realise that plums can be cooked, bottled and frozen.

Now, the only way he can sell traditional varieties of plum is through his farm shop; when in season he will have eight varieties of plum on sale and three types of greengage. As a result he now only has thirteen Early River trees left – he once had 2 acres and his Czars have fallen from 7 acres in the 1980s to just fifteen trees this year. In 2003 he had forty trees that he did not pick, as he simply could not sell this delicious and beautiful *small* plum. If he had picked his Czars, he would have received £1.50 a tray (12lbs) – he would have had to pay the picker £1, plus 30p for the tray itself, and 20–40p for transport – consequently Czars can now only be bought in his farm shop.

With apples it is the same. The world's best eating apple is a Cox – it is naturally a small apple, but the supermarkets want 70ml apples – so again the trees have to be pruned to reduce the crop so that the remaining apples grow larger, and the larger a Cox grows the more diluted its taste becomes. From this it seems that the average supermarket fruit-buyer knows as much about fruit as the average fruit grower knows about nuclear fission. As a friend said while reading the proofs of this book: 'Most people don't want large apples; why don't the supermarkets realise this? When you want an apple you want a snack – not a b...... four course meal.' It is again supermarket *choice* or lack of it – not customer *choice*.

Regrettably this is only the start of the madness – supermarkets now sell 80 per cent of all Britain's food. Yet it costs the producer between £10,000 and £25,000 to be put on the supermarket's computer. If produce is rejected the supermarket fines the producer for loss of profit and shelf-space – the *fine* is applied by simply deducting the fine from the money already owed – the supermarkets do not pay the producer for 90 days – consequently the supermarkets hold the producers in more that an 'armlock'. What would the supermarkets do if their customers failed to pay for 90 days?

At the end of the year the supermarket can then charge the producers 5 per cent of their turnover with that supermarket. Finally the producer is instructed by the supermarket where to purchase his fruit boxes (the nominated supplier) and what transport to use, with the supermarket taking yet more commissions from the box supplier and the haulier. No wonder supermarkets are making huge profits.

The enormous profits of the supermarkets – Tesco made £1.7bn in 2003/4 compared to £675m in 1995 – mean huge salaries for supermarket executives. While twelve farms go out of business every day, with one farming suicide every six days, and some dairy farmers and fruit growers earning as little as £2.90 an hour – for an 80-hour week – well below the rate of the National Minimum Wage – the Chief Executive of Tesco received ('earned' is an inappropriate word) £2.977m before tax in the year 2003/4. If he worked an 80-hour week,

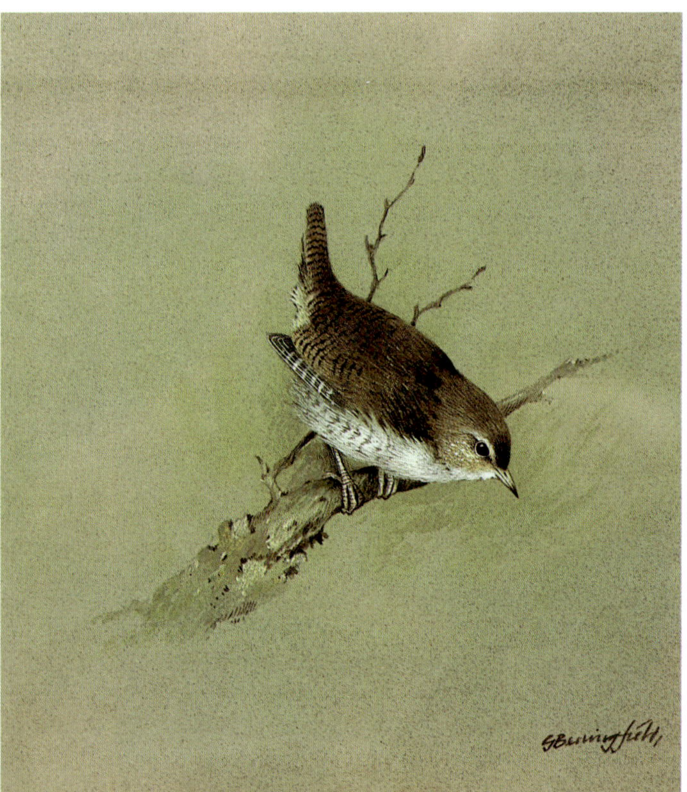

The wren – common on both the CRT Herefordshire farms.

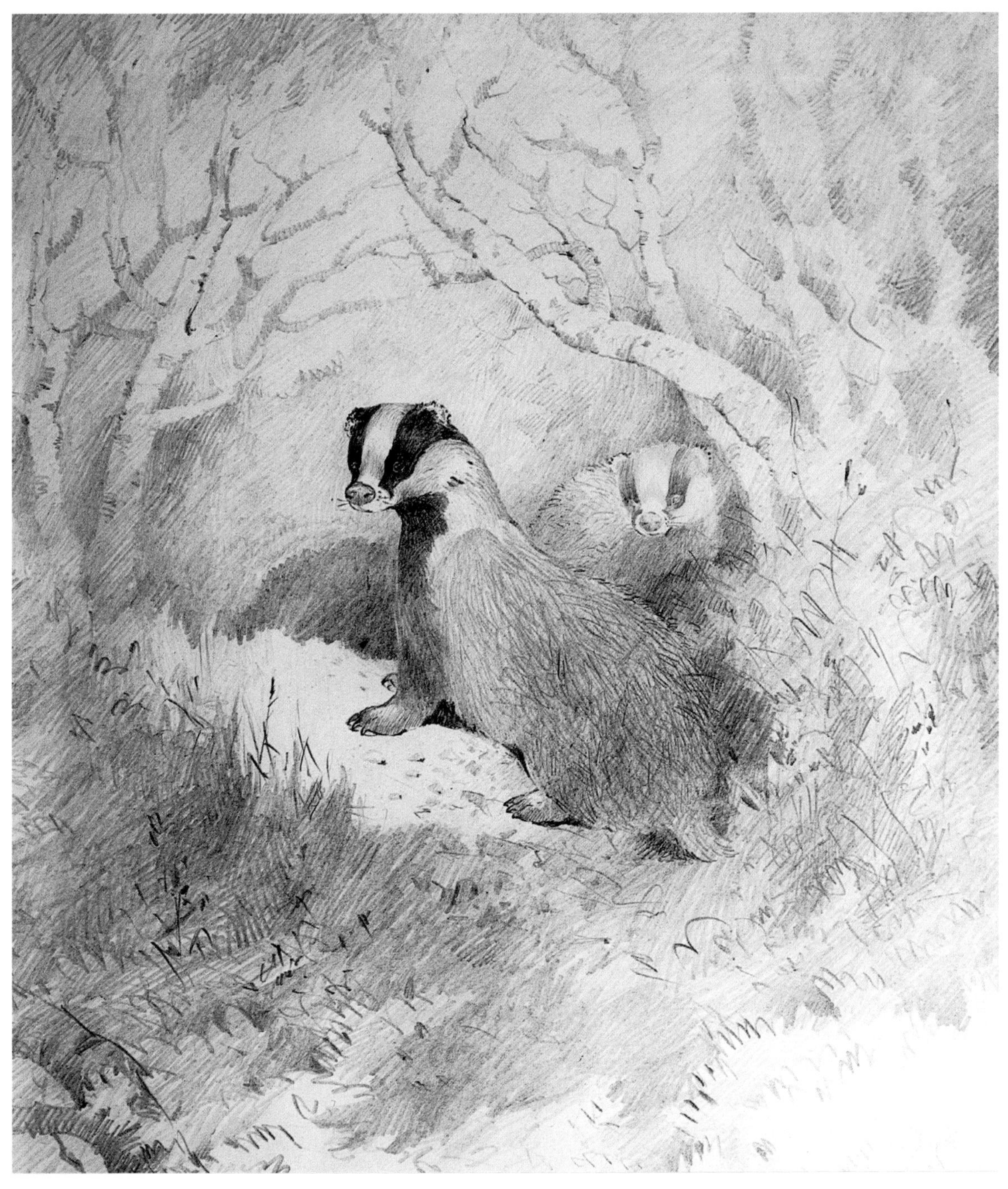

his rate of pay would be £715 an hour – nearly 250 times greater than some of those who supply him. But for only a 35-hour week his hourly rate would be £1634.28 – and I still have no desire to work for Tesco.

But my Fenland fruit grower's problems are not over – for in steps the great European Union. Most people – myself included like different sized fruit – some days I feel like eating a large apple – some days a small apple – and I would even prefer two small apples to one large apple. But with the supermarkets only buying large apples the customer's choice is again restricted. It is made worse by an EU Directive which declares that the size of all Euro-apples in a box have to be within 10 mls of each other. If the apples are wrapped or in a presentation box they have to be within 5 mls of each other.

My other fruit grower was also East Anglian. One day he had an urgent supermarket request for 2000 cases (30 tons) of apples – Discovery – with the price agreed beforehand. Between the order and delivery the market price dropped and so on arrival at the supermarket the apples were rejected on 'cosmetic grounds'. A DEFRA Inspector could find nothing wrong with them – but the supermarket still refused to accept them; the grower then had to pay for the independent inspection, for the transport back to his farm and for twenty women to remove the individual supermarket stickers so that they could be sold on the open market – which they were – as Grade One apples. The same supermarket expressed interest in a new variety of apple – a Red Pippin – which was a Cox cross. The grower planted 15 acres; yet by the time the trees began fruiting after four or five years, the supermarket refused to take any.

His orchard is now down to 40 acres from 300, and fifty local people have been made redundant. He too believes that the supermarkets' buying policy will gradually phase out the Cox. 'They don't talk about taste – just size and colour – appearance. Consequently there are Italian and French varieties that have colour – because of more sun – and size – but inferior taste, and they impose them on their customers.' As a result he now sells most of his twenty-five types of apples at local Farmers' Markets.

It is hardly surprising that in 1987 there were 1512 registered producers of desert apples in England and Wales. Today the number has plummeted to 512. Similarly in 1987 there were 33,937 acres of desert apples in England and Wales: now there are 13,214 acres.

One of my most vivid orchard memories occurred only four or five years ago when I was travelling through the Fens at plum harvest time. Although there were plums on the trees, there was no plum harvest. I passed at least a dozen orchards with no pickers and the plums just left on the trees where they grew, to fall and to rot. What a waste and what a tragedy. These beautiful English plums that somehow turn water, air and light into sweetness, were just left for wasps, foxes, badgers and hedgehogs.

Incredibly too, the government has a scheme to encourage children to eat fruit and each week there is free fruit in our schools – but no plums. Our nanny state considers plums to be a danger to small children – they may swallow the stones or choke on the stones – oh dear – a meteorite may fall from the sky, shouldn't they stay indoors? A politician might be struck by common-sense-syndrome – vaccinate, vaccinate.

There is still more – the health nannies of this ignorant urban government, in the guise of the Food Standards Agency, is now threatening to force farmers to exclude livestock from traditional orchards on health grounds. The Agency fears that fruit could become contaminated by manure. Clearly the Agency does not realise that cow and sheep droppings, drop, they respond to gravity and fall to the ground, whereas apples grow in the branches of trees, high in the air. Perhaps the Food Standards Agency anticipates cow pats being shot into trees by cows performing headstands. Several years ago I wrote as a joke that sooner or later some health freaks would want all farm livestock to wear nappies, and would declare 'farmyard muck' to be unhygienic for organic vegetables – that day of madness is evidently getting ever nearer.

The Countryside Restoration Trust of which Gordon was a Founder Trustee, and Vice-Chairman, has taken a more positive step to save our orchards. It has acquired two farms in Herefordshire – Britain's most traditional fruit-growing area – an area of orchards and apple blossom – of cider and perry pears.

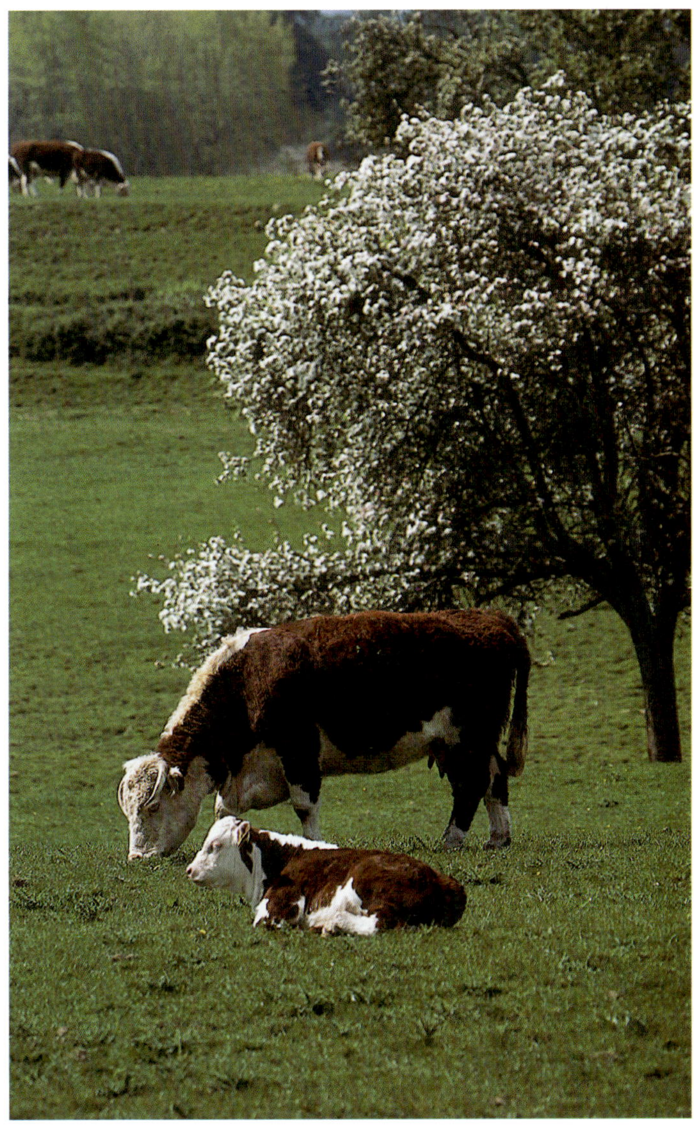

The first farm, Awnells, was given to the Trust by David Powell; with no children he wanted his beautiful, traditional, 235-acre farm to be safe for the future. For years he has produced wonderful Traditional Hereford cattle and in addition he has a fantastic cider and perry orchard. The name 'Awnells' is derived from Thomas Awenel who lived on the farm in the thirteenth century. It

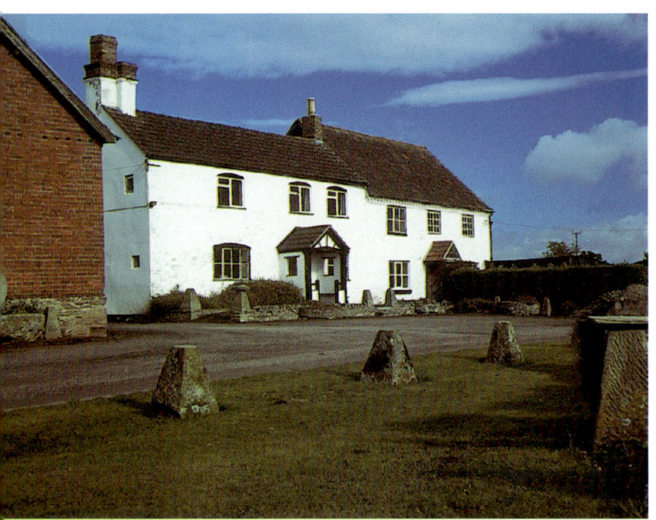

became known as Awnells farm in 1607, and so its roots go back centuries as do the roots of its orchard. David Powell's father bought the farm in 1922 and its old trees and blossom are a picture. It has cider apples and perry pears with many local varieties such as Helen's Early and Greg's Pit which are made into perry, and many varieties of cider apple including Bulmer's Norman, Dabinett, Yarlington Mill, Tom Putt, and Kingston Black. There are also a number of cider apple trees and perry pear trees which have not been identified.

Photographs of –
LEFT: *Awnells farm, the CRT's first Herefordshire farm.*
BELOW: *Some of the beautiful Traditional Herefordshire cattle (also on the previous page).*

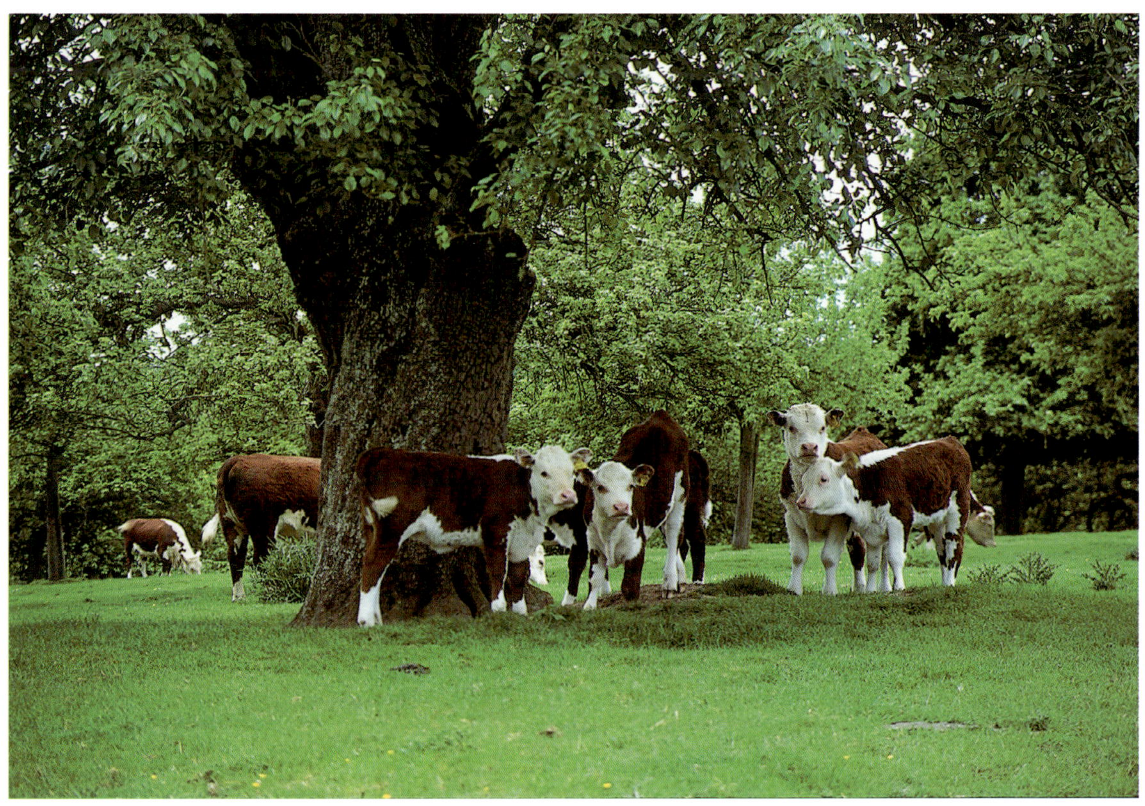

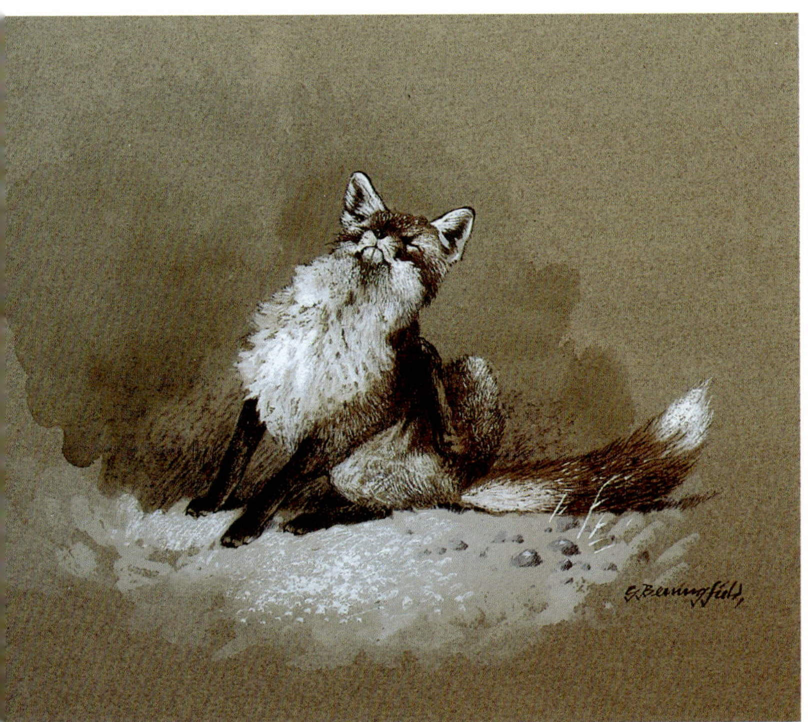 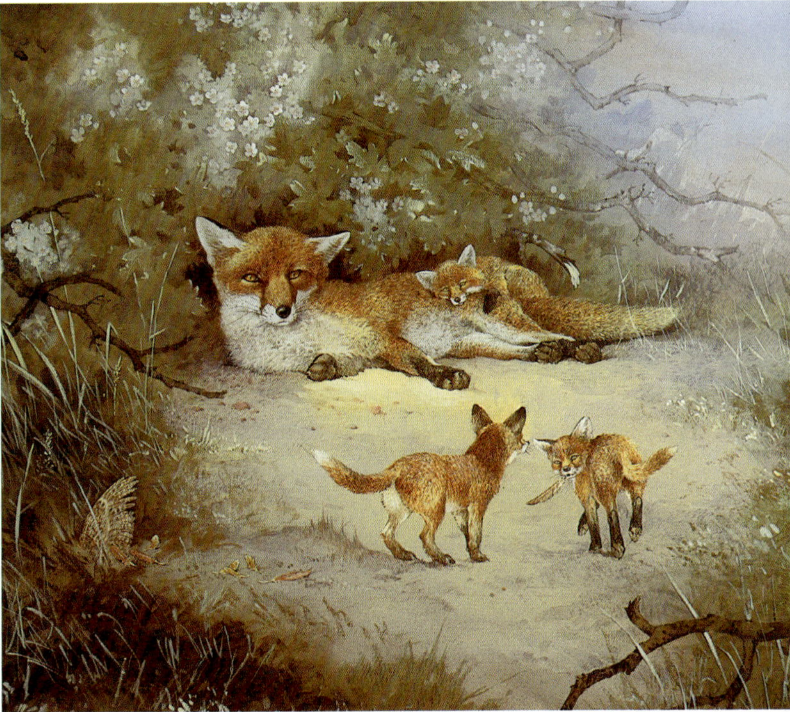

In one ditch on the farm foxes have bred for generations – perhaps one of the unidentified apples could be of the Foxwhelp variety. As we have seen foxes do make use of orchards and David certainly sees signs that foxes have been in his orchard and the perry pear tastes extremely good although it can upset the unfamiliar stomach. To make the work easier for the foxes the cider and perry harvest is simple. The apples and pears are allowed to fall to the ground and are then gathered for the local cider makers. Being in Much Marcle *Weston's Cider* uses some of the Awnells fruit as does David's next door neighbour, James Marsden, who has started his own little cider business which he calls *Gregg's Pit, Cider and Perry*. To make the Food Standards Agency happy, grazing animals are already removed from the cider and perry orchards 90 days before harvesting.

With desert apples the hope is:

September blow soft
Till the fruit's in the loft.

With cider apples it is wind and gravity that do the picking.

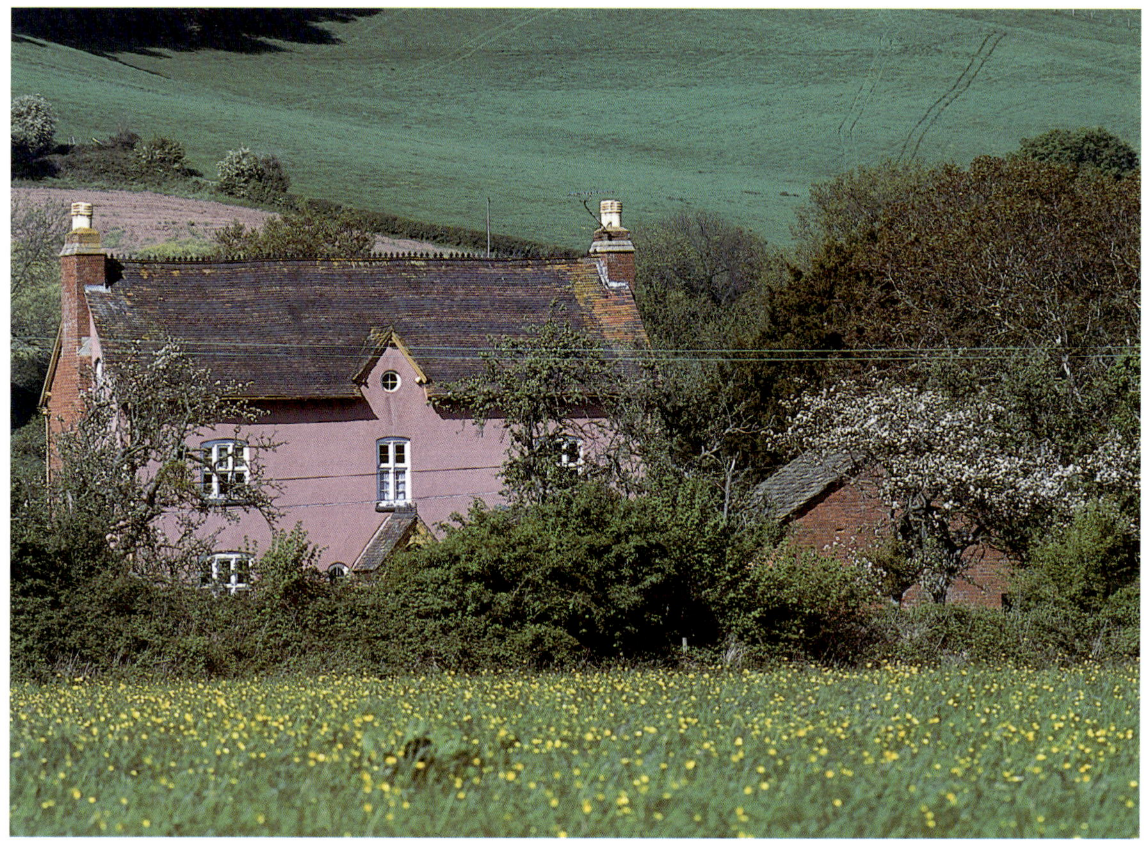

A photograph of Turnastone Court Farm, nestling into the beautiful Herefordshire countryside.

It is one of the most pastoral scenes possible to walk around David's farm looking at his trees and his cattle. The CRT realises its responsibility to see that both these old traditions continue, and part of that responsibility is to find a market for the produce and to ensure that ordinary shoppers develop a taste and an appreciation for quality local British food.

Common Ground is a charity that has done more than any other to re-awaken people to the quality and range of British apples. It has started and promoted 'Apple Day' – 21 October – and we hope that visitors will be able to visit Awnells farm on the weekend closest to Apple Day for many years to come.

Twenty miles away the CRT has purchased another farm. The journey from Awnells to Turnastone Court passes many more orchards some of them belonging to *Bulmer's Cider.* Turnastone Court itself was not as much purchased by the CRT, but saved by the CRT. Its 250

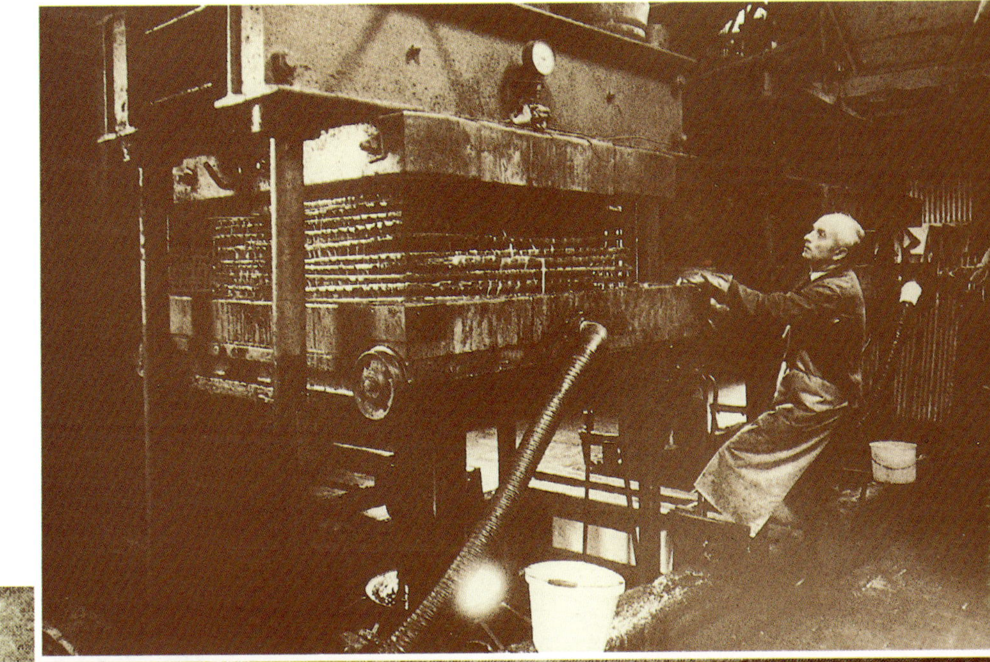

*Traditional cider making –
more pictures from Weston's
photographic archives.*

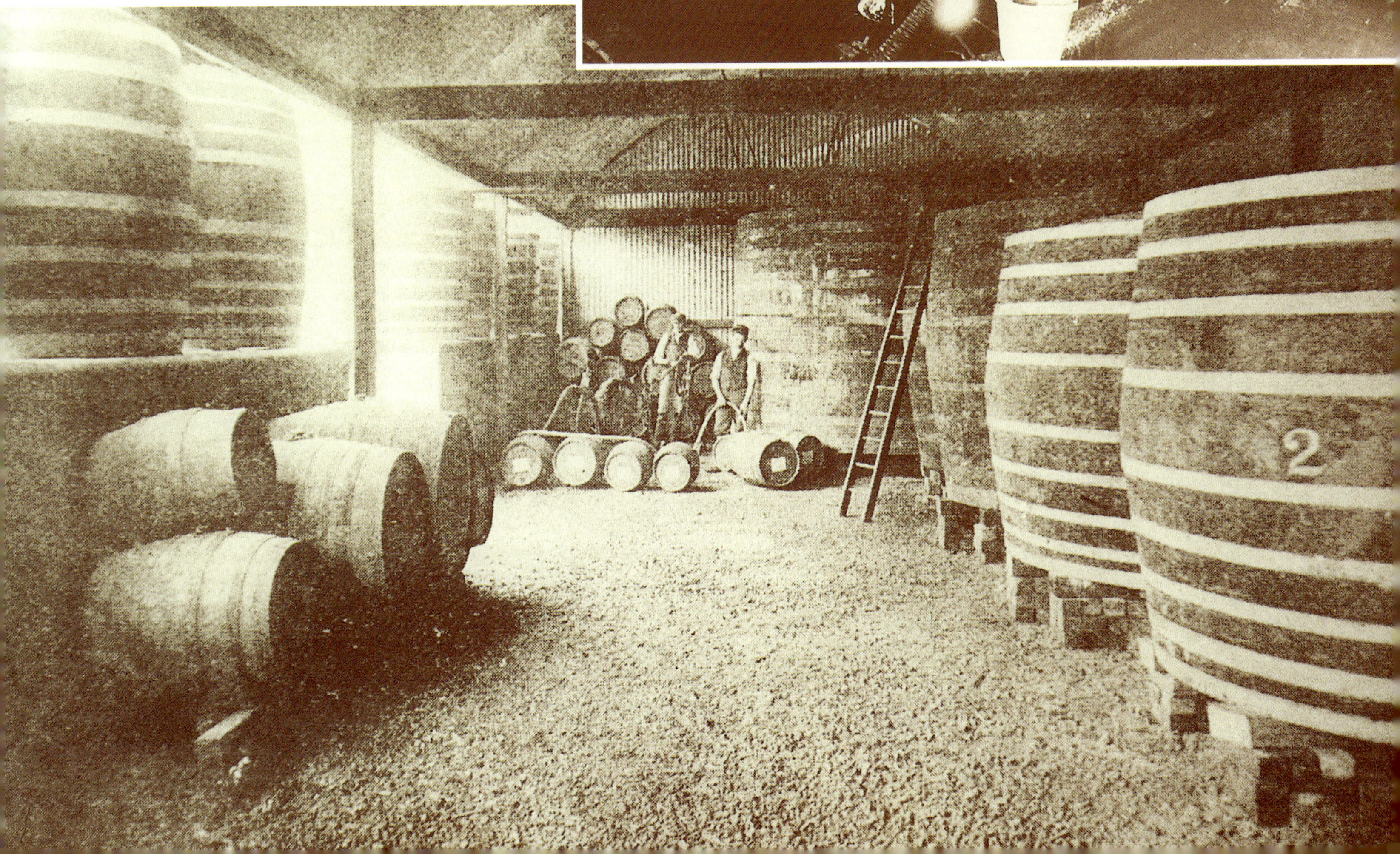

acres of ancient pasture were threatened with cultivation for potatoes. In addition it makes up part of the most important landscape in the Golden Valley and it seemed to the CRT that a major environmental crime would have been allowed if it had not been purchased. A local naturalist has said: 'Turnastone Court Farm is one of the most important farms in Herefordshire. It has traditional orchards; bio-diversity; a vital historic landscape with some fascinating agricultural archaeology and it produces organic fruit and beef.'

Otters are regularly seen along the River Dore as it flows through Turnastone Court Farm.

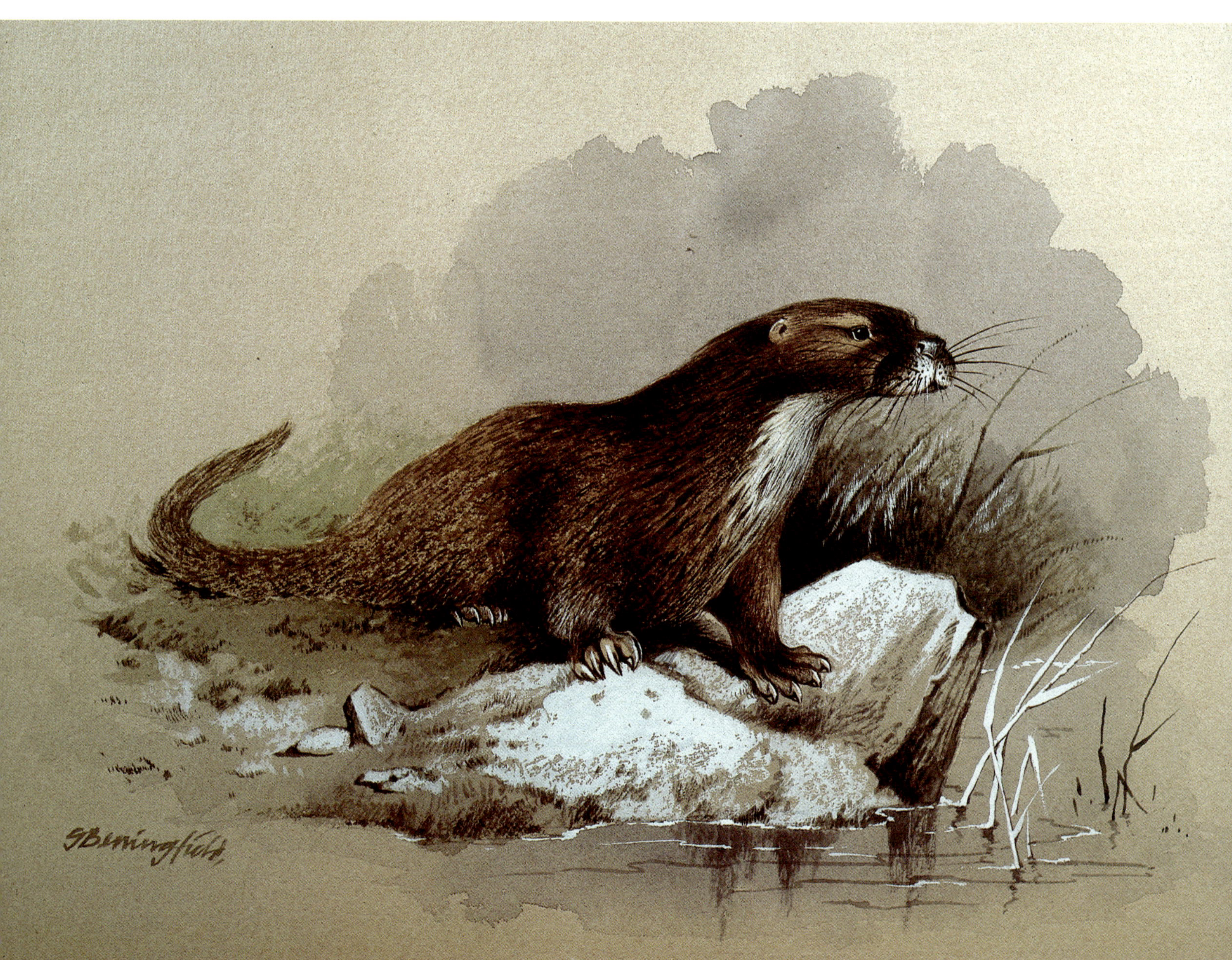

By saving Turnastone Court the CRT took on a large overdraft at an uncertain financial time, but the risk has been worth it for around the farmyard there is an ancient orchard with many old and unidentified trees. Some of the fruit is again taken by a local cider maker from Abbey Dore and the fruit can be drunk as a very strong *Gwatkin* cider. It is hoped to help reverse the decline of orchards in the near future by actually planting a larger orchard at Turnastone and in addition to the cider apples it is hoped that there will be one or two trees for desert fruit for local people to pick or to buy.

Strangely, that is one of the problems with orchards for eating – that these days in Britain physical labour is looked down upon and so it is very difficult for orchard owners to get fruit-pickers. In my teens, every school holiday in the summer meant fruit picking for pocket money – from blackcurrants through to late apples. Many of the local women and young people picked for pocket money and we were joined by gypsies who moved from area to area – season to season – undertaking agricultural work. Alas British young people no longer seem to want to get dirt on their hands and so pickers have to be allowed in from Eastern Europe who are familiar with man-ual labour and who actually seem to enjoy it. As British people get fatter, slower and more urban, so their appreciation of the countryside becomes less and less. In a sane world many people ought to jump at the opportunity of fruit picking – out in the fresh air and experiencing work of a differ-ent nature and at a different pace than sitting in front of a computer screen – but new comfortable habits die hard and the computer screen seems to be winning. The computer screen watchers then go shopping at Tesco to buy their fruit – Italian plums, Uruguayan apples and Californian pears – what a strange world we live in. When they buy 'organic' they even imagine they are being 'green' – they have evidently forgotten greenhouse gases. Self-delusion is one of the twenty-first century's most contagious and debilitating conditions.

The wildlife at Turnastone is typical of rural Herefordshire. In old buildings near the ancient orchard there are redstarts and in the River Dore there are both otters and the rare white clawed crayfish which survives in such numbers that the odd otter snack can be afforded. Grey wagtails, yellow wagtails and curlews are other birds of the grass meadows, and again traditional Hereford cattle contribute to the traditional life on the farm; traditional sheep, Shropshire and Ryland, are also produced. Perhaps one day farming officials will visit the CRT's farms in Herefordshire to see the important contribution they are making both to the environment and to the local communities.

So eat the fruit, drink the drink and help save our orchards. Read the book, enjoy the pictures and appreciate the work of Gordon Beningfield, a good man. He will be remembered for many years as a friend; as an artist who through his work helped to keep the countryside alive, and, as the man who loved butterflies.

R.P. Autumn 2004

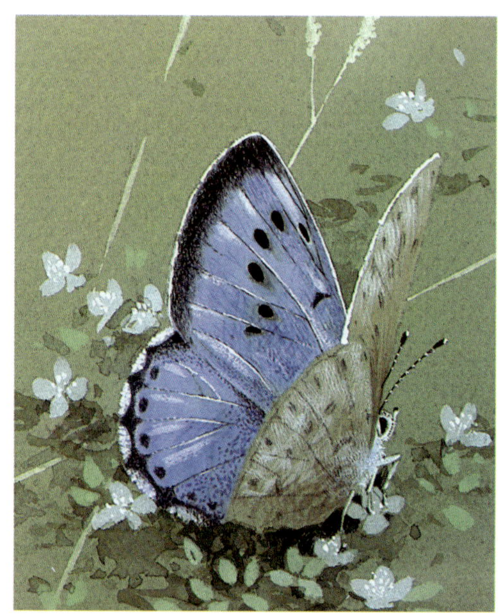

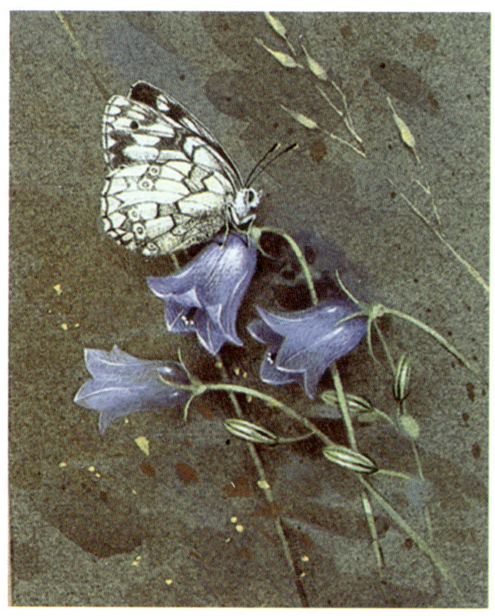

TOP: *Large blue.*   ABOVE: *Marbled white.*

Gordon Beningfield supported a number of important conservation and countryside organisations.

THE COUNTRYSIDE RESTORATION TRUST

The Countryside Restoration Trust was founded in 1993 with Gordon Beningfield as one of the key Founder Trustees. The CRT was probably the first Charity on practical farming and conservation to demonstrate the importance of sustainable farming. In order to do this the Trust purchased land so that it could show farmers, politicians and the public the way forward, not simply tell them the way forward. Those early stalwarts in the CRT had never intended to start a farming Charity, but felt compelled to do so as so many of the other major conservation Charities seemed reluctant to get involved with practical farming and reluctant to take on the challenges of conservation in the general countryside. The CRT now has about 1000 acres and its work has been rewarded by the sights and sounds of wildlife flooding back to its farms, which at the same time as producing larksong are also producing quality food. For those who want to join the CRT to help restore a living, working countryside for farming, wildlife and people please write for more details to: The Countryside Restoration Trust, Barton, Cambs CB3 7AG.

THE WOODLAND TRUST

The Woodland Trust is one of the few Charities that has been working hard in the general countryside. Whereas the CRT has been concentrating on farming, the Woodland Trust concentrates quite naturally on woodland. Since it began in 1972 it now owns approximately 50,000 acres of both young and mature woodland on 1000 sites. Gordon Beningfield was greatly honoured by the Trust planting a wood in his beloved Dorset and naming it Beningfield Wood. The wood can be found near West Milton, close to Bridport. The address of The Woodland Trust is: The Woodland Trust, Autumn Park, Dysart Road, Grantham, Lincs NG31 6LL.

BUTTERFLY CONSERVATION

Gordon Beningfield was at one time President of Butterfly Conservation and it was one of his most highly regarded Charities. He worked extremely hard for butterflies in general and Butterfly Conservation in particular. Butterflies are an indicator species and an abundance of butterflies means that the environment is healthy. Scarcity of butterflies means that there are problems of pollution and uncaring development. Butterfly Conservation has numerous reserves and it has performed miracles in raising the profile of butterflies and all the serious issues surrounding healthy butterfly populations. Gordon was passionate about his butterflies and a keen supporter of this worthwhile Charity. Butterfly Conservation, Manor Yard, East Lulworth, Wareham, Dorset BH20 5QP.

THE DORSET WILDLIFE TRUST
Gordon was a great supporter of local Wildlife Trusts, as they are the ones which are working at grass roots level to save important areas of local conservation importance. Because of his love of Dorset and of Thomas Hardy he was therefore a keen supporter of The Dorset Wildlife Trust. The Dorset Wildlife Trust, Brooklands Farm, Forston, Dorchester, Dorset DT2 7AA.

THE HERTFORDSHIRE AND MIDDLESEX WILDLIFE TRUST
Similarly Gordon was a great supporter of his local Wildlife Trust which has a number of important reserves and which works tirelessly for the conservation movement in Gordon's home area. The Hertfordshire and Middlesex Wildlife Trust, Grebe House, St Michael's Street, St Albans, Hertfordshire AL3 4SN.

Other conservation bodies that Gordon belonged to and felt strongly about include:
THE NATIONAL TRUST, 36 Queen Anne's Gate, London SW1H 9AS.
THE ROYAL SOCIETY FOR THE PROTECTION OF BIRDS, The Lodge, Sandy, Bedfordshire SG19 2DL.
THE GAME CONSERVANCY TRUST, Burgate Manor, Fordingbridge, Hampshire SP6 1EF.
THE KINGCOMBE TRUST, The Kingcombe Centre, Toller, Porcorum, Dorchester, Dorset DT2 0EQ.

As an organisation campaigning for rural culture in general Gordon was also a keen supporter of **THE COUNTRYSIDE ALLIANCE,** The Old Town Hall, 267 Kennington Road, London SE11 4PT.